CHRISTOLOGY:
MEMORY, INQUIRY, PRACTICE

CHRISTOLOGY: MEMORY, INQUIRY, PRACTICE

Anne M. Clifford
Anthony J. Godzieba

Editors

THE ANNUAL PUBLICATION
OF THE COLLEGE THEOLOGY SOCIETY
2002
VOLUME 48

ORBIS BOOKS

Maryknoll, New York 10545

Founded in 1970, Orbis Books endeavors to publish works that enlighten the mind, nourish the spirit, and challenge the conscience. The publishing arm of the Maryknoll Fathers & Brothers, Orbis seeks to explore the global dimensions of the Christian faith and mission, to invite dialogue with diverse cultures and religious traditions, and to serve the cause of reconciliation and peace. The books published reflect the views of their authors and do not represent the official position of the Maryknoll Society. To learn more about Maryknoll and Orbis Books, please visit our website at www.maryknoll.org.

Library of Congress Cataloging-in-Publication Data

Christology : memory, inquiry, practice / Anne M. Clifford, Anthony J. Godzieba, editors.
    p.   cm.— (The annual publication of the College Theology Society; v. 48)
    Includes bibliographical references.
    ISBN 1-57075-456-X (pbk.)
    1. Jesus Christ—Person and offices.   I. Clifford, Anne M., 1944-   II. Godzieba, Anthony J., 1951-   III. Series.

BT203.C48 2003
232—dc21   2003002294
                                        CIP

In memory of William J. Hill, O.P.
(March 30, 1924 - October 12, 2001)
Professor of Theology and Teacher of Christology
at The Catholic University of America

"From the fullness of the heart the mouth speaks."
(Matthew 12:34)

Contents

Acknowledgments   xi

Introduction   xiii
   Anne M. Clifford, Duquesne University
   Anthony J. Godzieba, Villanova University

PART I
MEMORY

What Does Jesus Have to Do with Christ? What Does
Knowledge Have to Do with Faith? What Does History Have
to Do with Theology?   3
   Paula Fredriksen, Boston University

Epistemology and the Theological Application
of Jesus Research   18
   James F. Keating, Providence College

PART II
INQUIRY

The Future of Christology: Expanding Horizons, Religious
Pluralism, and the Divinity of Jesus   47
   Roger Haight, Weston Jesuit School of Theology

The Clash of Christological Symbols: A Case
for Metaphoric Realism   62
   Robert Masson, Marquette University

Response to Robert Masson: The Clash of Christological
Symbols 87
  Roger Haight, Weston Jesuit School of Theology

The Power of Divine Presence: Toward a *Shekhinah*
Christology 92
  Gloria L. Schaab, Fordham University

The Spirit Christology of Piet Schoonenberg 116
  Michael E. O'Keeffe, Xavier University

Derrida's Use of Scripture 141
  Jacquelyn Porter, Marymount University of Virginia

Jesus Turns the Wheel of Dharma: Emerging Christologies
of Contemporary Buddhism 159
  Peter A. Huff, Centenary College (Louisiana)

PART III
PRACTICE

To Live at the Disposal of the Cross: Mystical-Political
Discipleship as Christological Locus 177
  M. Shawn Copeland, Marquette University

To Live at the Disposal of the Cross: A Response 197
  Mary Ann Hinsdale, Boston College

"At the Disposal of the Cross": Discipleship, Julian
of Norwich, and What Bartimaeus Saw 206
  Anthony J. Godzieba, Villanova University

Feminists' Christs and Christian Spirituality 214
  Linda S. Harrington, The Catholic University of America

The Practice of Teaching Christology: A Panel 237

  • The Evolution of an Undergraduate Christology Course 237
    Patricia A. Plovanich, University of San Diego

• Christology as Introduction 250
  Elena G. Procario-Foley, Iona College

• Teaching Christology: History and Horizons 265
  Terrence W. Tilley, University of Dayton

Contributors 277

Acknowledgments

This volume is the fruit of the combined efforts of all those who value the College Theology Society's contribution to scholarship in theology and religious studies.

We would like to thank the members of the CTS Board of Directors for trusting us to plan a stimulating annual convention and to edit this volume with care and dispatch. We are especially grateful for the contributions made by the convention's plenary speakers Paula Fredriksen, Roger Haight, Patricia Plovanich, Elena Procario-Foley, and Terrence Tilley. We wish to thank all those who delivered papers at the convention and submitted them for our consideration.

We are indebted to the following colleagues who graciously offered their time and expertise by serving as manuscript referees: Regina Boisclair (Alaska Pacific University), Walt Noyalis (Anna Maria College), Kenneth Homan (Aquinas Institute of Theology), Robert Daly, S.J., and Frederick Lawrence (Boston College), Mary Frohlich (Catholic Theological Union at Chicago), William Loewe and Peter C. Phan (The Catholic University of America), Mary Kaye Nealen, S.P. (College of Great Falls), Dennis Hamm, S.J. (Creighton University), Michael Cahill, James P. Hanigan, and Michael Slusser (Duquesne University), Raymond van Leeuwen (Eastern University), Mary Hines (Emmanuel College), Francis Schüssler Fiorenza (Harvard Divinity School), Joan Nuth (John Carroll University), Frederick Crowe (Lonergan Research Institute, Toronto), Shannon Schrein (Lourdes College), Ralph Del Colle (Marquette University), William Portier (Mount Saint Mary's College, Baltimore), J. Edward Owens (St. John's Seminary, Camarillo), Sally A. Kenel (St. John's University), Daniel Sheridan (Saint Joseph's College of Maine), Margaret Pfiel (St. Joseph's University), Phyllis Kaminski and Anita Houck (Saint Mary's College, Notre Dame), Mary Ann Getty-Sullivan (St. Vincent's College), Jack Bonsor (Santa Clara University), John Topel, S.J., and Donna Teevan (Seattle University), Michael H. Barnes and Dennis

M. Doyle (University of Dayton), Matthew Ashley and Kevin Hart (University of Notre Dame), Carol Dempsey, O.P. (University of Portland), Norbert Rigali, S.J., (University of San Diego), Suzanne Toton (Villanova University), Pamela Smith, SS.C.M. (Villa Sacred Heart), Kevin Burke, S.J., and Margaret Guider (Weston Jesuit School of Theology), David Hammond (Wheeling Jesuit University), and Joseph A. Bracken, S.J. (Xavier University). Thanks to each of you for this professional courtesy and service to our discipline.

On behalf of the CTS we wish to thank St. John's University (New York) and especially Loretta Devoy, O.P., and her colleagues for hosting the 2002 convention. Our deep gratitude also goes to Orbis Books for its continual support of the scholarly work of the College Theology Society and its publication of the annual volume. Finally, we are especially grateful to have worked with Susan Perry; no one could ask for a more knowledgeable, enthusiastic, and understanding editor.

Introduction

Anne M. Clifford and Anthony J. Godzieba

Just as a lens can focus the complex elements of a beam of light into a single point of intense illumination, so the College Theology Society chose Jesus Christ to be the focus of its 2002 annual convention, sought to sharpen this focus, and thus attempted to cast new light on Jesus' identity and significance. In this way, the papers presented at the convention, and especially those gathered in this volume, join a multifaceted conversation about Jesus Christ that began during the life of the earthly Jesus and continues with unabated vigor today. This conversation has sought to answer two fundamental questions (which are really two sides of a single issue), namely, "Who is Jesus Christ?" and "Why is he significant?" The CTS chose this central topic of christology, as it does all of its convention topics, in order to enrich the disciplines of our members and to benefit the faith life of the next generation of adults whom we all have the privilege to teach.

The current conversations about Jesus Christ among Roman Catholic scholars have been underway in earnest for at least a half-century, especially since 1951, the fifteen-hundredth anniversary of the Council of Chalcedon. The years since then have been marked by a veritable storm of scholarship that has plunged theologians into a closer study of the biblical sources and a reexamination of the person and mission of Jesus and the saving work attributed to him. The past fifty years have seen enormous, even breathtaking, developments in christology—some now seen as so "usual" and "commonplace" that their paradigm-shifting effects have been forgotten. During these fifty years our academic settings and intellectual circumstances have changed considerably as well, as new questions have emerged in an increasingly complex and pluralistic world. It would be impossible to provide an exhaustive survey of these questions and the responses to them.

It is our hope, however, that this volume may provide thought-provoking perspectives on at least some of them.

As we read the gospels, the primary sources for our knowledge of Jesus, it is impossible not to place into the foreground the simple yet startling question that Jesus puts to his disciples: "Who do the people say that I am?" (Mark 8:27; Matt. 16:15; Luke 9:20). The premise of this book is the conviction that at the heart of Christian faith lies not so much a set of abstract doctrines or theories but rather the living person of Jesus himself, about whom there is something qualitatively different that sets him apart from other teachers and thinkers. This difference demands careful consideration. It has led Christians to confess that Jesus is the human face of God and to hold the memory of Jesus sacred over the centuries.

An adequate theological response to the christological question requires a gathering of testimony from both past and present, with an eye directed to the future. The essays chosen for this volume have suggested an arrangement according to a tripartite division of *Memory, Inquiry,* and *Practice.*

Memory

By "memory" we mean much more than the simple acts of remembering the words and deeds of Jesus. "Memory" is concerned with recovering and understanding Jesus as a historical person whose life unfolded within a first-century A.D./C.E. Palestinian Jewish context. This requires the use of methodologies for making sense of the historical evidence for Jesus as well as the negotiation of the contested relationship between faith and contemporary historical methods.

In her essay, Paula Fredriksen approaches these issues from the historian's perspective and suggests certain ways that recent research on the historical Jesus and his context can (and should) impact on christology. She warns, in particular, against "anachronism" in both historical Jesus research and in christology—the misplaced desire for Jesus and his time to be immediately relevant to contemporary concerns. To combat this, she places issues of divinity, the personal identity of Jesus, and the vexed relationship between Judaism and Christianity back into their "thicker" historical contexts in the ancient world; she then examines the somewhat surprising results, and in the process shows how the "Third Quest" for the historical Jesus can invigorate christology by encouraging theologians to take history and the incarnation more seriously than they might normally do today.

James Keating, on the other hand, approaches the quest for the historical Jesus from the theologian's perspective. From his vantage point, the quest's status in theology remains unsettled: while some are attracted to the possibility that historical methods might uncover truths about what Jesus actually said and did, others worry that granting theological significance to the quest undermines theology's claim to a distinctive methodology. This concern is often expressed in foundational terms, with a stark declaration that historical research cannot provide the basis for either Christian faith or theology. Keating argues that "foundherentism," a recent philosophical attempt to get beyond the impasse between foundationalist and coherentist theories of knowledge, provides a model for upholding the capacity of credible historical claims to affect theology without giving such claims absolute preeminence over other theological sources.

Inquiry

Essays that highlight the present diversity of christological approaches and attempts at discerning the future shape of christological reflection constitute the second section, *Inquiry*. "Inquiry" in the broad sense is a process of formulating appropriate research questions, organizing the search for data, analyzing and evaluating the data found, and communicating the results in a coherent fashion for one's contemporaries.

No area of inquiry in christology is more difficult than trying to propose the contours of its future development. Roger Haight dares to do just that in his plenary essay, "The Future of Christology: Expanding Horizons, Religious Pluralism, and the Divinity of Jesus." Rather than project the future on the basis of statistical data, necessary axioms, or the laws of logic, Haight's strategy is to draw from common experience and common sense, with attention to development in the ideas and attitudes of educated middle-class Christians in mainline American churches. He first provides three "homely" descriptions of the dynamics at work in how people change their views. He posits that spatial contexts change, temporal contexts also change, and experiential or mental horizons expand. Having explored these, he then applies these patterns to two areas in the development of comparative theology, which he treats as a discipline closely related to the practice of interreligious dialogue as it involves becoming aware of the other religions and the impact this makes on a Christian's faith in Jesus Christ. Finally, he addresses the question of the divinity of Jesus and how this will likely be experienced and understood in the future.

Robert Masson's essay "The Clash of Christological Symbols: A Case for Metaphoric Realism" offers a critique of and a direct response to the theory of symbol that lies at the heart of Haight's recent work *Jesus, Symbol of God*. Haight has derived his fundamental understanding of symbol from the theologies of Paul Tillich and Karl Rahner, but Masson argues that attention must be paid to the fundamental differences that exist between Tillich and Rahner on the issues of religious predication in general and in christology in particular, despite any similarities in their phenomenological characterizations of religious symbols. In a constructive alternative to Haight's view, Masson argues that a description of religious discourse as metaphoric, rather than symbolic, provides a more effective way to explain the Christian affirmation of identity between Jesus and God. His essay provides a detailed analysis of "metaphoric realism" and demonstrates its applicability to dogmatic christological claims.

Haight's response to Masson focuses mainly on the issue of the nature and character of symbol as it is appears in Rahner, his own *Jesus Symbol of God,* and Masson's constructive alternative. On the one hand, he believes that Rahner's portrayal of the structure of symbol admits distinction between symbol and symbolized but emphasizes the unity between them. On the other hand, *Jesus Symbol of God* admits the inseparable unity of symbol and symbolized but emphasizes the distinction of the two and the dialectical character of their unity. All of this, he argues, is directly relevant to christology.

Intended as a theological thought experiment from a feminist hermeneutical perspective, Gloria Schaab furthers christological inquiry by proposing an alternative approach in response to significant critiques of traditional christological models. She names this alternative paradigm "*Shekhinah* Christology." She explores the possibility and fruitfulness of a paradigm that characterizes Jesus the Christ as the incarnation of the *Shekhinah* of God. As resources for this paradigm she draws upon the traditionally female personification and hypostatization of the immanent presence of God with the oppressed and suffering people of Israel, as commented upon in rabbinic and kabbalist literature.

Michael O'Keeffe extends the focus of our christological inquiry to continental Europe and the contribution of Piet Schoonenberg to "Spirit Christology." O'Keeffe examines Schoonenberg's christological works with special attention to his final major monograph *De Geest, het Woord en de Zoon* (1991, not yet available in English translation). First, O'Keeffe examines Schoonenberg's theological methodology with particular attention to his "post-exegetical unified reading" of the New Testament. Then he surveys Schoonenberg's major interpretations of enhypostasis, giving attention especially to his way of describing the substance of the human in the divine nature as a "reciprocal enhypostasis" that results in emphasis on the mutual involvement of the divine and human persons, expressed in terms of the union of two "personal" natures in one "divine-human" or "theandric" person. This leads him to explore Schoonenberg's unique way of speaking of the becoming of the Son in history through the work of the Spirit. In the essay's final sections O'Keeffe explores implications of Schoonenberg's Spirit christology for trinitarian theology and pneumatology, and offers suggestions for possible directions for Spirit christology in the future.

Jacquelyn Porter extends the focus still further by examining the impact of post-structuralist theory, in particular Jacques Derrida's deconstructive readings, on the religious use of scripture and especially the Christian reading of the word of God in the light of the coming of the Jesus Christ, the Word of God. Her essay sets Derrida's analysis of the concepts of hospitality and forgiveness (where he uses scripture as a catalyst) within the framework of his affirmation of the (open) "messianic" over against (concretized and thus closed) "messianisms." Although she is sympathetic to Derrida's concerns, her own analysis points out the tendency of Derrida and his followers to separate "the religious" from specific religions, a movement away from the particularity of religious traditions that she pointedly questions. She then considers the implications of Derrida's analysis for religion, especially Christianity, which professes faith in the incarnate Messiah, Jesus Christ. She brings to light new directions in the study of "the religious"—directions that are sensitive to the issues raised by Derrida and at the same time surpass his characterization of "religion." These show how the religions, from within their own scriptural resources, have not only the capacity to perform the kind of "ascesis" that Derrida advocates but also the capacity to recognize and to mediate the particular revelation of God and to respond to the call of the other.

In "Jesus Turns the Wheel of Dharma: Emerging Christologies of Contemporary Buddhism" Peter Huff provides an exposition and critical examination of the readings of Jesus offered in popular venues by two major Buddhist figures: Tibetan leader Tenzin Gyatso, the fourteenth Dalai Lama, and Vietnamese Zen master Thich Nhat Hanh. More than simply Buddhist appreciations of Jesus or imitations of Christian christologies, even Asian ones, these experiments in non-Christian christology demonstrate the degree to which Jesus has been appropriated as a symbol and at times as a source for popular Buddhist spirituality. Huff argues that while the Dalai Lama does not go far beyond translating Jesus into Buddhist terms, Nhat Hanh's christology represents a more venturesome attempt to transplant Jesus into Buddhist soil. Signaling an unprecedented christological "moment" in contemporary Buddhism, both imaginative exercises carry important implications for the future of christology, the future place of Jesus in interreligious dialogue, and the future meaning of Jesus in Buddhism's evolving view of the world.

Practice

"Practice," the third and final section of the volume, is divided into two parts. The emphasis on practice leads us to pose the question of Jesus' identity in a somewhat more personal way than in the previous essays. Here the emphasis is on Jesus' other question to his disciples, "Who do *you* say that I am?" (Mark 8:29). The "you" rather than "people" presupposes a desire for a vibrant relationship of discipleship and a spirituality that informs who *we* are as Christians. M. Shawn Copeland's essay "To Live at the Disposal of the Cross: Mystical-Political Discipleship as Christological Locus" speaks of who Jesus is as the revelation of the compassionate solidarity, the unconditional love of God. This revelation forms the ground on which the disciple lives at the disposal of the cross and seeks loving relationship with the crucified Jesus who is the "way" through the Spirit to union with the Father. In developing her thesis Copeland reflects on Catherine of Siena and Josiah Henson as conspicuous examples of such discipleship.

Mary Ann Hinsdale and Anthony J. Godzieba continue the conversation with responses to Copeland's provocative essay. Hinsdale views Copeland's essay as an invitation to reflect upon the vocation of disciple of Jesus, particularly what it means to "live at the disposal of the cross." From the vantage point of her vocation as an academic theologian, Hinsdale considers the demands of a mystical-political discipleship and how such a discipleship might serve as the *locus* for doing christology. In listening to many voices in addition to Copeland's, especially those of John of the Cross, Jon Sobrino, and Teresa of Avila, Hinsdale proposes that the locus be "christology from within." By adopting this approach she seeks a mediation of Christ not based merely upon external imitation, but one that "includes a profound sharing of Jesus' own consciousness."

Godzieba sees Copeland's essay as an invitation as well, this time to consider the cross and the suffering that it symbolizes as integral to Jesus' message and to the disciple's following of Jesus. While fully agreeing with Copeland's thesis, Godzieba seeks to supplement and extend it by drawing on additional resources (a "performance" hermeneutic of the kingdom of God, the Gospel of Mark's portrayal of Bartimaeus, Julian of Norwich's meditations upon the crucifixion) that call on the Christian not to rush past Good Friday in order to reach the happy resolution of Easter Sunday, but rather to remain "at the disposal of the cross," to experience its mystical pedagogy, and thus participate in a deeper way in the revelation of God's transforming love that is present in the crucified Savior.

The theme of practice is approached in a different fashion by Linda Harrington, who seeks in her essay "Feminists' Christs and Christian Spirituality" to make explicit the connection between christology and spirituality. Harrington's focal question is: What do the images of Christ and the descriptions of Jesus developed in the works of Rosemary Radford Ruether, Rita Nakashima Brock, Jacquelyn Grant, and Elizabeth A. Johnson offer a Christian believer? After providing a brief description of Christian spirituality, Harrington uses it to engage critically the christologies of four feminist and womanist theologians. In her assessments of each, the relationship between the historical person Jesus of Nazareth and the Christ as each imagines him plays a crucial role. Her overriding interest is how well their images of Christ function as a basis for personal and communal spirituality. Specifically, is the Christ described by these women the one through whom and with whom and in whom the Christian community worships God in union with the Holy Spirit? Further, do their contributions to the conversation about who Jesus is offer anything of value to the Christian who desires to develop a personal relationship with Jesus Christ, one that also contributes to a deeper relationship with God in the Holy Spirit?

Where the theological discipline of christology is concerned, "practice" encompasses more than active discipleship and an enlivened Jesus-centered spirituality. It also entails pedagogy exercised within the sacred trust of teaching. It is fitting, then, that a section of this volume be devoted to the teaching of christology, since the gospel writers (in over fifty instances) describe Jesus' work as teaching, and the most frequent title of address for Jesus in the gospels is "teacher." In Jesus' pedagogy he deeply engaged the people he encountered, often inviting them to reconsider old perspectives, while proposing new ones. The final mandate of Matthew's Jesus to his disciples was to teach, to practice the art they had learned from him (Matt. 28:16-20).

Good teachers of christology engage their students in the exploration of what "people" (especially noteworthy christologians) say about Jesus. They also invite their students to reflect and to answer the question "who do *you* say I am?" for themselves. This invitation is evident in Patricia A. Plovanich's plenary paper, "The Practice of Teaching Christology, the Evolution of an Undergraduate Christology Course," which describes the creation of a christology course in terms of building bridges between the teacher's scholarly research and the learning of students with highly diverse religious and ethnic backgrounds. Teachers of christology will likely find in her description of the four stages of her course's ten-year evolution dynamics similar to those at work in the design of their own courses.

In her plenary paper entitled "Christology as Introduction," Elena Procario-Foley explains how she facilitates her undergraduate students coming to grips with the question "Who is Jesus, the Christ?" She reflects on the methodology and content of two courses that she regularly teaches. In her basic introductory christological course, "Images of Jesus throughout History," her pedagogical approach is strongly influenced by the christological project of Edward Schillebeeckx, with the resulting emphasis on how students can approach christology as an integration of story, theology, and praxis. She compares this course with a second upper-level course "Jesus and Judaism," in which she pointedly addresses the question of the Jewishness of Jesus. She stresses that the experience of teaching this course leads her to recommend that any undergraduate christology course incorporate a critical assessment of the influence of anti-Semitism on how Jesus is presented in biblical and post-biblical writing.

Terrence Tilley's plenary essay describes a graduate christology seminar and displays the concerns of his current research program that centers christology in the imagination(s) of disciples. Beginning with the images in the New Testament, he turns to historical images of Jesus, including conciliar ones. Tilley concludes by evaluating contemporary images of Jesus as he emerges from the quests for the historical-Jesus and Jesus as savior among the living faith traditions. His approach claims that all christologies necessarily are "from below" and that the distinction of christologies as "from above" and "from below," while useful in the past, is finally misleading.

Part I

MEMORY

What Does Jesus Have to Do with Christ?
What Does Knowledge Have to Do with Faith?
What Does History Have to Do with Theology?

Paula Fredriksen

Memoriae Tony Saldarini sacrum[*]

My formal assignment for this meeting was to speak on the impact that recent work on the historical Jesus has had, or perhaps should have, on contemporary christology. I'd like to offer four items to serve, collectively, as our point of departure.

- Two ancient philosophical definitions of God, the first from c. 160 C.E., the second from c. 360: "That which always maintains the same nature, and in the same manner, and is the cause of all other things: that, indeed, is god." "All god is free from passion, free from change."
- A sixth-century mosaic of a uniformed Roman army officer, perhaps even an emperor. He holds aloft a military standard. The banner proclaims: *Ego sum via, veritas et vita.*
- A question-and-answer volley in the spring of 1998 during a three-day conference for lay people sponsored by Duke University's theology school on the question, "Who was Jesus?" Someone in the audience asked the panel (all reputed experts in historical Jesus research), "Did Jesus think he was God?" Tom Wright

---

*One of the best things about working at Boston University was having Tony Saldarini just a little further down on Commonwealth Avenue, at The Other Place (Boston College). I miss his humor, his erudition, his sharp intelligence, and his company. I am grateful to have known him and to have had him as my colleague. May his memory be for a blessing.

leaned into the mike to say "Yes" at exactly the same moment that I leaned into the mike to say "No." After a perfect pause, A. J. Levine then opined, "Jesus was not bi-polar."

• Another question-and-answer volley, this time among hardened professionals at a meeting of the Society of Biblical Literature, in 1992 or 1993. The ideas that would eventuate in my book *Jesus of Nazareth, King of the Jews* (1999) were just taking shape. I had presented a paper challenging one of the few orthodox doctrines still holding the field, namely, the historicity of what is known in the field as the "Temple tantrum," especially in its Markan mode as the trip-switch for the Passion. I compared Mark and John; I reexamined the redactional problems and issues of chronology; I surveyed the size of Herod's huge outer court and Josephus' population estimates of holiday crowds. I spoke of the sheer irrelevance of the gesture both to the evangelists' narratives and to Pilate's historical decision to crucify. I then took questions. The very first one to come from the floor—from another member of this scholarly body—was this: "Are you saying then that the Jews did *not* kill Jesus?"

Let's think with each of these points as a way to get into our topic.

Theology

The first sentence I quoted comes from one of history's great failed interfaith dialogues, Justin's *Dialogue with Trypho*, chapter 3. Other Christians of philosophical, practical, and exegetical persuasions different from Justin's lurk in the background, and occasionally pop to the surface: Justin writes from a field thick with Marcionites, Valentinians, Basilidians, and other "heretics" (c. 35), where gentile Christians, harkening to Jewish Christians, begin themselves to live according to Jewish practice (c. 47); where gentile pagans voluntarily Judaize and, indeed, where some convert fully to Judaism (c. 122-123). Justin presents his own position through a dialogue with a literary persona who embodies key elements of Justin's own commitments. Trypho, unlike Valentinus or Marcion, has a positive exegetical orientation toward the Septuagint; unlike most gentiles, he worships the god of Israel; like Justin and like other well-educated gentiles, pagan or Christian, he is committed to philosophy.

I will return to the impact that Justin's gentile Christian opposition had on orthodoxy's *contra Iudaeos* tradition when we consider my fourth point above. Here it suffices to note that Platonizing philosophical *koinē*, the vernacular of antiquity's middle-brow intelligentsia, structures the *Dialogue* and determines Justin's reading of the Bible.[1] His *logia* about *theos*—what other philosophers, pagan, Jewish, or Christian, call "the high god" or "the being" or "the One" or "the Father"—is purely pagan; hence the fourth-century quotation from Sallustius, *On the Gods and the World*, also adduced in my first point. His high god is Justin's high god is (for that matter) Valentinus's high god[2] is virtually any educated person's high god in this period. Immutable, transcendent, discernible only to or by the mind, without body of any sort: ὁ Θεός, *the* god.[3]

Christology is a form of theology, and I want to use both terms in the way that they would have been understood in their formative period, and occasionally still are in ours. By "theology" I *do not* mean something like "religious feelings and thoughts." By theology I mean specifically: ordered, rational discourse on the nature of god/divinity (*theos* translates both ways). As such, theology is *not* native to ancient religion, whether pagan, Jewish, or Christian. Its cultural and social matrix was the school; its project unabashedly intellectual, indeed, philosophical. "God" as defined stands as a discrete item within a larger rational discourse that seeks to coordinate *theos* with other ideas constitutive of "reality": cosmos, matter, *psychē, sōma*, mind/*noûs*, and so forth. The metaphysical distance between the highest *theos* and this material *cosmos,* reinforced by the concepts of ancient science, accounts for the hyper-development of philosophical ideas of mediation in Graeco-Roman *paideia*, among which, in both its docetic and non-docetic modes, is ancient christology.

Herewith, then, is one principle source of our current complications. Theology is philosophical. In principle, it coordinates "god"/ "divinity" with other elements within a larger—and, ideally, a systematic—discourse of meaning. But scripture is narrative. In the Bible, God is a character, not a rational principle; in the gospels, *encore plus*, so is Jesus. (That Jesus is an historical character as well as a literary one is, of course, a point to which I shall return.) We can read biblical texts—we can read *any* text—philosophically, should we so choose, but what results is a meta-textual interpretation. (Historically, typological allegory closed the gap between *mythos* and philosophy.[4]) Biblical texts themselves, in a first-order way, yield stories, not systems. They can be made to yield systems—or perhaps, to yield *to* systems—only through hermeneutical effort.

The fact that modern philosophy—since Wittgenstein? Spinoza? Descartes? pick your point—suffers (or should suffer) from metaphysical aphasia only adds another layer to contemporary theology's problems. But problems always attended the effort to make philosophical sense out of traditional religious texts, because of the intrinsic differences between these two forms of human reflection and expression. Posidonius had to sweat over Homer and Hesiod no less than Philo over Moses, no less than Justin or Origen or Athanasius over Isaiah and Matthew.[5] Current historical research may not oblige the intellectual concerns and commitments of traditional christology; but in its resistance to philosophical reformulation, history is little different from scripture itself. Put more simply, history is more like biblical scripture and biblical scripture more like history than either is like philosophy. The intellectual problems facing theologians who wish to avail themselves of the results of current historical research have already been rehearsed in the foundational Christian problem of reading the Bible philosophically, which is to say, theologically.

Context and Meaning

Next, our second item, the mosaic. Most people reading this have already decoded the Roman officer as an image of the Johannine Christ. My undergraduates, less at home in Latin, always gasp in surprise once I translate its banner. I wish I could get them to react the same way when I present them with Jesus the feminist, Jesus the countercultural performance artist, Jesus the advocate of peasant land reform, Jesus the social egalitarian, Jesus the post-Zionist anti-nationalist—alas, I could go on.[6] These later images—*forte à la mode* in current constructions of the historical Jesus—are no less anachronistic than this Johannine Christ from Ravenna.

In many ways, though, the sixth-century image has more intellectual rigor than many of its modern academic counterparts do. To the degree that the artist was familiar with the gospels, he would have been aware that the figure he presented was not an historical—that is, evangelical—image of Jesus of Nazareth at all. He was, instead, making a theological and political statement about ancient monotheism, divine mediation, and the imperium. One God; One Lord; One Empire; One Emperor. That the emperor ruled and protected the commonweal as heaven's special agent on earth was imperial boilerplate. In its Christianized form, the idea flowers fully for the first time in the writings of Eusebius. Native to Mediterranean piety, expressed in Hellenistic ruler cults, and then adopted by Rome, its specifically imperial expression begins when the empire begins, with Augustus, although Aurelian, Diocletian, and then Constantine give it a special spin.[7] Our mosaicist condensed and Christianized these ideas, elegantly offering as visual representation what the cult of the emperor and his image encoded behaviorally, from the first century B.C.E. to long after 312.[8] The image's anachronism stood in service to theology.

What do the modern anachronisms serve?[9] Primarily, I think, the idealized politics of their authors; too often, I fear, demeaning stereotypes about Jesus' native religion.[10] These images of Jesus, in their appeal to history, serve somehow to authorize their authors' beliefs— about genuine religion (no blood sacrifices, no messy rituals!); about Jews or Jewishness ("Judaism" is okay; but Jews, as Jesus and Paul realized, needed to drop "ethnic boundary-markers," circumcision, *kashrut,* and Sabbath observance); about good societies (egalitarian, thus, so goes the "argument"—anti-purity). The items on the list vary according to the concerns of the particular scholar. The images' moral "relevance"—their meaningfulness, their emotional familiarity—is exactly what makes them age rapidly, and reveals them for the un-history they are. Their fundamental interpretive context is the present. As this present drifts inexorably into the past, the images lose their resonance, appearing instead as the projections they are. As John Meier, musing (for thousands of pages) on the historical Jesus, has observed: Nothing ages faster than relevance.

Are *theological* images of Jesus intrinsically anachronistic? Yes, because the categories of meaning that structure the theological enterprise are not native to Jesus' historical context: to interpret him in light of them means taking him out of his "native" context and putting him somewhere else. But this is what theology—any theology—does. (The "historical" Moses would have been no less baffled by Philo's assertions about him in *de opificio mundi* than the "historical" Jesus would have been by the consensus document hammered out by the professional theological politicians at Chalcedon.) And theological categories of meaning are themselves also subject to the march of time. "Ground of being" and "ultimate concern" now creak; so do "substance" and "essence" and "person" (though more subtly, perhaps, their aging masked by the botox of ecclesiastical institutions). Time takes no holiday.

The anachronistic quality of theology is an inevitable consequence of its mission: the philosophical restatement of principles that can be supported by appeal to scripture. But anachronism in the historical enterprise collapses it, betraying its *raison d'être*. Put differently, theology, to be theology, will inevitably be anachronistic; history, to be history, can never be anachronistic. Those modern theologians who wish to incorporate the results of the Third Quest into their constructions of christology, then, must proceed with caution. Thanks to the problem of anachronism *in historical studies* (the place where it *is* a problem), stoked as it is by the desire that the ancient figure be immediately relevant to modern concerns (especially to modern ethical or political concerns), there are a lot of *doppelgänger* out there.

Anachronism in historical Jesus work is just bad history. Anachronistic Jesuses in theological works are worse than bad history, they are bad theology. The classical phrase for "bad theology" is "heresy." Anachronism in historical Jesus studies leads, for theology, to Docetism.

I speak now to the theologians. And I invoke not theology as such, but an essential doctrine of Christian theology, namely, the Incarnation. Historians can do and indeed do history without any thought to this doctrine or, indeed, to any other. Theological doctrine not only *is* irrelevant to doing history (any history, not just ancient Christian history), it *should* be irrelevant.

But the doctrine of the Incarnation cannot be irrelevant to Christian theology. Again, the theological enterprise is intrinsically anachronistic because of the sort of hermeneutical enterprise it is. But if christology draws on anachronistic constructions of Jesus—if the historical component of the theological effort is itself compromised—then it stumbles into heresy. A supposedly historical Jesus who is more at home in our century and in our culture than in his own is not a fully and truly human Jesus, one who lived and acted meaningfully and coherently in a particular place and time: in the Galilee and in Roman Judea, as a religious Jew, in the days of the late Second Temple. A truly "historical" Jesus can be no less constituted by his historical, social, and cultural circumstances than are we.

Whether good history can help yield good theology is a compli- cated question: We would need to know what "good theology" would look like. But bad history clearly yields bad theology. Presented in these studies as an ancient figure, such a Jesus is actually a displaced modern Christian, a man without a country. Unstuck in time, he is not a real person. An anachronistic Jesus is a docetic Jesus. And a docetic Jesus can only produce, in turn, a docetic Christ.[11]

Speaking strictly as an historian—but one who cares about christology and about Christianity—I would be sad to part with the doctrine of the Incarnation. I hope that my colleagues who actually are theologians feel the same way. Incarnation, for Christians, anchors the philosophical idea of "god" in human time, giving the biblical God—the creator of this time and of humans—and the biblical myth their purchase in Christian theology. Incarnation is what keeps Chris- tianity, in this sense—the biblical sense—Jewish. As a doctrine, it provides the reason for a point of contact between the Bible and the church, and between Jesus and Christ.

Incarnation as a concept and as a doctrine complicates all sorts of other issues, and we review some of those here: divinity, humanity, time, history, hermeneutics, meaning, identity. As angels go, it's a particularly tough one to wrestle with. But if being a Christian theolo- gian were easy, everyone would be doing it. To the theologians among us, then, I say: *Hazak, hazak*: Be strong, and go for it.

Concepts of Personhood

Did Jesus think he was God? Let's start with A.-J. Levine's pro- posal—Jesus was not bi-polar—and think from there.

Chalcedon, in 451, lay down the terms of classical christology: Jesus was "fully god and fully man without mixture or confusion." This formulation does not require of believers what Wright, in re- sponse to our questioner, affirmed, namely, that *Jesus thought* he was god. It was the bishops who thought Jesus was god. They found verses in scripture that supported their claim, but the reasons behind the claim itself had been generated long ago, by theological concepts of inter- mediation between *cosmos* and the high *theos*. What happens when we gather these issues as articulated in the fifth century—ideas about god ("theology") and about the human being ("anthropology")— around the historical figure of Jesus?

Theos in ancient monotheist imagination—pagan, Jewish, and Christian—was a much more flexible term than is "God" in its modern avatars. For moderns, conceptually "God" functions as a unique divine point. For ancients, divinity was on a gradient, from the high god at a defined pinnacle through the celestial and super-celestial intelligences populating and structuring *cosmos*[12] to the messengers (*angeloi*) who communicated between these different strata to, finally, special humans who functioned as heaven's agents, not least among whom, to either side of 312, was the emperor. Divinity did not imply ontological identity. The logos was god, that is, divine (θεὸς ην ὁ λόγος, John 1:1), but not the same as "God" himself (θεὸς ην ὁ λόγος).[13] Neither was Metatron. For pagans, Jews, and Christians, other gods existed along with—that is to say, "beneath," contingent upon—the high god. For Jews and Christians, but not for pagans, these other gods were not to be worshiped, yet their existence and their power were certainly acknowledged.[14]

Thus claims about Jesus' divine status originally appeared within a culture where such a thought was thinkable, without *eo ipso* calling into question either the integrity of Jesus' humanity[15] or the high god's (God the Father's) distinctive difference.[16] Theologically, the claim cohered with contemporary constructs of monotheism (one god at the top, others of varying degrees below). Chalcedon affirmed an extreme version of this more traditional concept of graduated divine personalities. It bordered on paradox. But it was not nonsense.

That was then. This is now. The classic christological formula remains, embalmed by institutional sanction; but both the universe and philosophy are much changed. With the advent of modern science, the world has grown progressively disenchanted. In consequence, Western ideas of godhead have grown more austere, while Western concepts of personhood increasingly focus on issues of identity, memory, and embodiment.[17] To affirm that a human being is god, howsoever moderns might try to do that, is not paradox. Without reworking or redefining the terms, it *is* nonsense.

All this has led the historical study of Jesus into a curious secondary fundamentalism. Despite the slough of post-modernist relativism, empirical science—the jewel in the crown of Western culture since the Renaissance—still sets many of the criteria of legitimacy or of meaningfulness for any sort of truth claim. This empiricism complicates theological claims about the historical Jesus by promoting a particular sort of fundamentalism, a fallacy of intention. To legitimate or authorize Christian beliefs about Jesus, these beliefs are imputed *to* Jesus himself. If Jesus himself did not think a thought, then the thought—usually, a theological thought—seems less than legitimate for the tradition.

Thus, if Christian doctrine holds that Jesus died for humanity's sins, then Jesus must have thought so too, and he arranged to die accordingly. If Christianity holds that Jesus was the messiah, then Jesus must have thought so too—despite the problem that even the evangelists, who clearly thought of Jesus as messiah, do not clearly represent him as having said so.[18] If Christianity developed as a law-free gentile church, then that is what Jesus must have intended to happen. And so on (and on).[19] Hence, again, Wright's response to our questioner at the Duke University conference.

To end where we began, then: Did Jesus think he was God? I do not know, but I doubt it. From what I can tell, on the basis of the gospels and of my knowledge of his social context, he seems to have operated more within the Jewish paradigm of prophecy. Within his culture, a prophet might be designated a "son of God," but that implied no ontological claim. This does not mean that Christian theologies might not have good reason to hold that Jesus was "divine" in whatever ways they choose to constitute the claim; but one of those reasons will not be what Jesus thought of himself.

After his lifetime, within the matrix of the Hellenistic synagogue, Christian theological reflection *about* Jesus—early, if we see Paul's letters as involved in this enterprise; certainly by century's end, if that indeed is the provenance of the final redaction of John, for example, or the period of composition for Hebrews, or Revelation—did make claims about Jesus' status as a divine agent in both senses: agent of God, more-than-human himself. These positions based themselves not on what the historical Jesus thought or said so much as on what followers thought about Jesus in light of their experience (direct or according to *paradosis*) of his resurrection.

Systematic theological reflections about Jesus as a divine entity had to wait for Christians with the education and ideological motivation to articulate them. Here we come to the roll call of second-century, formerly pagan intellectuals: Valentinus, Marcion, Ptolemy, Justin, and other early fathers. Their project was largely hermeneutical, its terms dictated by philosophical issues, biblically re-conceived.

The church, howsoever conceived or identified, is the matrix of Christian theology. Jesus of Nazareth was its necessary though insufficient cause. To impute later theological positions to the historical Jesus is anachronistic in a simple way. To sum up simply, then: Whatever the criteria of legitimacy churches use to validate their christologies—and different churches will judge by different criteria—what the historical Jesus "would have thought" cannot be one of them. Intentionalist fundamentalism is both silly history and bad theology.

Christianity and Judaism

Why was my unknown colleague at this long-ago meeting of the Society of Biblical Literature so alarmed by my arguments about Jesus and the Temple?[20] As a scholar, he would have already known that if Jesus died by crucifixion, he died by Rome's hand. My reconstruction had the ancillary effect, however, of reducing the priests' first-order interest in getting Jesus out of the way. No principled religious dispute or intrinsic religious antagonism between Jesus and the priests, I had argued, could be teased from the evangelical evidence. *This* point, not some inference about agency in the crucifixion, was what actually bothered my colleague.[21] But the way his query came out was: "Are you saying that the Jews did *not* kill Jesus?"

Modern scholars, of any denominational affiliation or none, cannot but see the Christian past through the prism of the orthodox *contra Iudaeos* tradition.[22] The "Jew" as a theological and hermeneutical idea—fleshly, hard-hearted, philosophically dim and violently anti-Christian—had assumed its familiar shape in the disputes of early second-century, formerly pagan intellectuals.[23] The concept helped them to articulate their convictions as readers of the Septuagint against the other biblical communities. In no ancient gentile theological system do Jews and Judaism seem to figure positively. For orthodox theology in particular, however, hostile characterizations of Jews became a defining characteristic.

Constantine's patronage ultimately empowered orthodox bishops, the conduits of the erudite *contra Iudaeos* tradition. In the West, with the collapse of Mediterranean civic culture and the consolidation of local power around the bishop, this tradition facilitated the eventual, progressive social separation of Jews and Christians; and separation facilitated targeted aggression. And this anti-Jewish hermeneutic con-

trolled the church's understanding of its own past, whereby the Hellenistic Jewish texts that composed its core canon—the gospels and the
letters of Paul—were read as *contra Iudaeos* themselves. Both Jesus
and Paul thus came to be seen as preaching and working *against* Judaism.

For centuries, then, Christian constructions of Christian identity
and of the formative Christian past have worked with this idea of Judaism as Christianity's opposite. We see this in patristic, intra-gentile
Christian polemic: this is how Tertullian can call Marcion a "Jew";
how Origen can call the millenarian *simpliciores* of his own church
"Jews"; how Athanasius can brand his opponents "Jews"; and
Ambrose, his; and Augustine, his. Combining with nineteenth-century theories of racial purity, the *contra Iudaeos* tradition contributed
to the efforts of German Protestant churches, which produced a de-
Judaized New Testament and an Aryan Jesus.[24] Combining with the
identity-politics of the modern academy, it has produced the darkness
of Jewish sexism and patriarchy against which the light of Jesus' feminism can shine; the oppressive, purity-rule-obsessed hierarchy of Second Temple Judaism against which the egalitarian Jesus gallantly takes
his stand; the nationalist, racially exclusivist Judaism, which the inter-
nationalist, inclusivist Jesus defies. Out with the old slogans (grace
vs. works; freedom vs. legalism; gospel vs. law) and in with the same-
old, same-old (compassion vs. purity).[25]

Does Christian identity have to depend on caricatures of Jews and
Judaism? Must the Jews always and everywhere be the ones who killed
Jesus, so that Christians can affirm with the comfort of clarity who
they (think they) are? I do not know. The most recent cycle of violence in Israel has exposed a level of Christian anti-Judaism that I had
never, in my lifetime, seen before. Spain's *El Periodico de Catalunya*
ran a cartoon of a young Arab boy, much like Simon of Trent, crucified on the Star of David on Israel's flag.[26] When armed Palestinian
militants barricaded themselves against Israel's army in the Church of
the Nativity in Bethlehem, a church in Edinburgh responded by un-
veiling, at Easter, a huge oil painting of Christ on the Cross, complete
with Roman soldiers and Israeli Defense Forces (IDF) officers at his
feet. A newspaper cartoon in Italy depicted baby Jesus (one supposes,
in his cradle in Bethlehem) looking at Israeli tanks and crying out,
"Oh, *no*. Do they want to kill me again?"[27] The *L.A. Daily News* featured a cartoon by Patrick O'Connor: IDF soldiers beating the (un-

armed) magi outside the numinous manger.[28] Synagogues have been torched in Europe and in North America. Criticisms of Israeli politics spill with vertiginous ease into anti-Zionism, thence anti-Semitism, thence into classic, christological anti-Judaism.

Will Christian anti-Judaism ever go away? I do not know. The pessimists among us argue that, if the Shoah did not shock Christian culture out of its anti-Judaism, nothing will. Again, I do not know.

What I do know is that, despite this noxious patrimony, Christian scholars have led the way in the Third Quest, the hallmark of which has been the recovery of Jesus' Judaism. In its challenge to simple— and hateful—constructions of Christian identity, the Quest has also invigorated modern christology.[29] I can do no better than to repeat the words of one of the most eminent toilers in the historical vineyard, John P. Meier:

> The third quest's emphasis on the Jewishness of Jesus has willy-nilly made a lasting contribution to christology. . . . To speak in Johannine terms: when the Word became flesh, the Word did not take on an all-purpose, generic, one-size-fits-all human nature. Such a view would not take seriously the radical historicity of both human nature and divine revelation. The Word became truly flesh insofar as the Word became truly Jewish. No true Jewishness, no true humanity. . . . I think that a proper understanding of the Chalcedonian formula, illuminated by the third quest, necessarily leads to a ringing affirmation of the Jewishness of the flesh the Word assumed. Even if the third quest has no other impact on contemporary Christology, the emphatic reaffirmation of the Jewishness of Jesus will make the whole enterprise worthwhile.[30]

I agree with Meier, which is to say, I would like to think he's right. Theologians: It's up to you.

Notes

[1]By which I (and Justin) mean the Septuagint (LXX). Justin's church has no "new testament"—that was Marcion's repudiated innovation—and Justin refers to specifically Christian writings as the apostles' "memoires" (105).

[2]"The nature of the ungenerated [i.e., non-contingent or self-existent] Father is

incorruption, self-existent, simple and homogeneous light," Ptolemy, *Ad Floram* 7.7.

[3] *Pagan Monotheism in Late Antiquity*, ed. Polymnia Athanassiadi and Michael Frede (Oxford: Clarendon Press/New York: Oxford University Press, 1999).

[4] See the essays collected in *Interpretation and Allegory: Antiquity to the Modern Period*, ed. Jon Whitman (Leiden: Brill, 2000), which treat the period from Homer to the mid-twentieth century.

[5] See Robert Lamberton, "Language, Text, and Truth in Ancient Polytheist Exegesis," *Interpretation and Allegory*, 73-88.

[6] Earlier and more orderly laments available in my *From Jesus to Christ*, 2d ed. (New Haven: Yale University Press, 2000), xiii-xxviii; *Jesus of Nazareth, King of the Jews: A Jewish Life and the Emergence of Christianity* (New York: Knopf, 1999), esp. 197-213; "What You See Is What You Get: Context and Content in Current Research on the Historical Jesus," *Theology Today* 52 (1995): 75-97.

[7] On Aurelian, solar monotheism, and Constantine, see Henry Chadwick's still valuable discussion, *The Early Church* (Harmondsworth: Penguin, 1967), chap. 8.

[8] See esp. S. R. F. Price, *Rituals and Power: The Roman Imperial Cult in Asia Minor* (Cambridge/New York: Cambridge University Press, 1984); H. A. Drake, *Constantine and the Bishops: The Politics of Intolerance* (Baltimore: Johns Hopkins University Press, 2000), on Constantine's orchestration of solar and Christian images in service to imperial politics; J. H. W. G. Liebeschuetz, *Continuity and Change in Roman Religion* (Oxford: Clarendon Press/New York: Oxford University Press, 1979), esp. 235-304 on imperial theology and (literally) the politics of divine mediation; G. W. Bowersock, "Polytheism and Monotheism in Arabia and the Three Palestines," *Dunbarton Oaks Papers* 51 (1997): 1-10. Bowersock points out that, as late as the fifth century, in Constantinople, Constantine was revered as a god (ὡς θεός; Philostorgius, *Hististoria Ecclesiastica* 28), and Theodosius II wrote about reverence to his *numen* and image at public festivals, *Codex Theodosianus* 15.14.1 (in 425).

[9] See E. P. Sanders' meditations on anachronism in academic portraits of a Jesus who stands aloof or opposed to blood sacrifices, purity rules, demonic agency, and apocalyptic constructions of redemption ("Jesus as the First Modern Man") in his "Jesus, Ancient Judaism, and Modern Christianity: The Quest Continues," in *Jesus, Judaism, and Christian Anti-Judaism: Reading the New Testament after the Holocaust*, ed. Paula Fredriksen and Adele Reinhartz (Louisville: Westminster/ John Knox, 2002), 31-55.

[10] With these concerns in mind, Sanders has incisively reviewed modern Pauline scholarship (*Paul and Palestinian Judaism* [Philadelphia: Fortress Press, 1977], 33-59 and 434-42) as well as work on Jesus (*Jesus and Judaism* [Philadelphia: Fortress Press, 1985], passim); before him, George Foot Moore's fundamental essay, "Christian Writers on Judaism," *Harvard Theological Review* 14 (1921): 197-254; also my works cited above, n. 6.

[11] On this point, Sanders, *Jesus and Judaism*, 340; Fredriksen, *From Jesus to Christ*, xxv-xxviii, 214-215.

[12]No matter what the denominational affiliation of this cosmos. For a pagan statement, again, Sallustius; a Jewish statement, Philo, *de opificio mundi* (where Philo unself-consciously refers to stars as *theoi*); a Christian statement, Origen, *Peri ArchÇn.*

[13]Any competent commentary will walk readers through the forest of Greek grammatical issues surrounding articles in the attributive position and their relation to John's prologue.

[14]Biblically, e.g., Micah 4:5 ("All the peoples walk, each in the name of its god; but we will walk in the name of the Lord *our* god forever and ever"); cf. Exodus 22:28 (LXX), where the injunction not to revile God (*elohim*) becomes, "Do not revile *the gods* (*theous*)." So too Paul, 2 Corinthians 4:4 (the "god of this cosmos" works against Paul); Galatians 4:8-9 (*stoicheia*); 1 Corinthians 15:25 (astral or cosmic entities). Inscriptions give details of practical arrangements between Diaspora Jews and these lower divine entities, respected and occasionally invoked (as in the manumission inscriptions from the Bosphorous) but in principle not worshiped. Evidence is collected and discussed in Lee I. Levine, *The Ancient Synagogue: The First Thousand Years* (New Haven, Conn.:Yale University Press, 2000).

[15]That is to say, "humanity" as defined in antiquity. In defense of gnostic and Marcionite christologies, I will point out here that while *soma* was a necessary component of all non-divine reality (for Origen, only "God" as Father, pre-existent Son, and Holy Spirit was absolutely asomatic), *sarx* was a detachable item for anthropology—hence, for christology as well. The docetic Christ did not truly have a fleshly body; but *pace* Tertullian, Irenaeus, and the other high-voltage heresiologists, this was *not* the same as claiming that Jesus was not truly "human." Docetism coordinated with concepts of redemption: while a *soma pneumatikon* would be rescued, the *sarx* would not be—as, indeed, Paul had long ago stated plainly (1 Cor. 15:50). In historical context, this anti-docetic rhetorical ploy defends, if obliquely, the resurrection of the flesh and, in the late second/early third century, millenarian ideas of redemption. See Paula Fredriksen, "Apocalypse and Redemption in Early Christianity: From John of Patmos to Augustine of Hippo," *Vigiliae Christianae* 45 (1991): 151-83.

[16]*Pace* Athanasius, this was Arius' point: not that Christ was a "creature," but that he was contingent, and that God the Father was the only self-existent, non-contingent entity. Arius had tradition right: the vocabulary of both the New Testament (father/son) and of philosophy (*theos/logos*) was hierarchical. I understand how Athanasius won; but he shouldn't have.

[17]On science and the disenchantment of the universe, Max Weber's classic essay, "Science as a Vocation," *Essays in Sociology*, ed. H. H. Gerth and C. Wright Mills (New York: Oxford University Press, 1946) 137-144, 150-156. Alfred I. Tauber, *Confessions of a Medicine Man: An Essay in Popular Philosophy* (Cambridge, Mass.: M.I.T. Press, 2000), gives a lucid and compelling overview of modern constructions of personhood both philosophical and legal, and how confusions there compound problems in medical ethics.

[18]Fredriksen, *Jesus of Nazareth,* 137-154.

[19]Wright's oeuvre, both on Paul and especially on Jesus, is a monument to this sort of intentionalist fundamentalism. See, most recently, *Christian Origins and the Question of God, Vol. 2: Jesus and the Victory of God* (Minneapolis: Fortress Press, 1996); see also Fredriksen, *Jesus of Nazareth*, 293-94.

[20]Summarized in *Jesus of Nazareth*, 207-59; now see my paper, "The Historical Jesus, the Scene at the Temple, and the Gospel of John," Society for Bibilical Literature Annual Meeting 2002, available from *tom.thatcher@cincybible.edu*.

[21]For a similar response, see the essay in this volume by Terrence W. Tilley, "Teaching Christology: History and Horizons," n. 18. Tilley observes, "Fredriksen's reconstruction nearly collapses Jesus into his background." Exactly my point: Jesus' native religion is not his "background," but his context. Why not look at Christianity—especially if we wish to trace the phenomenon into the lifetime of Jesus himself—as an extreme form of Judaism, rather than as something distinct from it?

[22]For an overview of the social and intellectual history behind this identity-confirming construct, see my essay, "What 'Parting of the Ways?' Jews and Gentiles in the Ancient Mediterranean City," *The Ways That Never Parted: Jews and Christians in Late Antiquity and the Early Middle Ages*, ed. Adam H. Becker and Annette Yoshiko Reed (Tübingen: Mohr, 2003).

[23]There is a valuable discussion in Judith Lieu, *Image and Reality: The Jews in the World of the Christians in the Second Century* (Edinburgh: T & T Clark, 1996).

[24]Susannah Heschel, *Transforming Jesus from Jew to Aryan: Protestant Theologians in Nazi Germany* (Tucson, Ariz.: University of Arizona Press, 1995).

[25]On anti-Judaism, Jewish patriarchy, and the feminist Jesus, see especially the essays in *Women and Christian Origins*, ed. Ross Shepard Kraemer and Mary Rose D'Angelo (New York: Oxford University Press, 1999); on some Third Questers' use of demeaning characterizations of Jews and Judaism to define the particular moral excellence of their Jesus, see my "What You See Is What You Get" (n. 6). Historically, socially, anthropologically, and religiously, compassion is to purity as fish is to bicycle. The slogan is Marcus Borg's, against whose reconstruction in particular my essay, "Did Jesus Oppose the Purity Laws?" (*Bible Review* XI.3 [1995]: 20-25, 42-47), is directed.

[26]October 6, 2000.

[27]"Non vorranno mica farmi fuori un'altra volta?!" *La Stampa*, 3 April 2002.

[28]December 12, 2001.

[29]See especially William P. Loewe, "From the Humanity of Christ to the Historical Jesus," *Theological Studies* 61 (2000): 314-331.

[30]"The Present State of the 'Third Quest' for the Historical Jesus: Loss and Gain," *Biblica* 80 (1999): 459-87, at 486.

Epistemology and the Theological Application of Jesus Research

James F. Keating

The quest for the historical Jesus occupies a peculiar place in contemporary theology. A category of theological activity unknown prior to the Enlightenment, it has preoccupied friends and foes alike ever since. Numerous Christian intellectuals have hailed the effort to reconstruct the historical reality of Jesus of Nazareth using the critical tools of historiography as a necessary and welcome step in the ongoing task to relate faith and reason. These supporters of the quest hope that historical research can provide either corroboration for traditional beliefs or new insights into the life, death, and resurrection of the figure at the root of authentic Christian faith.

Others, by contrast, have been much less sanguine about the value of such a project. For them, the quest represents a profound confusion of theology and history and the principles appropriate to each. They regard the religious significance of Jesus as a matter well beyond the competence of the historian, and the "historical Jesus" of little or no use in the task of theology. While the arguments marshaled on each side have varied with time and location, the vigor of the disputants has been a constant. In short, after more than two centuries of argumentation, the theological value of the quest for the historical Jesus remains unsettled—a paradox of attraction and hostility.[1]

The unsettled status of the quest for the historical Jesus confronts the theologian who works in christology or in a related area with a dilemma. To what extent if any should his or her reflections be guided by recent historical research into Jesus? A responsible resolution of the question involves not only an appraisal of the theological significance of the quest but the equally knotty issue of application as well. To decide in favor of relevance means that the theologian is led into a field of inquiry notorious for its lack of consensus, its ideological biases, and the tentative nature of its conclusions.[2] This essay attempts to assist theologians as they struggle with the questions of whether the quest is relevant to theology and how it might be integrated into the theological enterprise. The argument will proceed in two steps. First, explanations are offered for both the attractiveness of the quest for some theologians and the hostility to it on the part of others. Second, a position in contemporary epistemology will be proposed as a model for how Jesus research might be applied in a way that reflects the intrinsic theological value of the quest while at the same time responding to the concerns of its critics.

The Ongoing Attractiveness of the Quest for Theologians

Demonstration of the resilience of the quest for the historical Jesus need go no further than the mere mention of the "Third Quest." This label has been used by some commentators to distinguish the most recent group of Jesus historians from two previous generations of scholars occupied with the same pursuit. What is commonly called the "First Quest" arose with the work of Hermann Samuel Reimarus (1694-1768).[3] A professor of biblical languages and a deist, Reimarus employed the methods of historical inquiry practiced in the German universities of his day to expose what he saw as the unbridgeable gap between the New Testament accounts of Jesus and the actual truth of his life and death. Intending his work to one day assist the defenders of rational religion in a future battle against the upholders of Christian orthodoxy, Reimarus argued that the true Jesus viewed himself as a political messiah commissioned to rule Israel after the Jewish God had destroyed Roman power. Although Jesus played out his role with great determination and in accord with the rules of reason suitable to his time and place, no divine intervention arrived and his life ended on a Roman cross. Jesus' followers, unwilling to return to their normal lives, responded to this tragic disappointment by refashioning their leader as a risen savior and the founder of a new religion, with themselves as leaders. Thus the New Testament, according to Reimarus, is little more than apostolic propaganda and its witness to Jesus nothing less than a fraud.[4]

David Friedrich Strauss (1808-1874), the other great figure in the First Quest, continued the anti-orthodox posture of Reimarus but with a considerable difference.[5] While Reimarus equated the lack of historical truth in the Gospels with fakery, Strauss offered a more sympathetic reading of the evidence. The writers of the Gospels were not self-promoting liars, but religious enthusiasts who communicated the truths imparted by Jesus in the best way they knew how. Desirous of preserving the spiritual insights of their master, the evangelists employed the style of historical narrative as a means to impart the essence of his teachings to those less enlightened. Accordingly, Strauss labeled much of the New Testament witness to Jesus as "myth" instead of history and dedicated his great work, *The Life of Jesus Critically Examined* (1835), to extracting the spiritual kernels from their mythical husks.[6]

From the viewpoint of traditional Christian theology, the difference between Reimarus's belligerence and Strauss's condescension was not significant. As attacks on the historical veracity of the New Testament's witness to Jesus, both represented a serious threat to the integrity of the faith. The central truth of Christianity was at stake and a forceful response clearly necessary. Some theologians countered by defending the traditional Christian claim that as a divinely inspired text the Bible could be trusted in historical matters.[7] Others were motivated to join the quest and took up the tools of the historian not to undermine faith but to craft a portrait of Jesus that would be scientific enough to quiet the scoffers and traditional enough to calm the nerves of the faithful.[8]

This apologetic stratagem suffered a severe setback when Albert Schweitzer published a detailed and critical history of the quest from Reimarus to William Wrede (1859-1906).[9] His survey purported to show that with rare exceptions the historical Jesus who was discovered bore a striking and unsettling resemblance to his discoverer.[10] Furthermore, Schweitzer challenged the common assumption that guided the quest, namely, that once the real Jesus was retrieved, he would prove an instructive exemplar for the present age. In Schweitzer's opinion, to the extent that the historical Jesus could be located, his apocalyptic obsession with the Kingdom of God would continue to render him strange and irrelevant to contemporary hearts and minds. "He does not stay," Schweitzer warned; "[h]e passes by our time and returns to his own."[11]

Schweitzer's thesis quickly found a wide audience and the quest for the historical Jesus lost much of its momentum.[12] Nevertheless, the power of Schweitzer's argument did not long hold its own against the attractive possibility that historical research might be able to reveal some important truth about Jesus. Resistance gave way in a most unlikely place, a conference convened in 1953 by the students of the quest's foremost critic at the time, Rudolf Bultmann. In particular, Ernst Käsemann, a student of Bultmann, argued that his teacher's historical skepticism was excessive in view of increased exegetical sophistication concerning the layers of New Testament tradition.[13] While there was no returning to the naive confidence of the First Quest, the careful application of form and redaction criticism allowed researchers to attain some knowledge of Jesus by isolating the independent traditions behind particular interpretations of the basic *kerygma*. Moreover, they felt that such research had the implicit approval of the Gospel writers, since they themselves took care to ground their narratives in what Jesus actually said and did.[14] This combination of renewed historical confidence and theological legitimization inaugurated a new and fruitful phase in the search for all that can be known of Jesus by the methods of scientific historiography. Six years after Käsemann's speech, James M. Robinson labeled this movement the "New Quest."[15] Subsequently some have renamed it the "Second Quest" in order to distinguish it from the upsurge in books and articles on the historical Jesus that began appearing in the mid-1980s.

This more recent research has taken on the label of the "Third Quest." N. T. Wright, who coined the term and is himself a leading contemporary Jesus historian, views the work of E. P. Sanders as a watershed in this regard.[16] Sanders's *Jesus and Judaism* (1985), according to Wright, constituted a significant methodological development in recovering the Jesus of history. In contrast to the New Quest's tendency to privilege those aspects of the Gospel reports in which Jesus stood out from the world of first-century Judaism, Sanders insisted that only within that world could Jesus be found.[17] While Wright's delineation between the Second and Third Quests has not attained the level of consensus, his nomenclature has.[18] In any case, the leading themes and claims associated with the Third Quest have now become familiar to most theologians.[19]

Reasons for historians' continuing fascination with the quest are not difficult to discern. Not only is Jesus, by any measure, a pearl of great price for the historian, but technical advances and an expanding historical purview have sustained a level of intellectual excitement. When we ask why so many theologians have willingly followed the quest with its twists, turns, promises, and deadends, the explanation is more complex. One can point, of course, to apologetic considerations: the need to demonstrate in every generation that faith has nothing to fear from rational inquiry, including historiography. This concern clearly animated the first respondents to Reimarus and his anti-Christian successors, and it was also at work in a majority of Roman Catholic contributions prior to the Second Quest.[20]

Theological interest in the quest for the historical Jesus goes beyond apologetics, however, and touches the very heart of the Christian proclamation that in Jesus of Nazareth "the Word became flesh and lived among us" (John 1:14 [NRSV]). To have seen Jesus, to have heard his words, to have witnessed his actions and his fate was to have come into contact with the very self-presence of God and the ultimate intelligibility of the universe. Whatever else Christian faith claims to be, it is first of all a response to the intrinsic reality of Jesus. Consequently, if Jesus were to be a figure significantly different from the object of Christian faith, that faith would cease to be viable on its own terms. Moreover, what goes for the whole goes for the part. If Jesus were to have held a certain position in contradistinction to either scripture or tradition, it is they and not Jesus who must yield.

Although the harsh simplicity of the logic might jar, it is neither modern nor alien but internal to the Christian conviction that God is revealed in Jesus of Nazareth. All specifically Christian assertions must find their justification in him. In the words of Paul, "no one can lay any foundation other than the one that has been laid; that foundation is Jesus Christ" (1 Cor. 3:11 [NRSV]). In this sense at least, Reimarus chose his target wisely, and the apologists knew well what was at stake. A successful demonstration that Christian faith has no basis in Jesus would cause the whole edifice to crumble under its own weight.

In sum, the enduring allure of the quest for the historical Jesus for theologians can be traced to the Christian doctrine of the incarnation. Christian faith presents itself as the only appropriate response to this event, and Christian theology is, thereby, the disciplined reflection upon the fullness of its meaning. Accordingly, all Christian claims about God must find their legitimization in one or other aspect of Jesus' life, death, and resurrection. To the extent that the quest for the historical Jesus holds out the possibility of discovering some truth about these matters, theologians cannot stay away. Yet, if this is so, why such hos-tility to the quest on the part of some theologians?

The Rationale for Theological Hostility to the Quest

In light of the anti-Christian origins of the quest, it would seem that an explanation for the hostility of so many theologians may be ready at hand. Yet, most opponents have been motivated much more by theoretical concerns than by historical precedent. Theological resistance to the quest for the historical Jesus boils down to the fear that historiography will dominate all theological reflection. If historians claim to enjoy the surest means to the truth of Jesus, then their conclusions, and only theirs, will control what can and cannot be held by Christian faith. All other sources for theological reflection will become secondary and derive their validity solely from the basis of what the historians provide.

A fear of domination clearly animates the leading contemporary critic of the quest, the Catholic exegete Luke Timothy Johnson. His book *The Real Jesus* (1996) appears at first glance to be a broadside against some of the most radical proponents of the quest, especially those connected to the Jesus Seminar.[21] A closer look, however, reveals that Johnson's ire is directed against a pernicious impression that results when theological attention is lavished on the quest. "The most destructive effect of the Jesus Seminar and recent historical Jesus books," Johnson warns, "has been the perpetuation of the notion that history somehow determines faith, and that for faith to be correct, the historical accounts that gave rise to it have to be verifiable."[22]

Johnson relies upon a combination of historical and theological arguments to make his case against the quest. With respect to history, Johnson offers fairly standard arguments that the fragmentary and perspectival nature of the historical sources impose severe limitations on any attempt to reconstruct the life of Jesus and the origins of Christianity.[23] Of more particular interest is his conclusion that the limitations are such that the careful historian is confronted with a drastic dilemma: either accept the historically unsecured narrative framework of the Gospel of Mark or be content with disconnected and rather uninteresting facts about Jesus. The dilemma consists in the fact that, while our knowledge of the context, antiquity, and sources of Mark's witness must remain forever tenuous, that witness is absolutely necessary for arranging what is historically probable into a meaningful whole. Once the framework of Mark is rejected all historical controls slip away and the quest for the historical Jesus, even if carried out with sobriety and erudition, becomes an exercise in rank speculation. Thus, while the chronology of Mark cannot be substantiated historically without it, "the various elements in the story become free-floating 'pieces' that can be arranged according to whatever principle or grid or structure is imposed on them."[24] This argument allows Johnson to broaden his critique of the quest to include not only what he characterizes as the sloppy and self-interested scholarship of figures like Barbara Thiering and Robert Funk (the founder of the Jesus Seminar), who demand drastic changes in Christian belief in light of their discoveries, but also more scholarly and conservative practitioners like John P. Meier and N. T. Wright.[25]

Johnson's insistence on the importance of Mark for our knowledge of Jesus dovetails with his theological concerns. The Gospel of Mark represents for Johnson not fodder for historical investigation but a literary aftereffect of the impression made on an early Christian community by the reality of Jesus during and after his earthly life. Its significance lies more in how the entire narrative communicates the essence of Jesus' character as one of obedience to God and loving service to others than in the discrete events and sayings it records of his ministry and fate.

Moreover, the portrayal of Jesus' character in Mark does not stand alone but must be interpreted in light of the diverse narratives and portraits found in Matthew, Luke, John, and even Paul. Here Johnson relies on the church's wisdom to remember Jesus through four differing Gospels instead of one. The attempt of historians to flatten the diversity of these narratives and to bypass the faith-perspective that informs them constitutes a rejection of two millennia of Christian practice.

> [W]hat the questers for the historical Jesus seem never to have grasped, is that the church canonized separate *literary compositions* called Gospels. These texts *as* texts are read in the assembly as the word of God, are debated in council for the direction of the church, are used in theology for the understanding of faith. By canonizing four such versions of gospel, the church obviously also accepted them in all their diversity as *normative*. That is to say, their normative character is not found *outside* these texts and apart from their diversity, but *within* these texts in all their diversity.[26]

This diversity is not ultimate, however, and Johnson makes a strong argument that a common pattern links together all the New Testament portraits of Jesus.[27] It is within this pattern that the believer encounters the one whom Johnson calls "the real Jesus." This is not the Jesus accessible to the dispassionate probing of historians, but the Jesus whose living presence created the early church and still abides, transforming its members through the power of the Holy Spirit.[28] It is this "real Jesus" rather the "historical Jesus" who ought to occupy the attention of believer and theologian alike.[29]

Johnson's strategy to thwart the quest's reach into theology by insisting on a distinction between the historical Jesus and the object of Christian faith has an impressive pedigree going back to Martin Kähler (1835-1912). Like Johnson, Kähler had nothing but scorn for efforts to present historical reconstructions of Jesus as theologically significant.[30] In the place of an historically tenuous and uninteresting "historical Jesus" (*historisch*), Kähler counseled theologians to prize the "historic Jesus" (*geschichtlich*). While the "historical Jesus" is a figure of the dead past at the mercy of changing historical fashions, the "historic Jesus" transcends the momentary and lives through his continual impact on ongoing Christian tradition.[31] Since Kähler there have been a host of efforts to label that figure who is to be counterposed to the "historical Jesus," such as "the Christ of faith,"[32] "the existential historical Jesus,"[33] "the kerygmatic Christ,"[34] and Johnson's own "the real Jesus."

These distinctions, despite their unsettling variety, can be credited with upholding the integrity of theology as a discipline independent of history. They highlight the fact that the theologian employs particular methods and sources for discerning the truth of Jesus that go well beyond what is appropriate for the historian. The Jesus who is accessible to historical methods is simply not enough to sustain theological reflection. At the same time, these distinctions have proved much less helpful at delineating any positive value the quest might have or in explaining why it ought to be denied any such value. This is unfortunate because there is a clear conceptual difference between the desire to distinguish the historical Jesus from the object of Christian faith and the judgment that regards the former as irrelevant for theology. Apart from an appreciation of this gap, a justifiable distinction can turn easily into a simple refusal to deal frankly with the theological issues involved in a precise delineation of the quest's importance.

When this happens, a laudable attempt to gain greater clarity can end up creating more confusion. Two examples should suffice.

A first example of such confusion comes from John P. Meier, the leading Roman Catholic contributor to the Third Quest. His multi-volume and yet unfinished *A Marginal Jew* will surely stand as a lasting example of careful, erudite, and clearly written Jesus research.[35] Yet, for all Meier's clarity on the subject of the historical Jesus, it is difficult to gain a clear picture of the theological value he bestows upon his project. On the one hand, Meier can be quite forceful in distinguishing the goal of his research—the Jesus accessible to historical methods—from the object of Christian faith. One finds statements such as "the historical Jesus is not the real Jesus"[36] and "the constantly changing, often contradictory portraits of the historical Jesus served up by scholars . . . cannot be the object of Christian faith for the universal Church."[37] Yet, Meier asserts with equal vigor that while the historical Jesus has no direct relevance for faith, he "must be an integral part of modern *theology*."[38] In particular, he finds that the value of an historically secured reconstruction lies in its capacity to rein in overly mythical or ideological renderings of Jesus.

> The usefulness of the historical Jesus to theology is that he ultimately eludes all our neat theological programs; he brings all of them into question by refusing to fit into the boxes we create for him . . . equally offensive to right and left wings. . . . His refusal to be held fast by any given school of thought is what drives theologians onward into new paths; hence the historical Jesus remains a constant stimulus to theological renewal.[39]

It is hard to disagree with such an assertion, but it is equally difficult to square it with Meier's claims that the historical Jesus bears little relevance for faith. If theology is understood as "faith seeking understanding," as Meier explicitly holds, how could something so relevant to the understanding of faith as our knowledge of Jesus not be relevant to faith itself? Moreover, it is not clear whether Meier believes that the historical Jesus possesses a greater capacity for ideological correction than the Jesus presented in the canonical Gospels or explicated in church teaching. Do the particular methods the historian employs in order to recapture something true about Jesus give the results a potentially special power in this regard?

Similar questions haunt the theologian who seeks to limit the theological significance of the quest to its apologetic value. The apologetic power of historical research first became apparent to theologians in the wake of Reimarus's and Strauss's attacks on the historical veracity of the New Testament. Since their assertions about Jesus were in grave conflict with Christian faith, theologians had no other choice but to meet fire with fire. The novelty of the challenge hampered the speed of the response, to be sure, but a number of Christian intellectuals came to recognize that just at the time theology had learned to engage challenges arising from philosophy and science, history itself had become an unavoidable field of debate. Moreover, most who took up this challenge realized that only standardized historical methods would stand a chance of convincing the skeptic or the concerned believer.[40] In this way, the quest became viewed as a necessary part of the complete apologetic arsenal for the defense of the truth of Christianity's claims about Jesus.

The apologetic use of the quest clearly enjoys the support of Christian theology's longstanding commitment to the unity of all truth, whatever its source. If theology is to make claims relating the truth of Jesus to the truth of God, the legitimate claims of historiography concerning the truth of Jesus require no less attention than that given any other intellectual discipline. At the same time, there are reasons to believe that this particular intersection of faith and reason demands particular consideration and makes its difficult to place the quest comfortably within that realm of theology that is traditionally reserved for apologetics. While the claims of philosophy or natural science, for example, normally concern the reasonableness of the act of faith, the quest is concerned with the historical truth of Jesus and thus is inseparable from the truth of the faith itself. For this reason, no sharp separation between the historical Jesus and the object of Christian faith is possible without denying the capacity of the historian to attain any truth about Jesus whatsoever. Short of this extreme step, theologians must seek greater clarity on the precise place of the quest in their enterprise.[41]

A successful articulation of the role of the quest in theology must address the concern that bestowing any theological significance upon historical research into Jesus is tantamount to an abdication of the proper province of the theologian to the historian. It must incorporate the wisdom behind the commonly stated dictum that the historical

Jesus is not the real Jesus. At the same time, since there is a good deal of conceptual space between specifying the theological importance of the quest and denying its importance, it will be possible to include what many theologians find attractive in the quest. The following section seeks to illuminate some of that conceptual space by exploring a debate within contemporary epistemology over whether and to what extent experience can be foundational for human knowledge.

The Question of Foundations of Knowledge

To claim that epistemological debates concerning whether experience is foundational for knowledge can be helpful for the application of the quest for the historical Jesus may strike the reader as odd. Nevertheless, it is striking how often opponents of the quest formulate their critique in the language of foundations—specifically, raising the concern that the product of historical research might serve as a basis for either faith or theological reflection. An early and influential example of this approach is Wilhelm Herrmann. Aware of the necessarily tentative and probabilistic character of all historical conclusions, Herrmann warned that "it is a fatal error to attempt to establish the basis of faith by means of historical investigation."[42] Luke Timothy Johnson makes a similar assertion that "the historical Jesus is too fragile a base from which to make the Christian interpretation."[43] Even Elizabeth Johnson, who views the quest as necessary to allow the historical Jesus to challenge and refresh the Christian imagination, insists that "it is a misuse of the historical Jesus to employ it to ground or validate in whole or in part the kerygma."[44]

In each case, there is an implication that the real danger the quest poses to the integrity of theology lies not in granting it a place but in treating its conclusions as foundational. The history of the quest is, to be sure, replete with assertions that a specific reconstruction of Jesus is the basis upon which all justifiable theological claims from now on must rest. Nonetheless, since there is no necessary connection between conceding the importance of the quest and granting it foundational status, the possibility arises whether the quest can be conceived as theologically important without making it the basis for all claims about Jesus.

Pursuing this possibility entails an inquiry into recent philosophical reflection on the question of foundations in any branch of knowledge. In particular, there has been a debate within analytic philosophy over whether empirical experience provides a certain foundation for all justified beliefs or whether knowledge proceeds without foundations by relating beliefs to one another to attain a coherent whole. In the remainder of this paper I want to show how a particular resolution to this problem sheds necessary light on how theologians might appropriate historical research.

The Debate between Foundationalist and Coherentist Epistemologies

Philosophical criticism of foundationalism—the "doctrine that knowledge constitutes a structure the foundations of which support all the rest but themselves need no support"[45]—is prevalent, even fashionable. Most theologians by now are familiar with the notion that even the most mundane movement from sensory experience to the justification of a consequent proposition involves a complexity that rules out self-justifying and indubitable foundations for knowledge. Indeed, a number of prominent theologians have written books applying the problematic status of foundations to the question of theological method.[46] Less remarked upon in the theological literature are the difficulties encountered in attempting to replace foundationalism with a nonfoundationalist theory of knowledge.[47]

The most commonly championed successor has been the theory of coherence, which holds that "what justifies a belief is not that it can be an infallible belief with an indubitable object, nor that it has been proved deductively on such a basis, but that it coheres with a comprehensive system of beliefs."[48] This theory has much to commend it. Its rejection of a noninferential fundament upon which all knowledge rests not only avoids a host of problems but highlights the complex and open-ended process by which individual human subjects evaluate their beliefs. Moreover, an epistemology that operates only within systems of belief can better absorb the insights of hermeneutical philosophies that stress the importance of the subjective, social, and cultural factors at every stage and level of human experience and understanding. This compatibility with hermeneutical analysis has led some to champion the theory of coherence as the long-awaited bridge between the analytic and continental traditions of philosophy.[49]

Despite these strengths, however, the theory of coherence has been under constant assault by philosophers who find it unable to account adequately for the role we intuitively grant empirical experience in guiding us toward true beliefs and away from false ones. In particular, critics normally raise two types of objections. The first holds that the theory opens up the unacceptable possibility of two equally coherent but alternative descriptions of the same reality; the second warns of a fully consistent worldview, which would have no plausible claim to reflect reality.[50] In each case the root problem is the same: if a theoretical system is justified to the extent that it is internally coherent, there is no clear epistemological role for experiential input from extramental reality. Indeed, it is difficult to explain on purely coherentist principles why the possession of a tightly coherent system of beliefs would not justify ignoring an experience merely because it threatens the system's coherence. Critics argue that when coherence is given epistemic priority over experience the possibility of correction from outside disappears and relativism creeps in.

The relativist consequences of the theory of coherence have been explicated by Richard Rorty. His influential work *Philosophy and the Mirror of Nature* chronicles the fall of foundationalism and upholds coherence as typical of how most subjects justify their beliefs. Yet, Rorty makes clear that the adoption of coherence as the standard of justification means that there is no objective way to separate true beliefs from false ones. What may count as good reasons for belief is decided wholly with reference to previously established systems of theory and practice and will vary with the time, place, and personality of the judge. "Nothing counts as justification," Rorty states, "unless by reference to what we already accept, and . . . there is no way to get outside our beliefs and our language so as to find some test other than coherence."[51] Such an assertion appears to equate epistemology with foundationalism, and its collapse with the end of the epistemological project.

Rorty's equation of coherence as the standard for justified beliefs with relativism has received support recently from an unlikely source— Laurence BonJour, for years a leading defender of the theory of coherentism.[52] BonJour had been well known for insisting that if coherentist epistemology was to overcome the charge of relativism it had to add an "observation requirement." The theory "must require that in order for the beliefs of a cognitive system to be even candidates for empirical justification, that system must contain laws attributing a high degree of reliability to a reasonable variety of cognitively spontaneous beliefs."[53] Recently, however, concerns for the corrective role of experience have compelled BonJour to move away from the theory of coherence altogether and embrace a moderate form of foundationalism. While admitting that serious objections to foundationalism remain, he now believes that there is no viable alternative if relativism is to be avoided.[54]

A Middle Way: Foundherentism

Other analytic philosophers reject both the simplifications of foundationalism and the relativistic consequences of coherentism and opt for a third way. A particularly relevant example for our purposes is the "foundherentism" advocated by the philosopher Susan Haack.[55] While her attempt at a linguistic merger is admittedly awkward, it expresses well the conviction that a new epistemological approach is required that retains the strengths of both foundationalism and coherentism while avoiding their missteps. "We need," Haack asserts, "a new approach which allows the relevance of experience to empirical justification, but without postulating any privileged class of basic beliefs or requiring that relations of support be essentially one directional, in other words, a foundherentist theory."[56]

Haack presents foundherentism as a resolution of the tensions endemic to each of the leading theories of justification. The great insight of foundationalism—and one worth preserving, according to Haack—is that the more a belief is "anchored in experience" the more justified a person is in holding it to be true.[57] Experience of the world makes a claim on all who desire to know, and a convincing theory of what justifies our empirical beliefs must afford experiential evidence a central role. Yet, the role that foundationalism assigns to experience has provided an opening for critics. According to the pure model, foundationalism asserts that experience yields basic and incorrigible beliefs upon which other non-basic beliefs can be inferentially justified.[58] There are good reasons to believe, however, that the notion of a "basic belief" is profoundly confused. While experience is properly viewed as causally related to justified belief (e.g., seeing a green car makes me believe that a green car is present), an experience, regardless of how strong or simple, is not a belief. Beliefs are logical creatures and their justification requires not only an underlying experience but a host of intermeshing logical relations as well.[59] Even more damaging to the cause of foundationalism is its unrealistic portrayal of the structure of justification as uni-directional, always moving from basic to derivative beliefs.[60]

The theory of coherence's strongest card, according to Haack, is its much more realistic description of how human beings actually go about justifying their beliefs. Never a mere matter of working up from an undeniable experiential bedrock, justification is a complex interrelating of beliefs—some directly related to an experience, others more remotely—to form a logically coherent whole. At the same time, advocates of the theory of coherence have paid too high a price for their advantage over foundationalism. Their correct insistence that no belief is justified by experience alone ends with no way to account for the special role experience plays in epistemology. Absent such a role, beliefs are justified solely by their relationship to other beliefs without reference to anything outside the system. To expose this flaw in coherentist reasoning, Haack employs the image of two drunken sailors. Like two sailors leaning upon the other but each incapable of supporting his own weight, beliefs about the world with no specific experiential evidence lack any support from the world.[61] In other words, while justification is not solely about experience, neither can it proceed without it.

In order to articulate how foundherentism constitutes a viable alternative to foundationalist and coherentist theories of justification, Haack offers the analogy of the crossword puzzle. To solve a crossword puzzle, one must attend not only to the stand-alone clues provided, but also to how each proposed answer fits with the others.

> My approach will be informed by the analogy of a crossword puzzle—where there is undeniably pervasive mutual support among entries but, equally undeniably, no vicious circle. The clues are the analog of experiential evidence, already-completed intersecting entries the analog of reasons. As how reasonable a crossword entry is depends both on the clues and on other intersecting entries, the idea is, so how justified an empirical belief is depends on experiential evidence and reasons working together.[62]

Of course, anyone who does crosswords knows that a pencil works better than a pen. The ambiguous nature of some clues means that an answer that seemed right when calculated independently simply will not fit and must be reconsidered. Likewise, as crucial as experience is in justifying beliefs—one cannot hope to do a crossword without being right about some of the clues—it is never sufficient. Rather, information derived from experience cannot translate into a justified belief without the support of other beliefs, beliefs that in turn are on their own way to justification.

Haack seeks to capture the tentative nature of all justification by a particular formulation of what epistemology seeks to explain: "A is more or less justified, at t, in believing that p, depending on how good his evidence is."[63] The first thing to note is that justification becomes a matter of degree. A single piece of evidence is seldom conclusive but most often exists within a network of supportive and non-supportive bits of information. Together they lead the person to a sense of being more or less justified in holding a particular proposition as true. Second, one's sense for how justified a belief is will depend on the nature and extent of the evidence available at the time the judgment is made. Thus, someone may be more or less justified in believing a proposition at a certain time than she will be later on. Finally, all of these qualifications indicate that justification for Haack is personal. She rejects the more common epistemological formulation "p is justified if and only if . . ." because it leaves out of consideration the fact that experiences are had only by persons. What counts as "good evidence" will depend on who is asking the question and who will be affected by individual differences in intensity of interest, kinds and depth of background knowledge, and intelligence.

The inevitable personal character of justification, however, does not mean that it is subjective. Against the relativism of Rorty and others, Haack insists that while judgments concerning one's evidence are perspectival, the standards of what counts as good evidence are not.[64] For example, two individuals could share the same belief but one be justified and the other not. Mary is convinced that Tom stole her radio because she thinks he looks dishonest. Jane believes the same thing, but her evidence includes actually having seen Tom with Mary's radio. According to foundherentisim, Jane's belief is more anchored in experience and thereby more justified than Mary's. As Haack puts it: "quality of evidence is objective, but judgments of quality of evidence are perspectival."[65]

The strength of Haack's proposal lies in its ability to absorb the insights of foundationalist and coherentist approaches to epistemology while taking with equal seriousness the challenges that each poses to the other. Foundherentism, accordingly, takes up what is attractive about both to form a new synthesis. The necessity of experience for justification is acknowledged but in concert with an acceptance that beliefs are justified through their relationship to other beliefs. Just as the solved crossword is the result of answered clues being integrated with other answers, good evidence for justification consists in both experience and the interlocking of beliefs. Thus the project of epistemology is saved by a recognition that experience need not be foundational to be relevant.

Applying the Quest in Light of Foundherentism

Haack's effort to combine foundationalism and the theory of coherence illuminates, I believe, the central issue at play in the integration of the historical research into theological reflection.[66] It provides theologians with a way to proceed when they wish to apply credible historical results of the quest without thereby granting them complete power over all theological judgments. The first step lies in a clear rejection of any notion that the historical Jesus—the figure accessible to historiography—is the foundation upon which faith and theology rest. This assertion, however, says less about the theological value of the quest for the historical Jesus than it does about the problems inherent in conceiving any intellectual endeavor in foundationalist terms. Consequently, the quest can be important without being foundational. Its importance stems from the fact that Christian theology and the quest for the historical Jesus, despite real methodological differences, both seek to make assertions that are true because they are anchored in the truth of Jesus. Thus, to the extent that historical research can recover aspects of Jesus' reality once available to experience, its conclusions enjoy a status analogous to empirical experience in foundherentism.

Experience derives its epistemological significance in foundherentism from its potential to deliver information about an aspect of extramental reality. The responsible knowers desire this input because they realize that the more their beliefs are anchored in experience the more justified they are in asserting their truth. Experience, however, does not settle the matter because the justification of any proposition involves the support of other beliefs as well. While experience is important, the careful weigher of evidence knows that it is not sufficient. A similar logic is at work in the relationship between the quest for the historical Jesus and the Christian theologian. As an effort to uncover truths about Jesus, the quest has the potential to deliver information that the responsible theologian desires. Knowing the fundamental importance of Jesus for Christianity, the theologian realizes that the more her beliefs are anchored in what Jesus did and said the more justified they will be. Whether any particular historical assertion can provide such an anchor will be determined independent of theological concerns and on historiographical grounds alone.[67] Yet, the theological value of a credible assertion will prove its value for theology only as part of a theological system.

The desire of all Christian theology to formulate beliefs that attain ever greater adequacy to an aspect of reality—the life, death, and resurrection of Jesus of Nazareth—means that it is bound to treat historical research into Jesus as potentially decisive input. This evidence will come to the attention of the theologian in the form of historical assertions about Jesus' actions and teachings, assertions which by their very nature will be partial, tentative, and influenced by the perspective of the historian. Yet, since the possibility exists that one of them may have captured a truth about Jesus, the theologian must go through the difficult task of assessing levels of historical credibility. In the majority of cases no strong impression will be made because either the information is not new or the evidence is too shaky, and the theologians, unperturbed, will proceed with their work. Occasionally, however, an historian's assertion is judged to be both highly credible and novel enough to affect an area of theological reflection.

It is at this point that the epistemological stance of the theologian becomes significant. If a foundationalist approach is adopted, the historical judgment will be treated as a secure basis upon which to build a new theological understanding. All other sources of knowledge proper to theology will become subservient to the new fact. A coherentist approach, on the other hand, will decide whether or not to accept the new claim in light of its fit with previously held beliefs about Jesus. In this case, a particularly troublesome assertion may be rejected on that basis alone, but at the risk of losing theology's anchor in Jesus. A stance tutored in foundherentism, in contrast to both, will recognize that the importance of historical research into Jesus is not lessened by the fact that even a highly credible assertion is something other than foundational. Consequently, a claim about Jesus will not be dismissed because it is a threat to the system since the system is only as good as its overall connection to a reality outside itself. A highly credible assertion will be incorporated into the system in order that the entire system be more adequate to the reality of Jesus, even if that requires a systematic realignment.

By way of example, let us imagine a theologian working on the question of whether there ought to be an evangelical mission directed to those of the Jewish faith. If the project is to have any validity for the Christian church, it will be informed by a variety of theological sources: the biblical witness, church doctrines, the painful history of Christian anti-Semitism, and so on. In addition, the theologian will wish to consult historical research into what can be known about Jesus' attitude to the Judaism of his time. Given the Third Quest's emphasis on the Jewishness of Jesus and the desire of its practitioners to get beyond the rather polemical portraits found in the Gospels, she will find much that is potentially useful. Gratitude, however, most likely will turn into exasperation upon the discovery of a lack of consensus. For example, she will be informed by E. P. Sanders that while Jesus was critical of the Judaism of his day that criticism was centered on his belief that God would destroy the Temple as a prelude to the restoration of Israel.[68] A slightly different position will be found in N. T. Wright, for whom Jesus' criticisms were more theological in nature and focused on Israel's failure to embrace its universal mission.[69] Further inquiry may bring her to the Jewish quester, Paula Fredriksen. In contrast to both Sanders and Wright, Fredriksen argues that there was little substantial disagreement separating Jesus and the Jewish leaders of his time.[70]

These differences may convince our theologian that the historical issue is too controverted and that she best rely upon other theological resources. Indeed, she might use the lack of consensus on the nature of Jesus' position to weaken the hold of the anti-Jewish polemics found in the Gospels and allow a break with traditional attitudes. Another possibility is that she will find one of the reconstructions more likely than the others and incorporate it in her proposal. What role it will play will depend on how convinced she is concerning what Jesus believed or did. If she is only mildly convinced, the historical claim will require a good deal of support from other trusted beliefs. If she is very convinced, other theological sources will have to be adjusted in order to attain a better fit with this new piece of evidence. In each case, her degree of confidence in what Jesus actually did and said will determine what role the quest plays in her particular resolution of this theological problem.

Conclusion

This essay has proposed that the issue of foundationalism is relevant for understanding how the quest for the historical Jesus can be so theologically attractive to some and so worrisome to others. Those who find the quest beneficial to the task of theology view historical research as a means to arrive at some truths about what Jesus did and said. The quest's attraction, therefore, is organically tied to the proclamation that in Jesus God has been revealed. To learn more about Jesus is to learn more about God. Those who worry about incorporating the quest into theology fear that historiography will come to dominate theology, distort its particular methodology, and crowd out its traditional sources.

While the history of the quest shows the legitimacy of this concern, it need not blur the distinction between bestowing foundational status on the quest and allowing significance to its credible results. The conceptual space created by acknowledging this distinction has been explored by a recent proposal in epistemology. Susan Haack's foundherentism provides a model for viewing empirical experience as significant, even decisive, for the justification of empirical belief without denying the role that others' beliefs play. In an analogous way, it can be said that just as experience is necessary but not sufficient for the justification of empirical belief, credible historical assertions about Jesus are necessary but not sufficient for the formulation and justification of theological statements and theories.

Notes

[1]Leander E. Keck has put the matter well: "If Jonathan Edwards's sinners had cause to worry about their fate in the hands of an angry God, the historical Jesus might well have been uneasy about his destiny among critics and theologians. Still, he has remarkable resilience and endurance. Ironically, today it is the critic who is insecure, for two centuries of work have not made it safe to speak of the place of the historical Jesus in preaching and in theology" (*A Future for the His-*

torical Jesus: The Place of Jesus in Preaching and Theology [Nashville: Abingdon Press, 1971], 17).

[2] One of the best-known Jesus scholars, John Dominic Crossan, openly acknowledges that the diversity of results runs the danger of making the quest a "bad scholarly joke" and that "it is impossible to avoid the suspicion that historical Jesus research is a very safe place to do theology and call it history, to do autobiography and call it biography" (*The Historical Jesus: The Life of a Mediterranean Jewish Peasant* [New York: HarperSanFrancisco, 1991], xxviii).

[3] This is the judgment of Albert Schweitzer in his *The Quest for the Historical Jesus: A Critical Study of Its Progress from Reimarus to Wrede*, trans. W. Montgomery (Baltimore: The Johns Hopkins University Press, 1998 [1906]), still the best survey of the First Quest. For discussions of possible predecessors see Raymond Martin, *The Elusive Messiah: A Philosophical Overview of the Quest for the Historical Jesus* (Boulder, Col.: Westview Press, 1999), 30-35, and *The Historical Jesus Quest: Landmarks in the Search for the Jesus of History*, ed. Gregory W. Dawes (Louisville: Westminster/John Knox Press, 1999), 1-53.

[4] Reimarus died without publishing any of his work on the historical Jesus. Fragments of his very large manuscript (over 4,000 pages) were published without attribution by G. E. Lessing between 1774 and 1778. A selection of these can be found in *Reimarus: Fragments*, ed. Charles H. Talbert, trans. R. S. Frazer (Philadelphia: Fortress Press, 1970).

[5] For a thorough treatment of Strauss's position on the historical Jesus see Gregory W. Dawes, *The Historical Jesus Question: The Challenge of History to Religious Authority* (Louisville: Westminster John Knox Press, 2001), 76-121.

[6] *The Life of Jesus Critically Examined*, ed. Peter C. Hodgson, trans. George Eliot (Philadelphia: Fortress Press, 1972). The English translation is taken from the fourth edition (1860).

[7] See George P. Fisher, *Essays on the Supernatural Origin of Christianity* (New York: Scribner & Co., 1865, rev. ed. 1870), and J. B. Lightfoot, *Essays on the Work Entitled 'Supernatural Religion,'* 2nd ed. (New York: Macmillan, 1893).

[8] Prominent examples include F. W. Farrar, *Life of Christ* (New York: E. P. Dutton, 1874) and Alfred Edersheim, *The Life and Times of Jesus the Messiah*, 2 vols., 8th rev. ed. (New York: Longmans, Greenman, 1904). For analysis of this period see Daniel L. Pals, *The Victorian "Lives" of Jesus* (San Antonio: Trinity University Press, 1982).

[9] Schweitzer, *The Quest for the Historical Jesus*, n.3.

[10] "It is nothing less than a misfortune for modern theology that it mixes history with everything and ends by being proud of the skill with which it finds its owns thought . . . in Jesus, and represents Him as expressing them" (ibid., 400).

[11] Ibid., 399.

[12] Walter Weaver has shown that the common view that Schweitzer brought the quest to an end needs qualification. See his *The Historical Jesus in the Twentieth Century (1900-1950)* (Harrisburg, Penn.: Trinity Press International, 1999), 45-71. Significant works of this period include: Joseph Klausner, *Jesus of Nazareth*, trans. Herbert Darby (New York: Macmillan, 1925); Shirley Jackson Case, *The*

Historicity of Jesus (Chicago: University of Chicago Press, 1912); *Jesus: A New Biography* (Chicago: University of Chicago Press, 1927); and Maurice Goguel, *The Life of Jesus*, trans. Olive Wyon (New York: Macmillan, 1933).

[13]"The Problem of the Historical Jesus," in *Essays on New Testament Themes*, trans. Theodore M. Greene (London: SCM Press, 1964), 15-47.

[14]"A primary concern of the Gospels is unmistakably the particularity with which the eschatological event is bound to *this* man from Nazareth, to the arena of Palestine and to a concrete time with its special circumstances" (ibid., 31).

[15]The definitive survey remains James M. Robinson, *A New Quest of the Historical Jesus and Other Essays* (Philadelphia: Fortress Press, 1983).

[16]Stephen C. Neill and N. Thomas Wright, *The Interpretation of the New Testament 1861-1986*, 2nd ed. (New York: Oxford University Press, 1988), 379-403.

[17]E. P. Sanders, *Jesus and Judaism* (Philadelphia: Fortress Press, 1985). Sanders lays out his method and its distinction from the New Quest in the book's introduction.

[18]A significant dissenter is John Dominic Crossan. He adopts Wright's term but describes the development differently: "This Third Quest is programmatically different on three fronts: its *materials* involve both intra- and extra-canonical documents; its *methods* integrate a crosscultural anthropological or social-scientific, a historical, and a literary level or vector; and its *philosophical bases* are more postmodern than positivistic, rationalistic, romantic, or existential" ("The Historical Jesus in Earliest Christianity," in *Jesus and Faith: A Conversation on the Work of John Dominic Crossan*, ed. Jeffrey Carlson and Robert A. Ludwig [Maryknoll, N.Y.: Orbis Books, 1994], 160). It might be significant that Wright has categorized Crossan and the rest of the Jesus Seminar as belonging to the out-dated Second Quest. For Wright's discussion see his own contribution to the quest in *Jesus and the Victory of God* (Philadelphia: Fortress Press, 1996), 28-82.

[19]Good surveys of this scholarship include Mark Allen Powell, *Jesus as Figure of History: How Modern Historians View the Man from Galilee* (Louisville: Westminster/John Knox Pres, 1998); Bruce and Craig A. Evans, eds., *Studying the Historical Jesus: Evaluations of the State of Current Research* (Leiden: Brill, 1994); and Ben Witherington III, *The Jesus Quest: The Third Search for the Jew of Nazareth* (Downers Grove, Ill.: InterVarsity Press, 1995).

[20]Prominent examples include Hilarin Felder, *Christ and the Critics: A Defense of the Divinity of Jesus against the Attacks of Modern Skeptical Criticism*, trans. John L. Stoddard (New York: Benziger Brothers, 1924) and Léonce de Grandmaison, *Jesus Christ: His Person, His Message, His Credentials*, 3vols., trans. Basil Whelan, Douglas Carter (New York: Sheed & Ward, 1935-1937).

[21]Luke Timothy Johnson, *The Real Jesus: The Misguided Quest for the Historical Jesus and the Truth of the Traditional Gospels* (New York: HarperSanFrancisco, 1996).

[22]Ibid., 141.

[23]Ibid., 81-104. See esp. 121-22, where Johnson lists the facts about Jesus that have a high degree of probability.

[24]"Every quest for the historical Jesus begins to have credibility problems when

scholars try to push beyond this [Gospel] framework. . . . Once one begins with the recognition that the Gospel narratives are not constructed according to principles of chronology or causality, then the various elements in the story become free-floating 'pieces' that can be arranged according to whatever principle or grid or structure is imposed on them" (ibid., 127).

[25]For Johnson on Meier, see ibid., 128-9. Johnson's critique of the work of N. T. Wright is found in "A Historiographical Response to Wright's Jesus," in *Jesus & the Restoration of Israel: A Critical Assessment of N. T. Wright's "Jesus and the Victory of God*," ed. Carey C. Newman (Downers Grove, Ill.: InterVarsity Press, 1999), 206-24.

[26]Johnson, *The Real Jesus*, 148-9.

[27]Ibid., 146-50.

[28]Ibid., 151.

[29]Johnson has provided an example of this approach in his *Living Jesus: Learning the Heart of the Gospel* (San Francisco: HarperSanFrancisco, 1999).

[30]"I regard the entire Life-of-Jesus movement as a blind alley" (Martin Kähler, *The So-Called Historical Jesus and the Historic Biblical Christ*, ed. Ernst Wolf, trans. Carl Braaten [Philadelphia: Fortress Press, 1964], 46).

[31]Ibid., 64.

[32]This common phrase has its origins in D. F. Strauss's *The Christ of Faith and the Jesus of History: A Critique of Schleiermacher's "The Life of Jesus"* [1865], trans. Leander E. Keck (Philadelphia: Fortress Press, 1977).

[33]Schubert Ogden, *The Point of Christology* (London: SCM, 1982), 16.

[34]*The Historical Jesus and the Kerygmatic Christ*, ed. Carl E. Braaten and Roy A. Harrisville (New York/Nashville: Abingdon Press, 1964).

[35]John P. Meier, *A Marginal Jew: Rethinking the Historical Jesus*, 3 vols. (New York: Doubleday, 1991, 1994, 2001).

[36]Ibid., vol. 1, 21.

[37]Ibid., 198.

[38]Ibid., 199.

[39]Ibid., 200.

[40]The following statement of Hilarion Felder is emblematic of this approach: "If we, however, summon the opponents of the Christian revelation before the bar of fair, unclouded history, we, on our side, must of course be equally scrupulous. In this case, we must not, as apologists, presuppose either the faith or the scientific credibility of Christianity" (*Christ and the Critics*, 13).

[41]John P. Galvin has noted that while theologians have by and large acknowledged the importance of the quest for their work, "many important theological dimensions of issues relative to the Jesus of history remain disputed and obscure" ("From the Humanity of Christ to the Jesus of History: A Paradigm Shift in Catholic Christology," *Theological Studies* 55 [1994]: 257).

[42]Wilhelm Herrmann, *The Communion of the Christian with God, Described on the Basis of Luther's Statements*, ed. Robert T. Voelkel, trans. J. Sandys Stanyon and R. W. Stewart (Philadelphia: Fortress Press, 1971), 76.

[43]*The Real Jesus*, 14.

[44]Elizabeth Johnson, "The Theological Relevance of the Historical Jesus: A Debate and a Thesis," *The Thomist* 48 (1984): 41. Most recently she has written: "Correlating history and faith . . . allows a kind of mutual light to be shed back and forth between historical reasoning and truth in God through Jesus Christ. Here it is not thought in some simplistic way that history 'grounds' faith or gives rise to faith, which is always a gracious gift from God" ("The Word Was Made Flesh and Dwelt among Us: Jesus Research and Christian Faith," in *Jesus: A Colloquium in the Holy Land*, Doris Donnelly, ed. [New York: Continuum, 2001], 148-9).

[45]William Alston, "Two Types of Foundationalism," *The Journal of Philosophy* 73 (1976): 165.

[46]Among the many examples are Francis Schüssler Fiorenza, *Foundational Theology: Jesus and the Church* (New York: Crossroad, 1984); John Thiel, *Nonfoundationalism* (Minneapolis: Fortress Press, 1994); Ronald Thiemann, *Revelation and Theology: The Gospel as Narrated Promise* (Notre Dame: University of Notre Dame Press, 1987); and William Placher, *Unapologetic Theology: A Christian Voice in a Pluralist Conversation* (Louisville: Westminster/John Knox Press, 1989).

[47]A notable exception is the work of J. Wentzel van Huyssteen. In a series of books he has championed the usefulness of a movement within philosophy that he calls "postfoundationalism." In what follows I am indebted to many of his ideas. See *Theology and the Justification of Faith: Constructing Theories in Systematic Theology* (Grand Rapids: Eerdmans, 1989); *Essays in Postfoundationalist Theology* (Grand Rapids: Eerdmans, 1997); *Duet or Duel? Theology and Science in a Postmodern World* (London: SCM Press, 1998); and *The Shaping of Rationality: Toward Interdisciplinarity in Theology and Science* (Grand Rapids: Eerdmans, 1999).

[48]Ernest Sosa, "The Raft and the Pyramid: Coherence versus Foundations in the Theory of Knowledge," *Midwest Studies in Philosophy* 5 (1980): 3-25, at 7.

[49]This arguement is made, albeit briefly, in Jonathan Dancy's *Introduction to Contemporary Epistemology* (Cambridge: Oxford University Press, 1985), esp. 227-42. One finds the same conviction in the work of Nicholas Rescher, such as in *The Coherence Theory of Truth* (Oxford: Clarendon Press, 1973), and *A System of Pragmatic Idealism*, vol. 1 (Princeton: Princeton University Press, 1992).

[50]These criticisms and others are well summarized in Richard Fumerton, "A Critique of Coherentism," in *The Theory of Knowledge: Classical and Contemporary Readings*, 3rd ed., ed. Louis P. Pojman (Belman, Calif.: Wadsworth, 2003), 215-21.

[51]*Philosophy and the Mirror of Nature* (Princeton: Princeton University Press, 1979), 178.

[52]Laurence BonJour, *The Structure of Empirical Knowledge* (Cambridge: Harvard University Press, 1985).

[53]Ibid., 141.

[54]"My conclusion for the moment is twofold: (i) coherentism is pretty obviously untenable, indeed hopeless; and (ii) a very traditional version of experiential foundationalism can be successfully defended against the most immediate and

telling objection, even though it then faces a very familiar and serious problem for which no developed solution is yet available." Laurence BonJour, "The Dialectic of Foundationalism and Coherentism," *Blackwell's Guide to Epistemology*, ed. John Greco and Ernest Sosa (Malden, Mass.: Blackwell Publishers, 2001), 139.

[55]Haack's most complete articulation of her position to date appears in *Evidence and Inquiry: Towards Reconstruction in Epistemology* (Malden, Mass: Blackwell Publishers, 1993). More recent statements can be found in her response to critics in "Reply to Commentators," *Philosophy and Phenomenological Research* 56:3 (1996): 641-56; and "A Foundherentist Theory of Empirical Justification," in *The Theory of Knowledge: Classical and Contemporary Readings*, 3rd ed., ed. Louis P. Pojman (Belman, Calif.: Wadsworth, 2003), 237-47.

[56]Haack, "A Foundherentist Theory," 239.

[57]Haack, *Evidence and Inquiry*, 19.

[58]Ibid., 14. Haack is well aware of the variety of options both within foundationalism and the theory of coherence. Her justification for dealing with pure models of each is that the moderated forms in which each side has borrowed insights from the other are inherently unstable and "lean" in the direction of her proposal. She makes this point most sharply in chapters dedicated to the moderate foundationalism of C. I. Lewis (34-51) and BonJour's earlier coherentist position (52-72).

[59]Haack, *Evidence and Inquiry*, 29.

[60]Ibid., 31-32.

[61]"The fundamental objection is this: that because coherentism allows no non-belief input—no role to experience or the world [*sic*]—it cannot be satisfactory; that unless it is acknowledged that the justification of an empirical belief requires such input, it could not be supposed that a belief's being justified could be an indication of its truth, of its correctly representing how the world is" (ibid., 27).

[62]Haack, "A Foundherentist Theory," 242.

[63]Ibid., 240.

[64]Haack's case against relativism can be found in *Evidence and Inquiry* (182-202) and *Manifesto of a Passionate Moderate: Unfashionable Essays* (Chicago: University of Chicago Press, 1998), 149-166.

[65]Haack, "A Foundherentist Theory," 244.

[66]My use of Haack is limited to the formal aspects of her proposal. Haack herself has yet to address the issue of religious experiences and seems to consider them as irrelevant for epistemology (*Evidence and Inquiry*, 214). Van Huyssteen has criticized Haack for this seemingly arbitrary exclusion (*The Shaping of Rationality*, 232-33).

[67]I must admit that I can find no rationale for asserting a special Christian historiography that is guided by the contents of faith. Such an approach collapses into fideism as soon as an historical assertion is dismissed solely on the grounds that it disagrees with Christian teaching. While it may be permitted to say that a faith-guided historiography can say *more* than a reason-guided historiography, it is always fideistic to claim that it can say something *different*.

[68]"Jesus looked for the imminent direct intervention of God in history, the elimi-

nation of evil and evildoers, the building of a new and glorious temple, and the reassembly of Israel within himself and his disciples as leading figures in it" (Sanders, *Jesus and Judaism*, 132).

[69]"Jesus was claiming to be speaking for Israel's god, her scriptures, and her true vocation. Israel was trusting in her ancestral religious symbols; Jesus was claiming to speak for the reality to which those symbols pointed, and to show that, by her concentration on them, Israel has turned inwards upon herself and was being not only disobedient, but dangerously disobedient, to her god's vision for her, his vocation that she should be the light of the world" (Wright, *Jesus and the Victory of God*, 442).

[70]See the discussion of Jesus in the temple in Paula Fredricksen, *Jesus of Nazareth King of the Jews: A Jewish Life and the Emergence of Christianity* (New York: Alfred Knopf, 1999), 207-14.

Part II

INQUIRY

The Future of Christology:
Expanding Horizons, Religious Pluralism, and the Divinity of Jesus

Roger Haight

Every talk that deals with the future begins with an apology that says, essentially, that when we talk of the future, we don't really know what we are talking about: the future does not exist and, when it becomes present, it always turns out differently than we imagined. But since everyone knows this, we can relax about the quality of this speculative discourse. In effect we may say, because none of us knows the future, we are all free to talk about it.

But some disciplines can do better than others in extrapolating from the present into the future. Statistical sciences can come pretty close to determining some things: for example, except for New England, in predicting the weather. For my part, I want to enter this discussion with a method or at least a strategy. This consists of extrapolating or projecting the future on the basis of present experience together with certain familiar patterns that measure or channel changes in human thinking and valuing. I do not draw these models from academic theory, but from common experience and common sense.[1] I remain on this common-sense level in order to highlight where the development I refer to is occurring. My attention focuses upon development in the ideas and attitudes of educated middle-class Christians in the mainline churches who are being drawn along with the times and culture in which we live. In other words, development here is being carried by the Christian faithful at large insofar as they reflect on the matters under discussion.

I am aware and you will become aware of the tentative character of this effort. This projection into the future is not controlled by statistical data, or necessary axioms, or the laws of logic. So let me state my

47

method and procedure in the pointed way in which I understand them. This is an effort at reading the signs of the times in the American churches, and my evidence rarely transcends an appeal to our experience today. I make this appeal in two stages. I will first point to three general patterns that help illumine what goes on in the process of how people's thinking develops or changes. If such patterns obtain generally, they should also apply in religious matters. These descriptions of how development occurs will thus serve as a night-light for peering into the future. In other words, in the second step, on the basis of these three ways of understanding how development occurs, I will guess how christology might develop. What you will have to judge is whether these descriptions of development have any merit, and whether the data I feed into them yields the projections that I foresee.

Let me summarize the structure of the argument: the development has two parts. Part one contains three homely descriptions of the dynamics of how people change their views. Part two applies these patterns to the development of christology in two areas. The first is the area of comparative theology, which may be considered as a discipline closely related to the practice of interreligious dialogue, but which I treat on the level of becoming aware of the other religions and the impact this makes. The second is the question of the divinity of Jesus and how this is to be experienced and understood in the future.

Three Patterns of How Development Occurs

Development in people's thinking occurs in three different ways: *spatial contexts* change, *temporal contexts* also change, and *experiential or mental horizons* expand. These terms do not constitute theories of development, but are meant as phenomenological descriptions that appeal to experience. But I will also make reference to sources that could be mined in an effort to build these descriptions into theories. It will also become evident that these three descriptions are not completely distinct, but overlap. I do not propose these patterns as being in any way exhaustive: one can find other logics of the development of understanding.[2] I set up these particular descriptions simply because I find them commonplace and useful.

Appearance within a New Spatial Frame of Reference

The first pattern of development that I wish to highlight may occur when something appears within a new spatial context. The metaphor of putting an old picture in a new frame is particularly simple and instructive. As the picture takes on all sorts of new perspectives in the various new frames into which it may be inserted, so too traditional understandings or propositions may take on new meaning when located in a new "spatial" context.[3] I remember visiting a small church in northern Spain: the former church had been razed and replaced by a new brick and glass structure that was light and modern. But the architect had preserved the baroque altar piece and inserted it into the bright sanctuary where it filled the space behind the altar and rose, with all its wooden nooks and crannies, high above it. The clash and the fit of the modern and baroque welded into one unified piece could stimulate a debate as to whether the altar piece was preserved in the new mid-twentieth-century modern church, or whether the architect had created something utterly new by situating the old piece in a new place.

Applying this metaphor of spatial change, of putting a picture in a new context, to theology may appear to be something of a reach. But what if we speak in terms of an imaginative framework for understanding? By this I mean a set of assumptions or presuppositions about reality that provides the context of meaning, or one's image or picture of the world. Most of our classical doctrines were formulated within the imaginative framework of a pre-Copernican universe, a relatively small earth and cosmos created all at once by God. Our language of redemption usually presumes that the first human beings were created in a whole and integral way, in a state of perfection, from which they fell, setting up a situation of sin, which in one way or another caused a break or alienation from God and which required a redeemer. The new picture of the universe that has evolved in the course of the nineteenth and twentieth centuries is quite different: an unimaginatively long period of creation of the cosmos, a stunningly long and intricate period of the formation of the planet earth, and finally the gradual evolution of life, and then the human species. Although these imaginative frameworks have not been completely determined, still the overall picture provides little space for an original pair, created in wholeness, or a fall, or original sin in the Augustinian sense that we have inherited in the West. The whole background cosmic picture of and story of the rise of humanity has provided a new imaginative context within which Jesus Christ and christology must be set, and this new setting will provide new meanings and understandings.[4]

A variety of current areas of study might provide theoretical resources to move beyond this loose, impressionistic allusion to this form of development. The topic of inculturation has become a major area of discussion since the Second Vatican Council. What happens when doctrines transmigrate into new cultures, worldviews, and language systems? One can depict postmodernity as an intellectual culture, as distinct from a set of doctrines, in which Jesus Christ will be understood differently simply because of inculturation into a new imaginative framework.

Appearance within a New Temporal Frame of Reference

Development also occurs as people's objective ideas, convictions, and commitments move through time. Many theories of development through time mark the theological landscape. Here I want to appeal more loosely to the basic metaphor of the narrative, which always moves forward into new contexts. Nothing human—no idea, value, theology, or doctrine—can be understood outside of a narrative context because human existence is historical existence. Existence always moves in time; nothing is stable in time; nothing is unchanging in time; to be a human being is to move irreversibly through time. This narrative always involves continuity and change, some dimension of sameness and always change. Meanings are not and cannot be stable, but one can find something within them that remains constant over history, at least insofar as the human subject that is changing retains a basic identity and entertains the same object.

Consider this example of radical change and continuity proposed by Sandra Schneiders:

[L]et us imagine a six-year-old child whose distant and financially irresponsible father dies. For the child and her mother the event is an unmitigated tragedy. They have lost the only support they know, however minimal it might have been. A couple of years later the widow meets and marries a man who loves her and the child and fills their lives with an affection and material security they have never known. The death of the natural father which produced the possibility of this new set of relationships is no longer a tragedy in their lives but a liberating grace. The effective history generated by the originating event, namely the death of the natural father, makes the event itself of the death, now experienced as integral to a new life and interpreted within a new horizon, a genuinely different reality. In a very real sense the event, although unchanged in its material facticity, . . . is completely different in significance, that is, in its historical reality and meaning because of its integration into the history that it effected.[5]

Besides the standard modern theories of the development of doctrine, hermeneutical theory also provides resources for giving this kind of development a solid theoretical grounding. The interpretation theories of Hans-Georg Gadamer and Paul Ricoeur both take historical consciousness seriously, and they formulate ways in which continuity, sameness, and relevance to the present can be retrieved from past classics precisely in the face of recognition that history can mediate radical change that threatens the past with irrelevance. More importantly for our day, John Thiel offers a postmodern theory of development that fully acknowledges the discontinuity of the present from the past and yet finds a way in which the past is drawn up into a new present-day narrative framework.[6]

Understanding in a New Expanded Horizon of Experience

One's understanding of reality also develops through an expanding horizon of experience and knowledge that all knowing subjects spontaneously undergo. This would apply as well to theological matters. Developmental psychology provides a wealth of categories and theories that illumine how a person, and perhaps also groups, develop through the broadening of horizon of experience within which they situate that which is understood.

Each person has recourse to his or her own experience of this pattern of a developing understanding: we simply understand things in new and different ways as we move through the life cycle and as we collect and process new experiences that shape the way we understand reality. The metaphor of an expanding horizon suggests visually how new understanding occurs. The physical horizon is the line where earth and sky appear to meet; the psychological horizon is the visual space or scope within which we perceive objects. As a horizon broadens, more objects are included within the picture, their positions and values change in relation to each other, and they take on new dimensions and significance. As one's existential horizon becomes broadened and opened up, one's own identity develops, mediating changes in insight and judgment that may be quite radical. But at the same time the knowing subject remains continuous despite change, and the elements and causes of change can be analyzed and justified. One thus possesses in this phenomenon of human development an excellent example of how sameness and difference, continuity and change, congeal in the process of change.

The common experience of human development has been studied extensively, and one need only mention the names of thinkers such as Erikson, Kohlberg, Gilligan, Fowler, and Kegan, who represent various theories of human development. These theorists provide the categories and distinctions that enable one to analyze the development of doctrine from the perspective of the psychology of the knowing subject. James Fowler's analyses, because they focus specifically on faith development, are particularly apropos here.[7]

Let me summarize what I have presented thus far: these are not theories of development, but three descriptions of and appeals to common experiences of how development occurs. These experiences could be more adequately accounted for by theories of development that are already in place, or they could be enhanced by more rigorous application of one or other of the resources that I have noted. I shall use them as lenses or heuristics for reflecting on how christology might develop, or has already begun to develop, into the future.

Two Areas of Christological Development: Other Religions and Jesus-Divinity

More specifically I want to apply these rough descriptions of development to two areas of christology. These are the status of Jesus Christ in relation to other religious mediations, and the question of the divinity of Jesus. Today the two questions are mutually intertwined. The issues are sensitive, and yet the questions raised are open questions. Both areas have generated some intense discussion, but the discussions themselves promise no simple or easy answers. Insofar as these issues will continue to come under intense discussion, it would be hard to imagine that there would be no development in the Christian community's appreciation of them. Perhaps the deployment of the three approaches to development as formal or structural categories might help us to project the direction development will take. I am not predicting the content of the development of christology in the future, but only trying to get some handle on the direction it might take. In fact, I assume that any development will leave the intention of the traditional doctrines intact, while the way they are explained may change considerably.

Attitudes toward Jesus in Relation to Other Religions

In mainline Christian theology, if one could determine a point of departure for development within the topic of the relation of Jesus Christ to other religious mediations, it would probably best be described as inclusivism. By inclusivism I mean the belief that readily grants that God saves people of other religions, and uses their religions to do so, but in the fundamental scheme of things Jesus Christ remains the ultimate cause of their salvation. Karl Rahner's explanation of what he called "anonymous Christianity" provides a clear example of this position. Generally speaking, it represents the current position of the Roman Catholic Church, probably most people in the mainline churches, and a majority of Christian theologians. The question I ask, then, is whether the three ways in which development transpires, outlined above, can shed light on how development beyond this position might unfold.

In the new spatial frame of the cosmos. I drew the first metaphor describing development in spatial terms, as when a picture is placed in a new frame. Analogously, what happens when one transfers the story of redemption by Jesus Christ into the imaginative framework of the evolving universe, planet, and species, which affords little or no place for a story of creation, fall, and rescue that has been the traditional Christian story? And as far as I can see, all educated people will gradually come to internalize this new picture of the origins of our cosmos, world, and selves. In the same measure the traditional story of origins, even when recognized as a religious symbol, will remain a possibly negative puzzle.

By contrast, one way the new picture of the world might provide a positive impulse toward a new constructive understanding revolves around the themes of creation and the immanence of God to all reality. The scientific story of creation redirects attention to the Christian doctrine of creation. In itself, the scientific conception of the origin of the universe, the planet, and the human species appears awesome and religiously charged: potentially it bears religious power. One can read in this picture the ongoing creation of God, or God as Spirit as an internal divine presence and creative force in the process itself. The sheer size of this imaginative vision expands beyond the Jewish creation myth; it dwarfs and compacts the human race and thus takes on a more explicitly universal character. Gradually one begins to think in a theocentric frame of reference as distinct from a christocentric framework. This refocusing of attention on God as creator, allowing God to be operative in all people and in all world religions, may well be accompanied by and perhaps will require an adjustment of our understanding of Jesus Christ within this larger frame of reference.

In the new story of the human race. The second context for projecting development is narrative, the one-way passage through time in which old meanings take on new valences and enhanced significance. In the "process" understanding of reality that history and the hard sciences have forced on our imaginations, we now have to understand the human phenomenon in narrative terms. Moreover, in that open-ended story, I think most would agree that we are entering a new stage of the history of the human race, where more and more we are becoming one world. In a way that has never happened before, all the "others" have now become members of my human community in a new concrete and practical way; the alien "enemy" has become a neighbor and a possible "friend." In this situation we cannot in principle provide a metaphysical grounding for competition and imperialism by defining Christianity as the only true religion, thereby relegating other religions as inferior to Christianity.[8] More and more thoughtful Christians are seeing the deep problems, both intellectual and moral, with the current self-understanding. The new stage of the human story, which in various settings and places involves the intermingling of religious people from different faiths, is gradually forbidding an *a priori* stance of superiority.

In place of regarding the other as inferior, one might envisage another possible although somewhat idealistic scenario of how peoples of different faith might gradually begin to interact. The attitude of the dialogue partners progresses from a relationship that might be characterized as an objective "us and them" to a more personal encounter described as an "I-Thou" relationship. But this is not the final goal. The movement into closer relationships in the human community and the broader context of an ongoing creation-centered picture of the world encourage us to hope that our relationship to other religions will develop into a "We" relationship in which, as we face our common world, we share our distinctive religious experiences in a non-competitive way.[9]

Summing up this second diagnostic: in comparison with the former isolation of the religions from each other, the new stage in the human story will not allow *a priori* self-definitions of superiority. And this will gradually engender new attitudes of *a priori* acceptance of what God is doing in other religions as roughly on a par with what God has done in and through Jesus.

In a new expanded horizon of experience. The spontaneous development of personal human existence and consciousness provides the third dynamic for understanding development in christology. All people continually revise their positions on everything as they constantly draw in new experiences and expand the horizons within which they situate the object under consideration. One of the catalysts expanding Christian horizons correlates with the shrinking of our globe, partly mediated by communications, and the expansion of our consciousness, which is ingredient to it. This leads to gradual acceptance of pluralism, including religious pluralism, a positive evaluation of it, and finally to a positive view of other religions. On the one hand, God as Spirit is working in their constituents; on the other hand, a plurality of religions provides more revelation of God than could a single religion in its finitude and particularity. Let me be clear about the object of understanding in this expanding consciousness: it is Jesus Christ as the mediator of God's salvation to me and to all those who share in the Christian faith and thus confess the same thing. That remains constant. What shifts, therefore, is not the object of christology, but the assessment of how, as a mediator of God, Jesus stands in relation to other religious mediations that bind the constituents of the various religions to what they understand to be absolute or ultimate. The direction of this shift will be away from an *a priori* taking it for granted that Jesus alone causes the salvation of all, that is, including those

who are not consciously related to him at all, in the direction of a
perception of other religions as also vehicles for, in Christian terms,
God's immanent presence to the human. This will lead to various theories in which people view the religions in a less competitive way. Relative to christology, the development will be toward a view of Jesus as
God's real and efficacious bringer of salvation but not necessarily in a
superior and competitive way.

To conclude this part, we can say that these three prognosticators
all point in the same direction with slightly different logics. Let me
now turn to development around the topic of the divinity of Jesus.

The Divinity of Jesus

How would one describe the conception of Jesus' divinity currently
in place in the mainline churches? I do not intend to set up an easy
caricature as a target on which we can train our guns. But a couple of
features of the general understanding of the divinity of Jesus Christ
flow from basic doctrine and catechetics. Most people and a majority
of theologians presuppose the doctrine of the Trinity as a metaphysical background for the incarnation of the Son or Logos. Jesus is divine
because the historical figure Jesus of Nazareth is the incarnation of
the second person of the Trinity. For a number of decades it has been
commonly admitted by theologians that this language of traditional
christology tends to undercut the integrity of Jesus' being a human
being. This, I believe, will change as Jesus Christ will be understood
more and more "from below," that is, beginning with and presuppos-
ing that Jesus is a person of history. In the following discussion of
how this might occur, I presuppose that the formal divinity of Jesus
Christ is a constant, the object of the development, but that this divinity will be understood and affirmed in new ways. How do the three
ways in which development transpires help to illumine how that development might go forward?

In the new spatial frame of the cosmos. When we situate the Christian story of incarnation into the new picture of the world as provided
by science, it occasions some shifts in understanding. One possible
shift may be a new recognition of the power of the doctrine of creation. I am inspired at this point by Edward Schillebeeckx's theology
of creation, and I can reduce the logic of this possible development to
three insights. The first is that creation is an ongoing process and real-

ity; God is always creating. Second, highlighting the doctrine of creation allows one to conflate the natural and supernatural spheres. God creates out of love and God's gratuitous love never withdraws from God's creation, even when it appears to be absent, as in the story of Job. Third, God is never distant from God's creating and as a result from God's creation, but always directly and personally present to all creatures, especially those who can personally respond, as in the human species.[10]

How does this affect a conception of Jesus' divinity? One would have to say, greatly—if the tacit supposition in understanding Jesus' divinity lay in a view that God is absent or withdrawn from the world. The doctrine of creation allows for no distance between the creator and the creature that needs to be overcome.[11] Are there degrees of God's being present? Or should we imagine differences in God's presence from the side of creation? Answers to these questions and an understanding of incarnation can be construed as occurring through the dynamics of God's creative activity itself and within the new conception of our cosmos. The premise is not that God is distant, but that God is within and personally present to every human being. But Jesus appears as a proleptic concentration of God's creating presence and activity that mirrors the intention and goal of creation itself.[12] What makes Jesus divine? Nothing on the side of Jesus as creature can make Jesus divine. Jesus is divine because of God's presence and action in him in a supereminent way.

In the new story of the human race. The second axis of how development might occur revolves around the idea of the passage of time and narrative. In the discussion of the question of the relation between Jesus Christ and other religions, I proposed that the human race is entering a new temporal context of global solidarity in which the religions of the world are rubbing shoulders with each other. Add to this the conviction just outlined, that God self-communicates to all people and thus becomes operative in their religious lives, and it will generate an atmosphere in which the idea of the uniqueness of Jesus Christ as it is currently understood will be challenged. In classical christology the uniqueness and the divinity of Jesus were correlative terms; divinity understood in terms of an incarnation of God as Logos explained an absolute and qualitatively different uniqueness of Jesus. In the physical and historical world as it is currently understood, it becomes more and more difficult to affirm that absolute and qualitative difference.

Jesus' divinity will be understood as correlative with the genuine divine revelation and mediation found in other religions.

Now I take it that such a development is underway at the present time and will continue as a matter of fact. But how is it to be reckoned theologically? Most often, theologians view such a development negatively. Critics often use such terms as "flattening out" or "reduction" in describing what is going on. One reason for this lies in the fact that the development moves from a literal imaginative sense of incarnation into a broader framework for understanding the presence of God at work in Jesus and its comparison with other religions. But from the perspective of christology from below, one can still claim the uniqueness of Jesus in the different but real sense of an historically distinctive presence of God to the world through Jesus. One may also insist that Jesus is truly divine, even though he is not solely or the only divine mediation.[13] As long as Christians remain Christian, they will be attached to God through Jesus in such a way that they find God's salvation in and through him. Thus one may understand the development as one that extends the divine reality that Christians encounter in Jesus to an affirmation that God also addresses other people in analogous ways in other religious mediations. The new conception, should it arise, would not subtract from Jesus, but would potentially raise up other religions to the level of Jesus within the Christian imagination. In effect, this new understanding would be saying that we Christians, through Jesus, have learned about what God is doing in the whole world through various religions.

In a new expanded horizon of experience. I turn now to the third path of development mediated through an expanded horizon of the perceiving and believing subject. Analysis of development from this perspective corresponds to and confirms the former scenarios. Once again, the constant in the development lies in the foundational experience of Christian faith: the Christian is one who encounters God in Jesus. On the one hand, this existential encounter of the revealing presence of God in Jesus for our salvation provides the basis for affirming Jesus' divinity. On the other hand, this consistent encounter occurs within an expanded horizon that includes a recognition of God's closeness and immanence to all of creation, a conviction that God works for salvation in the whole of creation, and an inquiring human spirit that expects to find other true manifestations (incarnations) of God in history. The result is an affirmation of Jesus' divinity that is realistic but not exclusive. The affirmation of Jesus' divinity says both that God is at work in Jesus in a distinctive and historically unique way, and that God can also be present and at work in other historical symbols of God that are also unique.

How will theology judge a development that says that Jesus is divine in a way that allows for the divinity of other religious mediators? The response to this question, I believe, reveals just how our horizon has changed. In a situation of relative isolation in which one religion correlates with one culture, pluralism appears as a threat. Thus to recognize the possibility of other "incarnations" of God is to relativize and so neutralize the one in Jesus. But the situation of religious pluralism mediates another consciousness: all mediations of God are themselves finite; one finite religious mediation or one single historical religion cannot fully reveal the mystery of God; no human argument or conviction can limit or contain the possibilities of the transcendent God; finally, no reason requires that the possible existence of other divine mediations necessarily undermines in any way the true presence of God actualized in Jesus. Even more strongly, a consciousness of pluralism in the future may judge that restricting divinity to Jesus would be unfaithful to the revelation of God mediated by him.

Conclusion

How will christology develop in the future? Let me conclude this reach into the future with a few brief summarizing propositions.

The first thing we can be sure of is that christology will develop; theology never remains the same. People in developed industrial cultures sense this movement in history as never before. The problem of development today lies not in explaining how change can legitimately occur, but in trying to find some continuity and stability amid the rush into an open future.

Second, relative to how it will develop, I have suggested some mechanisms that are meant to help understand how change is occurring. What I have done with this construction of types of development merely sets forth frameworks that help to take notice of and describe what is going forward. These imaginative structures also help to appreciate what, without such formal schemes, would have no human coherence. But these types are not technical or explanatory theories.[14] They serve only in helping common sense to situate what is going forward.

Third, however, we do not really know what the content of christology in the future will be, or even where the mainline center of gravity
will be located. No one can know the future. In reality, anyone who
speaks of the future does so by projecting certain aspects of the present
ahead. The developments I have described have already been set in
motion. This whole essay simply uses these frameworks to imagine
and project that what is already happening among many Christians
and will continue to work its way. But these developments may not
command the field; other aspects of our situation may elicit developments that coexist with or even supercede the tendencies I have selected. But whatever the predominant tendencies may be, it is hard to
imagine a future that will not be pluralistic.

Thus, fourth, it follows that we can be absolutely certain of one
thing, namely, that what I have suggested as the future of christology
will neither ring true nor be accepted by all. Therefore we may hope
that the conversation dealing with these issues will continue, and that
the pluralism that is already in place among Christians that pertains to
the understanding of our most central doctrine will become more explicit and refined.

Notes

[1]Although drawn from common experience and common sense, these constructs may either reflect methodically developed theories or be raised by disciplined reflection to such a state. But I shall prescind from those issues here.

[2]For example, reactionary developments that recoil from the incursions of
new data and their effects that impel a reappropriation of the past in much more
traditional but still transformed terms.

[3]The sense of the term "spatial" is analogous in the comparison: the literal
sense of space is broadened to include the imaginative framework for cognitive
apprehension.

[4]This theme provides the leading edge of the discussion of christology by
Michael Morwood, *Is Jesus God? Finding Our Faith* (New York: Crossroad, 2001).

[5]Sandra M. Schneiders, "Living Word or Dead(ly) Letter: The Encounter between the New Testament and Contemporary Experience," *Proceedings of the
Catholic Theological Society of America* 47 (1992): 51.

[6]John E. Thiel, in his *Senses of Tradition: Continuity and Development in
Catholic Faith* (Oxford: Oxford University Press, 2000), 56-95, develops a "retrospective," as distinct from a "prospective," theory of tradition and development of
doctrine. Theories of development that employ an "organic" root metaphor conceive of development moving forward into the future from the perspective of a

seed-like given that contains virtualities that open up in the course of the dialectics of history. A retrospective theory of development admits more discontinuity: the standpoint is a present time that constantly changes as it moves forward, but which consistently looks back to the past to discover relevant truth. The community continues to create new bridges across which it draws the past forward into ever new contexts.

[7]See James W. Fowler, *Stages of Faith: The Psychology of Human Development and the Quest for Meaning* (San Francisco: Harper & Row, 1981).

[8]To understand Christianity as the only true religion would be "a virtual declaration of war on all other religions" (Edward Schillebeeckx, "The Uniqueness of Christ and the Interreligious Dialogue," a paper delivered to the Catholic Academy in Munich, Bavaria [April 22, 1997], manuscript, 5).

[9]I borrow this scheme from Wilfred Cantwell Smith's sketch of stages in the progress of interreligious dialogue in *Towards a World Theology: Faith and the Comparative History of Religion* (Philadelphia: Westminster Press, 1981), 101, 193.

[10]See Edward Schillebeeckx, "God the Living One," *New Blackfriars* 62 (1981): 357-70, and "I Believe in God, Creator of Heaven and Earth," *God Among Us: The Gospel Proclaimed* (New York: Crossroad, 1983), 91-102. For interpretation of Schillebeeckx on this issue, see Dorothy Jacko, *Salvation in the Context of Contemporary Secularized Historical Consciousness: The Later Theology of Edward Schillebeeckx* (Ph.D. Dissertation, Toronto: University of St. Michael's College, Toronto School of Theology, 1987), 83-136.

[11]Jacko, *Salvation in the Context of Contemporary Secularized Historical Consciousness*, 94-99.

[12]"Therefore 'christology' is *concentrated* creation: belief in creation as God wills it to be" (Edward Schillebeeckx, *Interim Report on the Books Jesus & Christ* [New York: Crossroad, 1981], 128).

[13]Paul Knitter succinctly sums up his position that Jesus is "God's truly but not only saving word" in his essay "Five Theses on the Uniqueness of Jesus," *The Uniqueness of Jesus: A Dialogue with Paul Knitter*, ed. Leonard Swidler and Paul Mojzes (Maryknoll, N.Y.: Orbis Books, 1997), 3-16, at 14.

[14]The discussion of Thiel in *Senses of Tradition* contains a technical analysis of development, and among the theories he outlines, the retrospective, postmodern theory is the most adequate explanation of the dynamics of development among those he considers.

The Clash of Christological Symbols:
A Case for Metaphoric Realism

Robert Masson

In musical composition, a clash of cymbals signifies a dramatic moment in a passage. But its significance can vary. The force of brass plates can simply call attention to a phrase, voice, anthem, or transition in the arrangement. It can emphasize a thematic development, a musical notation anticipating a later twist or crescendo—or indicate that climax itself. It can signal a harmonious resolution of previous chords, or a rhapsody of dissonant voices. There are the occasions when a clash of cymbals heralds an extraordinary expression of musical creativity and genius: an adventitious musical gesture that brings together quite different voices in a way that enables the composition to express itself in a new idiom. At such moments cymbals announce a new musical vocabulary, a new form of expression. It is not just that something unexpected is said. The juxtaposition of the disparate voices creates a way to say something that could not have been said before. What it expresses is made possible only through the arrangement's invention of new possibilities of meaning created by its forcing a combination of musical phrases that until this composition had not been envisioned. The audience hears something it has never heard before—and could not have been expected to hear until this musical passage itself created the space for the hearing.

Such compositions can be extremely demanding for the audience. Understanding these pieces requires a stretch of sensibilities, a flexibility of affection, and suppleness of comprehension—even a reformation of one's register of meanings. Some in the gallery might not get the point. Others might not appreciate it. But for those who do, the clash of cymbals signals the advent of new meaning. The disparate voices are not reduced to one or the other—not harmonized in a familiar resolution. The uncalled-for juxtaposition is much more than a cacophonous celebration of dissonance. The composition is inspired, a revelation. That is what happens, for example, in great symphonies and great jazz. Indeed, symphony and jazz as distinct genres are themselves inventions of such musical genius.

The clash of christological symbols signals comparable dynamics in the movements of Christian thinking and discourse. The New Testament attests to a variety of images and potential trajectories for comprehending the significance of Jesus. Clashes among them preoccupied theological concerns for the first four centuries. The "official libretto and score" views the resolution of the christological and related trinitarian debates as a thematic progression—in Catholic parlance, as a development of doctrine. The earlier clashes call attention to distinct voices whose disparate and incomplete insights are harmonized at Nicaea and Chalcedon. The councils' determinations of phrasing provide the foundational chords and so are normative for subsequent advances. Still, progression is possible, even necessary, because of the inherent tension between the chordal elements. The councils resolved that the human and divine notes must be played together, but in the definition of Chacedon, "unmixed and unchanged, undivided and unseparated."[1] The terms are inescapably contrapuntal and analogous. Hence, as Rahner famously emphasized, Chalcedon is a beginning rather than an end for further theological meditation and development.[2]

Roger Haight's *Jesus Symbol of God* argues for an emended libretto and score.[3] As he sees it, the official rendition glosses the plurality of discordant voices in the New Testament. The scenario is not attentive to the genesis of the phrases intoned at Nicaea and Chalcedon, and so mistakes the movement's finale for the originating notes that it was meant to express. Haight contends that attention to the history of the controversies establishes that the original meaning that generated the christological formulas of the councils was not—and is not—identical to the formulations themselves, and indeed should be distinguished from them. Moreover, the official story line takes the movement toward that particular paradigm, the incarnation of the divine *Logos* in the human as *sarx* or *anthropos*, as a necessary and normative development. So doing precludes as orthodox any interpretations of Jesus' significance that appeal for inspiration and resources to voices in the New Testament that do not fit this pattern.

Haight challenges the notion that these developments were inevitable. This scenario is especially problematic, he alleges, because it does not render an account that can speak credibly to the historical sensibilities of postmodern consciousness. He insists that the problem is not with what Chalcedon intended and affirmed (the divinity and salvific significance of Jesus) but with the theoretical tools the council had at its disposal to express its intention. While the council played the divine and human notes as contrapuntal, Haight claims that the incarnate Logos paradigm did not provide the means to insure that the counterpoint would be clearly heard in subsequent generations and theologies. Indeed, the attempted counterpoint appears inevitably to resolve to a diminished humanity. Hence, if one is to take seriously Jesus' humanity and contemporary conceptions of what full humanity entails, the official score poses impossible conceptual dilemmas.

Haight's revisionist libretto and score put forward a detailed, multifaceted, and provocative strategy for defending in our present context the affirmation that Jesus is divine and savior. I propose a third libretto and score as a clarification of the official analogical reading and as an alternative to Haight's dialectical and symbolic reading. The third possibility is a metaphoric reading. Metaphoric, as distinct from metaphorical, refers to an epistemological process that creates the possibility for new meanings, illustrated, for example, by the previous description of the creation of a new musical idiom.

The role of the metaphoric process in generating such new understandings in science and theology has been analyzed in some depth by Mary Gerhart and Allan Russell.[4] Metaphoric process, in the specific sense in which they define it, offers a more effective way to explain the Christian affirmation of identity between Jesus and God—more effective because it suggests how to maintain credibly the realism of both the identity claim and the affirmation of Jesus' full humanity, while also accounting for the ways in which these affirmations stretch language to new uses and stretch believers to new horizons of understanding and action.

While I acknowledge, then, the considerable merit in Haight's contention that the issue of how language, concepts, and realities signify God is a decisive one for contemporary christologies, my considerations vie for a different libretto on that same issue. Haight's extended, systematic analysis confronts a number of issues that are problematic today for many thoughtful people and that are not convincingly explained by academic theology or adequately addressed by church pronouncements. But my aim is not an appraisal of these broader issues in Haight's proposals, or of his christology as such or as a whole. Reservations about key aspects in only one of the many lines of argumentation he advances prompt my suggestions and provide the context for developing them. My purpose is narrow: to sketch an outline of a constructive alternative for understanding the logic of Christian talk about Jesus' significance.

For our purposes, three moves are crucial in Haight's efforts to retrieve the authentic meaning behind Nicaea and Chalcedon, and to articulate an alternative orthodox christology. First, he argues that symbolic mediation provides the key for interpreting religious language and for explaining Jesus' significance. Second, he assumes that the coherence between Paul Tillich's and Karl Rahner's theologies of the symbol is sufficient to warrant a relatively undifferentiated appropriation of their positions in support of the first thesis. Third, he argues that a genetic interpretation of scriptural and patristic christological formulations precludes unwarranted extensions of their senses beyond the meanings that generated them.

There is something of a circularity to Haight's argument—legitimately so—and he acknowledges it. That applies to the three conceptual moves at issue here. His appropriation of Tillich and Rahner determines his understanding of symbol, which in turn shapes his genetic interpretation of christology, his critique and revision of Rahner's christology, and his constructive argument for a Spirit christology. To this I add that Tillich's and Rahner's theologies of symbol are both instances of what Gerhart and Russell have described as metaphoric process. This addition enlarges the interpretive circle and complicates further the question about the most appropriate point of entry into the discussion. Haight's conflation of Tillich's and Rahner's theologies of symbol suggests itself as an opportune ingress. It is not the most important of these issues, nor is it illegitimate to appropriate compatible insights from otherwise contrary arguments. But the conflation does offer a direct path to the divergence between my metaphoric and Haight's symbolic librettos.

Conflation of Tillich's and Rahner's Theologies of Symbol

Although Haight's theory of the symbolic draws on numerous sources, it appeals particularly to Tillich and Rahner. There is no ques-

tion that there are striking parallels in their phenomenological characterizations of symbol and the symbolic. The issue that demands attention is the fundamental difference between their approaches. In *Dynamics of Theology*, Haight admits that he brings "together in what
may appear to be a too smooth and easy way elements" from their
theologies of symbol.[5] He adds, though, that "despite these differences,
I see no fundamental antithesis between these two theologies of symbol. Rather I see Rahner much more willing to emphasize the 'is' side
of the dialectic between symbol and symbolized, especially in the case
of the concrete symbol Jesus."[6] The important point, he insists, is that
"the dialectical structure is still present in Rahner's christology, despite his tendency to emphasize Jesus' being the actuality of God in
the world. Moreover, this must be the case for his christology to be
judged consistent with Chalcedon which . . . is a strictly dialectical
confession."[7]

But there is more to this difference than a question of emphasis.
There is a fundamental antithesis between these theologies of symbol.
Haight's comment begs the real issue of how to understand the dialectic between symbol and symbolized, between, as he puts it, the "is"
and the "is not." Both theologies of symbol were developed to address
that very issue. The difficulty is that Tillich's notion of symbol, and
Haight's appropriation of it, rules out—and is intended to rule out—a
priori the very conception of symbol and symbolic that Rahner's theory
seeks to legitimate.

For theological, ontological, and christological reasons, Tillich
maintains, and Haight with him, that the symbolized points beyond
itself *to something else*. This precludes any sort of proper identity between symbol and symbolized. There can be no direct or literal sense
in which one could say that the symbol "is" the symbolized. The "is
not" always trumps the "is." Properly speaking, Jesus is a man not
God. For Tillich, both the Protestant principle's stricture against idolatry
and the infinite qualitative difference between finite beings and the
ground of being require this. "That which is the true ultimate," Tillich
emphasizes, "transcends the realm of finite reality infinitely. Therefore, no finite reality can express it directly and properly."[8] Both Haight
and Tillich insist that the integrity of Jesus' historical existence requires an uncompromising affirmation of his humanity. To say that
christology is dialectical means for them that the identity between Jesus
and God can be no more than the sort of transparency by which any

finite reality, in principle, can point beyond itself to the ground of being.

Neither Haight, nor Tillich, intends by this restriction to deny the appropriateness of affirming that Jesus is truly symbol of God. Haight takes pains to stress that it is indeed God who is encountered in Jesus; that God is uniquely—even though not exclusively—encountered in him; and that the point of explaining how Jesus, as symbol, mediates God is to facilitate the worship of God in him, not to undermine it. Nevertheless, it is only in pointing beyond himself and his humanity that Jesus mediates God. It is only in that qualified sense that he can be called divine or worshiped. Haight is emphatic: "One must recognize immediately that as a human being Jesus is Jesus, is not God, but points away from himself to God. Only then can the human mind begin to recognize certain contours of God within the reality of Jesus."[9] Hence, Haight, following Tillich, uses "symbol," "symbolic," and "dialectical" restrictively. The terms designate "mediation" of the divine but always with the qualification, in Tillich's language, of the "absolute break" and "infinite jump" between symbol and what it symbolizes.[10]

One can find wording in Rahner that might appear equivalent to Haight's definition of a symbol "as something that mediates something other than itself."[11] Likewise, Rahner's language might also seem to suggest that "a symbol makes present something else."[12] Rahner's conception of the symbol, however, is not derived from a phenomenological account of the relation between symbol and symbolized. Penetrating the point of Rahner's notion is clearly a situation where Haight's principle of genetic hermeneutics should apply. A genetic approach interprets a concept's sense by tracing the development of the meanings that generated it. Explanations that contradict the intentionality of the originating logic are deemed unwarranted.

So what explains the genesis of Rahner's notion? "What is going on in this development? Why is this move being made rather than another? What is at stake in this theological decision?"[13] Rahner was quite explicit about this in his seminal essay on "The Theology of Symbol."[14] He was looking for a more original explanation of the relation between symbol and symbolized than the phenomenological traces of its mediation that Haight and Tillich chart. He believed he found such an explanation in the insight that beings themselves are— and even being itself is—symbolic.

Every being, he argued, consists of a plurality in unity. The plural elements can be distinguished from the underlying unity that they express, and in that sense the plurality can be considered a kind of "other" or "otherness." But it is an "otherness" intrinsic to the unity and expressive of it—the way embodiment (the body itself and bodily gestures) expresses a person. On the one hand, the only access to persons is in their embodiment. We are our bodies. On the other hand, there is something fundamentally dialectical about personal embodiment. We are not simply our bodies. One can—and indeed must—distinguish between persons and their embodiments. In extreme situations (for example, such as deception, mental illness, the influence of pain, drugs, or stress, or in death) bodily expressions are in varying degrees no longer properly speaking a person's self-expression or embodiment. Hence there are genuine and proper senses in which what confronts us in the body and embodiment both "is" and "is not" the person himself or herself. Rahner contends that something like this is true of the relation between plurality and unity in all beings.[15]

For Haight and Tillich, symbol mediates something other than itself. For Rahner, symbol, in the most original and basic sense, is the otherness of a being itself through which the being is expressed. The "otherness" is not, as Haight says undialectically, "something else." This most basic "otherness"—what Rahner calls *Realsymbol* to distinguish it from more derivative instances of the symbolic—both "is" and "is not" identical with the symbolized. Ironically, Rahner's position is more complex, more dialectical than Haight's and Tillich's. His aim is to explain how the identity both "is" and "is not" at the same time. He argues against expectations that for such *Realsymbols* unity and diversity correlate in like, not inverse, proportion.[16] Hence his point is to legitimate a kind of identity between symbol and symbolized, which Haight and Tillich bar on principle.

Rahner argues further, appealing to the doctrine of the Trinity, that divine be-ing itself is symbolic in this sense. This is clearly the antithesis of Tillich's theological and philosophical convictions. God is not symbolic for him. Being itself is beyond the polarities of finite beings that enable one thing to symbolize another, and that enable all things, in so far as they point beyond themselves to their ground, to symbolize the ground itself. Rahner, too, stresses that God is not another being in the world, alongside it, or even beyond it. But Rahner does not conclude that the qualitative difference between God and creature restricts the logic of symbol in the same way. Hence, he does not endorse at all the kind of "symbolic realism" advocated by Haight. Rather, the point of Rahner's theology of symbol is to provide a philosophical rationale for conceptions of "dialectic," "symbolic," and "symbolic realism," which clearly differs from and stands opposed to what Haight intends by these notions. Rahner's point is not simply to emphasize the "is" at the expense of the "is not." His point is to argue that a very different logic (or dialectic) applies in this situation—one in which symbolized and symbol, unity and distinction, divine and human, contrary to expectations, are not reduced to one or the other, not harmonized in an artificial resolution, and not played in opposition to one another as properly "other" and different.

Given the genesis and contrary thrust of Rahner's theology of symbol, I conclude that although Haight uses language that often is similar to Rahner's, Haight cannot legitimately appeal, at least without further and substantial clarification, to Rahner's position, or the many theologies inspired by it, to warrant his position. This also raises more fundamental questions about Haight's critique and reinterpretation of Rahner's christology than Haight acknowledges in his publications. Likewise, it requires much clearer distinctions between the various senses of "symbol," "symbolic," "symbolic realism," and "dialectical" in our ongoing discussions of the logic of Christian talk about Jesus' significance. Otherwise our theological discussions will result in an obfuscation of what Christians are about in such discourse rather than lead to the sort of clarification for which Haight rightly calls.

Symbolic and Metaphoric Readings

Although such qualifications bring us to the nub of contention between Tillich's and Rahner's theologies of symbol, this does not yet elucidate the difference between Haight's symbolic libretto for christology and the case for a metaphoric reading. Nor does it clarify the most basic difference between Tillich's and Rahner's understandings of the logic of theological predication. The terms Rahner typically uses to describe such discourse are "analogical," "transcendental," and "mystagogical," not "symbolic." These preferences signify further divergences that need explanation. As Haight remarks, symbolic knowledge can be defined and distinguished from metaphor and other forms of speech in a variety of ways. There is no standard usage.[17] A more differentiated account is required.

When Christians seek to articulate the significance of Jesus, they are forced inevitably to stretch the available language and conceptual frameworks. That happens already in the scriptures. Followers of Jesus have an arsenal of linguistic tools at their disposal for this: not only symbol and literal speech but metaphor, parable, allegory, analogy, personification, paradox, myth, poetry, narratives of various kinds, and so on. The later christological controversies can be viewed in part as efforts at dealing with this diversity. They attempt to distinguish when language is stretched too far and when not far enough; to discern when the stretching is revealing and when obfuscating; and to decide what stretching of language, generated in particular communities and circumstances, is acceptable to broader communities of belief in different contexts, and what is not tolerable. It should be admitted that any attempt to account for this exceedingly rich play of language and arduous communal discernment under a single rubric, whether "symbolic" or "metaphoric," risks oversimplification and distortion. Such theories must be advanced with reservations and modesty. But still an accounting of how language and thinking can be legitimately stretched is necessary, and unavoidable. We must have such an account if we are to make judgments about the logical limits of such linguistic and conceptual moves, or to settle interpretative questions about the "point" of particular terms and formulations, or to develop a hermeneutics to help adjudicate between alternative ways of speaking and thinking about God and Jesus.

Gerhart and Russell

The advantage of the theory of metaphoric process advanced by Gerhart and Russell is that it focuses particularly on the epistemological moves in religion and science in which genuinely new possibilities for understanding and meaning emerge. Put very simply, their theory envisions situations in which a novel analogy is forced between two notions in our available world of meanings.

Their argument presupposes that our inquiries about the world and ourselves take place in what can be imagined as cognitive spaces or worlds of meanings. These worlds of meanings are made up of networks of interrelated concepts. Physics, theology, a religion, and common sense as defined by a particular time and culture are examples of such fields of meanings. The concepts within these fields do not stand directly for things in themselves, but for our notions of these things. These notions are defined by their interrelation with other notions. For example, to get some conception of "house," one must have other notions available (lumber, bricks, wall, window, roof, and so forth). These other notions are variable, as well as the relations between them, so meaning "arises out of the interaction of concepts and relations, and is expressed in the topography of the field. Necessary concept changes, such as those which might arise from a new experience, alter relations; and changes in relations, such as occur when one attempts to understand an experience in a new way, relocate old concepts." [18]

Gerhart and Russell speak of an analogy as "forced" when it involves an affirmation of an identity between two "knowns" that, given current understandings, is unwarranted. In the world of Copernicus, for example, the affirmation that the sun and not the earth is the center was uncalled for. In Newton's world, to affirm that the laws of heaven and the laws of earth are the same was unreasonable. In the world of meanings available to Palestinian Jews at the time of Jesus' death, the warrants for identifying him as the Messiah were questionable at best.

The first thing that distinguishes these particular analogies is that, despite their apparent unreasonableness, forcing them does not result in nonsense. Quite to the contrary, twisting accustomed meanings in these situations opens up possibilities for understanding that had not been available before, just as stretching the elements of musical composition can create a new idiom such as jazz.

The second thing that distinguishes such uncalled-for analogies is the disruptive effect on the fields of meanings associated with them. Copernicus's insistence that the sun is the center, or Newton's insistence that the laws of terrestrial motion are identical with the laws of planetary motion, changed related notions within physics in most fundamental ways.[19] So the force of the analogies did not simply add new information to the world of physics, expanding it the way the discovery of a new planet or a new mechanical law might have. Nor did it clarify the given world of meanings, the way an apt analogy between something known and something unknown might have. By Newton's time both Galileo's and Kepler's laws already were known. The uncalled-for analogies had a more "tectonic" or "metaphoric" effect because they forced a reconfiguration in the until-then accepted fields of meanings. The result was newly shaped fields of meanings that constitute a better understanding of what we know of reality.[20]

This effect—the creation of significant changes in fields of meanings—I take to be the fundamental characteristic of the metaphoric analogy. That is what distinguishes it from rhetorical moves we more commonly label "metaphor" or "metaphorical" in which forcing a new analogy extends the meaning of terms within a field of meanings but does not reshape the field of meanings itself. (In Gerhart and Russell's theory "metaphoric" and "metaphorical" are not equivalent. And on their accounting many metaphors are not genuinely metaphoric because they do not create the possibility for new meaning by creating fundamental shifts in our fields of meanings.)

For example, the affirmation that "Jesus is the Messiah" effects such a change in fields of meanings. Given the images current in the eschatology of the day, affirming that God was victorious in the crucified son of a carpenter from Nazareth was uncalled for. In fact most of the key eschatological images by which Jesus is identified in the gospels have something of this metaphoric dimension. By ordinary logic he was not a victorious King of Israel; he was not a Son of Man who descended gloriously from the heavens; he was not acknowledged by his people nor did he vanquish their enemies. To affirm that Jesus is the Messiah is to force an analogy between him and Israel's expressions of hope and trust in God. This in turn requires a different understanding of God, Israel's hope, and Jesus. Affirming that Jesus is the Messiah, if taken seriously, forces a thoroughgoing revision of the field of meanings operative in Palestinian Judaism, or at least those operative in the narrative worlds of the New Testament.

This leads us to the third factor that distinguishes the metaphoric process. The shifts of meaning entailed in it typically make a new logic available. Conceptual moves are possible in Einstein's world that were inconceivable in Newton's, and moves in Newton's world would not have made sense in Galileo's. Likewise, the affirmation that Jesus is Messiah reconfigures the meaning of "Messiah," the identity of Jesus, and the field of meanings associated with messianic hope. This makes possible a logical move otherwise unavailable and lays the groundwork for later moves otherwise unthinkable.

Several entailments of this conceptual step are noteworthy. First, there is no hedging of the "is" in the claim "Jesus is Messiah." The logic of this move loses its force if Jesus is not in some sense properly and literally the Messiah. I use "literal" here purposefully but advisedly. The conception of metaphoric process destabilizes the meaning of "literal" itself and warrants this qualified use. Although reference to the literal meaning often presupposes that exact and primary meanings are univocal and constant, and that fields of meanings are stable, the metaphoric process demonstrates that this is not always the case. In a metaphoric affirmation words come to have new exact and primary meanings. Moreover, these meanings can be semantically proper, logically warranted, and factually the case—three further important denotations of "literal." After Thompson and Joule, heat *is* motion. After Einstein, it is literally true that the speed of light is the same for all observers. For those whose world of meanings has been transformed by the gospel, Jesus *is* the Messiah.

Second, this is possible only if one allows for the fundamental shifts in fields of meanings. For those who got the point of the surprising affirmation, Jesus redefines what it is to be Messiah, just as the concept Messiah redefines Jesus' identity. Moreover, the fields of meanings associated with messianic expectation, Jesus, and God's relation to humanity are transformed. Hence, reception is always a crucial dimension in the metaphoric process. The point of the affirmation will be missed if the hearer is unable or unwilling to recognize the intrinsic changes in these fields of meanings.

This would be the case, for example, if a secular historian understood the predication univocally and so concluded that it is an analogy that in some ways is justified, in other ways not. This would also be the case if the affirmation is taken, whether by an historically naive believer or skeptic, as asserting a univocal, non-metaphoric identification of Jesus and the Messiah. Both people would miss the affirmation's logical significance. A univocal and literal reading in that sense—a reading that does not negotiate the entailed shifts in fields of meanings—will mistake the logic of the predication. Therefore, recognizing Jesus as the Messiah requires what the prophets had called *teshuva*, a fundamental "turning" or conversion in thinking and in identity.[21]

It was a shift in conception and identity that many at the time could not see or accept, a shift that many of Jesus' followers apparently found difficult, and a shift whose far-reaching implications plainly were not at all clear, at first, even to those who affirmed it. The logic was not patently explicit, conscious, or transparent. Nevertheless, the

metaphoric point of this predication is neither to deny the identity nor
restrict its significance but to open up a logical space that enables us to
say more than would be possible if the predication were interpreted as
either merely univocal (is) or merely dialectical (is not).

The Metaphoric Character of Rahner's Thought

Gerhart and Russell's conception of the metaphoric process provides an illuminating explanation of the logic entailed in Rahner's
appeal to the "analogical" and "transcendental" character of God-talk.
His performance is more subtle, innovative, and effective than his own
explanations. Inattention to such unarticulated but fundamental moves
in his thought is the source of significant misunderstanding among
some commentators and critics. For one thing, Rahner holds that "analogy" and "transcendental" are themselves analogous and transcendental conceptions. Pinning down their precise meaning and demonstrating that it is metaphoric requires attentive and extended analysis.
For the present purposes a brief overview of this claim and its justification must suffice.[22]

If one steps back from what Rahner says about analogous and transcendental statements and then examines how he actually uses such
language, it becomes clear that he is forcing an analogy. The effect is
to open up new fields of meanings and so a new logical and grammatical space in which it is possible to speak meaningfully of God, though
in a qualified, indirect, and somewhat apophatic way. Rahner insists
that this does not entail any grasping of God in concepts. His move is
a metaphoric act grounded in a very different understanding of how
we think and signify God in the first place. This does not entail affirming that God is in some ways like and in some ways different from
some putative analogue. Like Tillich and Haight, he resists the claim
that concepts can grasp God in that way at all. But unlike Tillich's and
Haight's restrictive views of the range of predication, Rahner's argumentation reveals that he thinks we can force language as we normally use it to different purposes, shifting our fields of meanings as
they apply to God, so that conceptual room can be open for saying
something meaningful and substantive that grasps at God without
grasping God.

More specifically (although Rahner does not put it this way himself) the transcendental argument in its most basic conceptual move

forces an analogy between two known elements that require a shift in our fields of meanings. This opens up possibilities for predication otherwise unavailable and unthinkable. The first known is what Rahner calls "transcendental" intentionality—the reflexive, indirect, and dynamic presence-to-self and anticipation (*Vorgriff*) of the horizon of knowing, love, and freedom. The second known is the more direct grasp of specific objects as known, loved, and affirmed in freedom, what he calls "categorial" intentionality.

Rahner forces an analogy by insisting that the model for knowing and speaking of God is transcendental intentionality rather than categorial intentionality, and by insisting that the former is not a derivative, secondary, or inferior activity, but the primary and grounding manifestation of the human spirit. Forcing this analogy—that is to say, speaking of God as "transcendental reality"—creates a logical space for talking about God, while insisting that God is the goal and presupposition of human intentionality and never its object, and underlines that God is always beyond our grasp. The logic of God-talk, for Rahner, is governed by the intrinsic reflexivity and indirectness of this metaphoric signification. If this is forgotten, one falls into the mistaken notion that transcendental reality is a transcendental "object" that can be known, spoken of, or described in the way we know and speak about categorial objects.

Rahner is able to show that a similar logic applies to other transcendental "realities," such as the self or freedom, that are real and that can be the grammatical objects of our predications even though they are not entities perceptible by the senses. People do indeed speak of such "things" as if they were objects in that sense. Moreover, people take them as "real." But even though people might not be able to explain why, most would recognize the inappropriateness of questions about the physical location of the self, its size, weight, color, taste, or smell. There is something metaphoric going on in much of our everyday talk about realities such as the "self," even though we do not normally call attention to this "stretching" of language and are not discomforted by its peculiar logic.

Rahner's use of "Holy Mystery," "nameless whither," "horizon," and "asymptotic goal" as terms for God is meant to call attention to such a metaphoric shift in signification and logic. Moreover, characteristic of metaphoric signification, the act of affirming that God is transcendental reality effects fundamental and global changes in the available theological and philosophical fields of meanings. Rahner seeks to exploit these meanings in his various theological investigations. We have already seen him do this in his theology of symbol. His affirmation that beings, and indeed being itself, are symbolic is itself a metaphoric proposal. Accepting his suggestion forces a reconfiguration of what symbol is, of how beings and being itself are, and of the fields of meanings associated with each of these notions. Moreover, this reconfiguration of fields of meanings makes available a logic in which, contrary to expectations, symbol and symbolized are not opposed, indeed in which unity and diversity correlate in like, rather than inverse, proportion.

It is true that Rahner explains and achieves this metaphoric move within the context of his rather cerebral transcendental metaphysics. He was inspired by Aquinas, who achieved a similar innovation in an earlier philosophical context, quite different from our so-called postmodern world of meanings. Aquinas also required a significant reconfiguration of the intellectual idioms of his day. Following Gerhart and Russell, however, it can be argued that the metaphoric process that their theologies exemplify is a more general epistemological activity entailed in the expansion of religious and theological understanding as well as other forms of scientific and artistic understanding.

Such moves are not a priori inimical to the sort of "intelligibility in today's world" that Haight argues must be a crucial criterion for christology. Contemporary belief structures, particularly those that have created the possibility for new horizons of human understanding, are built on such cognitive shifts in our fields of meaning. This argues for a significant qualification of Haight's insistence that "one cannot logically affirm a belief that stands in contradiction with what one knows to be true in a wider context" and that "the principle of non-contradiction rules out a compartmentalization of christological beliefs held in a private sphere that do not correlate with what we positively know to be the case from other spheres of life."[23] This norm can be granted, but only so long as one takes into consideration those significant metaphoric acts in other spheres of life that reveal knowing as a process in which our fields of meanings can be meaningfully stretched to unexpected uses, and our logic twisted in uncalled-for but warrantably productive ways. This qualification must be part of the equation, as well, in the application of Haight's positive articulation of the criterion: that "one's christological faith should find expression in belief structures or ways of understanding that fit or correspond with the way reality is understood generally in a given culture."[24] A restrictive theory of the symbolic that a priori rules out the metaphoric in theology and religion, or that relegates it to the non-cognitive and poetic, ignores the significance of the metaphoric as a legitimate cognitive process in the sciences and arts.

As I read them, Tillich and Haight also seek to force an analogy when they claim that all talk of God is symbolic. Establishing this reading is not necessary for the further development of the case I am making for a metaphoric reading of christological symbols, but it does provide an occasion to stress that making a metaphoric move does not require an awareness that one is doing so or a commitment to a theory such as Gerhart and Russell's. It also calls attention to the difference between recognizing a move as metaphoric and judging it true or as the most helpful conceptual move. Clarifying precisely how christological predications logically function, whether as metaphoric or symbolic in the various senses we have examined, is a crucial step toward interpreting their meaning, but it is still preliminary to determining their truth. Our concern is with the question "What kind of truth?" and so bears more indirectly on the question "Is it true?"

Hermeneutical Implications of a Metaphoric Reading

If the logic of christological predication is metaphoric in the sense I have argued, rather than restrictively symbolic, Haight's genetic hermeneutics loses much of its force. He acknowledges that his interpretation presupposes his theory of symbol as the only viable alternative either to literal readings, which he contends are today historically implausible, or to highly speculative metaphysical readings, which he maintains are at best problematic for postmodern consciousness. But a metaphoric libretto such as I have proposed here makes possible yet another construal. The scope of this essay permits little more than this bare suggestion itself and some of its hermeneutical implications. The significant historical issues related to this claim or to Haight's christological interpretations must be left to other occasions and to those with appropriate expertise.

The focal point of contention follows directly from what has been argued. If metaphoric acts in religion, theology, or other sciences can

sometimes adventitiously create the possibility for affirming an identity claim (a metaphoric analogy) that otherwise would have been unavailable and unthinkable, it has to be asked if similar conceptual moves
could not have been entailed in scripture and in the early reflections of
the church that prepared the grounds for the formulations of Chalcedon
and Nicaea.

This contrasts with Haight's interpretation of Jesus as the "Wisdom of God" and "Logos of God." The wisdom christology, he observes "is often considered a bridge to a fully three-stage, incarnational
understanding of a pre-existent Jesus Christ."[25] The logos christology
"both resembles the other wisdom christologies and transcends them
in the direction of an explicit statement of the incarnation of an hypostatized being."[26] He maintains that "what is happening in the development of the earlier wisdom christology is evident: 'What Judaism said of Sophia, Christian hymn-makers and epistle writers now
come to say of Jesus.' "[27] This conceptual move paved the way for
later assertions of Jesus' pre-existence, but in Haight's scenario those
later moves were not justified by the intentionality of the scriptural
texts that generated them. The originating meaning was very different
and contradicts the later, since the referent of these affirmations was
the historical Jesus of Nazareth seen symbolically as a personification
and revelation of God. The referent was not a pre-existent being in
identity with God.

> And what do these assertions mean? . . . James Dunn, for ex-
> ample, recognizes that in his wisdom christology Paul wanted to
> show that Jesus is the new and exhaustive embodiment of divine
> wisdom. He admits that Matthew transcends his source Q, where
> Jesus is a messenger of wisdom, and identifies Jesus with
> wisdom. It is clear that Jesus is being equated with the personi-
> fication of God's wisdom in the hymns like that of Colossians.
> Moreover, this metaphorical language of personification finally
> led to a christology in which Jesus is different in kind from other
> mediations of God, and enjoys a metaphysically divine status of
> personal pre-existence. But Dunn fails to find in the Jewish
> tradition prior to Jesus any consideration of wisdom as a hyposta-
> sis or divine being; this would not fit with Jewish monotheism.
> Wisdom language remains figurative personification. It is thus at
> least ambiguous that pre-existence represents the intention of

these wisdom christologies, because one cannot really show that this is more than the figurative language of metaphor and personification. Is there a way out of this impasse?[28]

Haight responds "yes" and proposes that the issue can be sorted out hermeneutically. His first move is to argue that the historical Jesus of Nazareth is the primary referent of such affirmations. He next notes that in such wisdom sayings the central theme is Jesus' role as one who "reveals both the true nature of human existence and also the nature of God."[29] Haight reasons that the personification borrowed from wisdom language should be interpreted in this light. "These texts are not providing unknowable information about transcendent realities from some secret source of knowledge. The epistemology of these christologies begins from below, with Jesus, and their content is based on the encounter of God in and through Jesus."[30] So, he concludes, the affirmations are symbolic: Jesus points to God but is not literally identified with God and does not pre-exist in identity with God. The affirmations are symbolic in this restrictive sense for two reasons: first, because it is language about transcendental reality and, second, because "this is consciously developed language of personification."[31]

On more careful analysis, the second reason is little more than a variation on the first. Throughout Haight's work, it is clear that he understands metaphor and personification in terms of his theory of the symbolic. He notes early in the book that "descriptions of how metaphor functions resemble the dynamics of symbols."[32] In his understanding, the logic of metaphor and personification presuppose the fundamental non-identity between the realities compared. They are analogies in the common sense—not metaphoric. One term (or perhaps both terms) communicates information about the other. In so doing, the analogies may introduce paradox, tension, and ambiguity into the meanings of the terms themselves, but the analogies do not create fundamental changes in the fields of meanings or create the possibility for new logical relations between them. They do not force a new identity. So Haight tells us:

> I indicated earlier how in a metaphor one thing is identified with something different, as in "My husband is a bear." What immediately strikes the listener or reader is the non-identity between the implicitly pared items. The creative imagination is thus set in

motion to formulate the similarity or point of identity: is he a teddy or a grizzly? So too, analogously, to say that Jesus is a parable of God introduces paradox, tension, and ambiguity in Jesus' mediation of God. One must recognize immediately that as a human being Jesus is Jesus, is not God, but points away from himself to God.[33]

A similar logic applies in his interpretation of personification in the Hebrew scriptures:

In some instances these metaphorical symbols in the Hebrew scriptures are personified, and this personification became a very significant factor in the development of christological and trinitarian doctrine. Personification is a figure of speech: the literal meaning of a personification, that is, the meaning intended by the author of the personification, is not that the "hands of God" refer to two actual hands, or that the Word of God is something really distinct from God. When the metaphorical character of personification is not respected, when it becomes hypostatized, that is, conceived as objective and individual, in the same measure the power of the symbol tends to be undermined. The symbol can then be made to point to something distinct from God, which in its turn acts as an intermediary between God and the world. God's transcendence and immanence in the world become separated and competitive; God, as holy and transcendent, cannot be mixed up in this world but needs a messenger, an angel, a Word. This goes against the primitive intention of the symbol as referring in its first instance simply to God experienced in the world.[34]

But do such metaphors always refer simply to God as experienced in the world in that restrictive way? I suggested earlier that identifying Jesus as Messiah is not a metaphor in the manner Haight defines, but metaphoric in Gerhart and Russell's sense. It opens up and requires a new way of conceiving Jesus, messianic hope, and God's relation to humanity. With this shift in fields of meanings, a new logic applies; one can say properly and literally that Jesus is Messiah. Christians proclaim nothing less. They do not proclaim him as a "sort of" Messiah.

It is reasonable to suppose that a similar logical move is involved in Philippians, Colossians, and the prologue to the Gospel of John—their authors were forcing new analogies stretching the available fields of meanings and logical relations between them. If they were doing something of the sort, it would not require that Jewish tradition prior to Jesus had available this sense of wisdom as a pre-existent hypostasis or divine being; nor would it require that the authors intended to appeal to such meanings. The point of a metaphoric analogy is to create conceptual room to say what could not have otherwise been said by forcing language and logic to a new use. There is as much evidence for the claim that the disciples' reflection on a deeper level of their experience of Jesus forced such a metaphoric expansion of the available language and logic, as there is for Haight's assumption that what followers of Jesus could have intended to say was restricted to the fields of meanings available before such a metaphoric act or limited to what would have been conceivable to those whose experience did not force and warrant such a metaphoric process.

The tension between the historical Jesus and what is affirmed of him in worship and scripture—and eventually in creed—supports the metaphoric reading just as much as it supports Haight's restrictive symbolic reading; it explains better the realism of the claims that Jesus is Lord, the Word made flesh, and the image of the invisible God, the firstborn of all creation. A metaphoric realism, like Haight's symbolic reading, would insist that the logic of christology begins from below with Jesus and with the historical encounter of Jesus. By invoking such realism, we would concur with Haight:

> It is mistaken to read this wisdom language as though it were straightforward descriptive language that told the story of a divine being that descended to become Jesus. To understand this language as descriptive language about a being who is "on the side of the creator in the creator-creature distinction" is to misinterpret the kind of language that is being used and its epistemological provenance. These texts are not providing unknowable information about transcendent realities from some secret source of knowledge. The epistemology of these christologies begins from below, with Jesus, and their content is based on the encounter of God in and through Jesus. Their revelatory character in epistemological terms is ascending. To

the question about God and what God is like, these texts testify that Jesus mediates an answer. God is encountered in Jesus; God is revealed in Jesus; God is like Jesus; the wisdom of God is made manifest in Jesus; Jesus is the wisdom of God. Jesus himself responds to the questions, what is God's wisdom and where is it found?[35]

But a metaphoric reading would not concur with the conclusion that talk of Jesus as God's word incarnate is thereby illegitimate. Nor would a metaphoric reading require us to conclude that subsequently drawing implications for our understanding of God as triune is unwarranted. If such claims are metaphoric and if this metaphoric act is justified, then within that context there is a warrant for the proper use of such language and justification for predications that involve more than the symbolic meanings envisioned by Haight. While Haight's symbolic reading enables a vigorous affirmation of Jesus' historical reality, that reading severely restricts the divine. God and God's relation to creation seem bound by the logic that constrains beings and the relations between beings. This appears to be at the root of his objection that Rahner's Logos christology undermines the affirmation of Jesus' full humanity:

But despite his intentions and his strong affirmations of Jesus' real humanity, the suspicions arise at several points. Jesus is not like us insofar as God is present to Jesus as Logos and God is present to us as Spirit. In other words, God's presence as Logos to Jesus is a qualitatively different mode of presence than God's union with human beings generally. It seems metaphysically inconceivable that this different presence to Jesus would not make a substantial, ontological difference in him relative to God's presence to us. It would be an odd metaphysics that could imagine God assuming a human nature without ontologically transforming that human nature.[36]

It is an odd metaphysics only if one assumes that the same logic applies between God and beings as between beings themselves, only if one assumes that God is a competing part of nature or of the world, and only if one assumes that God's agency in the world is like other kinds of agency. Despite Haight's and Tillich's strong affirmations to the contrary, their symbolic reading of incarnation has the similarly odd character of treating the distinction between God and creatures as if it were like other distinctions. They insist that in the case of God, as in other cases, the "is" and "is not" must be either harmonized or different.

But are those the only two choices? A metaphoric reading would say no, and question whether Haight's symbolic realism takes seriously enough the uniqueness of the distinction between God and what is not God. The metaphoric libretto would argue along with Robert Sokolowski that the Christian sense of God entails a unique distinction between the divine and non-divine and that "once this new context is reached, new 'kinds' of differences become available" that were not available within philosophical and religious conceptual frameworks prior to Christianity.[37] It is precisely this distinction in the notion of divinity and this new conceptual framework, and not just the status of Jesus, that Sokolowski argues was at stake in the christological controversies. The councils required a new understanding of the logic of Christian talk about God and Jesus:

> . . . They tell us that we must think of God as the one who can let natural necessity be maintained and let reason be left intact: that is, God is not himself a competing part of nature or a part of the world. If the incarnation could not take place without a truncation of human nature, it would mean that God was one of the natures in the world that somehow was defined by not being the other natures; it would mean that his presence in one of these other natures, human nature, would involve a conflict and a need to exclude some part of what he is united with. . . . But the Christian God is not a part of the world and is not a "kind" of being at all. Therefore the incarnation is not meaningless or impossible or destructive.[38]

Does Haight worry about God's transcendence and immanence in the world becoming separated and competitive in hypostatized symbols because he has missed, and indeed precluded as possible, the distinction (the metaphoric shift) that Sokolowski discerns as a key insight emerging from the classical christological controversies? Is it not reasonable to view the innovations of wisdom and logos christology in the first centuries as forcing an analogy and warranting a logic that open up the possibility for affirming both the identity between Jesus and God, and the integrity of Jesus' humanity?—both the "is" and the "is not" at once?

This short paper cannot settle the question. It has barely sketched the outline of a constructive alternative for explaining the logic of Christian talk about Jesus' significance. An adequate critique of Haight's response to the question would require more substantial analysis, as would a defense of a metaphoric realism. I can only hope that I have played out enough of the overture to suggest the crucial themes in the proposed metaphoric libretto and score.

Notes

[1]". . . inconfuse, immutabiliter, indivise, inseparabiliter," #302, Heinrich Denzinger and Adolf Schonmetzer, *Enchiridion Symbolorum: Definitionum et Declarationum de rebus fidei et morum* (Barcinone: Herder, 1966), 108.

[2]Karl Rahner, S.J., "Current Problems in Christology," in his *Theological Investigations*, vol. 1, trans. Cornelius Ernst, O.P. (Baltimore: Helicon Press, 1969), 149-200, first published in 1954 with the title, *"Chalkedon—Ende oder Anfang?"*

[3]Roger Haight, S.J., *Jesus Symbol of God* (Maryknoll, N.Y.: Orbis Books, 1999). Hereafter cited as *Symbol*.

[4]Mary Gerhart and Allan Melvin Russell, *Metaphoric Process: The Creation of Scientific and Religious Understanding* (Fort Worth: Texas Christian University, 1984); and *New Maps for Old: Explorations in Science and Religion* (New York: Continuum, 2001).

[5]Roger Haight, S.J., *Dynamics of Theology* (Maryknoll, N.Y.: Orbis Books, 2001), 280, n.17.

[6]Ibid.

[7]Ibid.

[8]Paul Tillich, *Dynamics of Faith* (New York: Harper & Row, 1957), 44. In the first volume of his *Systematic Theology* (Chicago: University of Chicago Press, 1951-1963), 237, Tillich emphasized that "Being itself infinitely transcends every finite being. There is no proportion or gradation between the finite and the infinite. There is an absolute break, an infinite 'jump.'" Tillich explained the implications for christology in his essay "Theology and Symbolism," in *Religious Symbolism*, ed. F. Ernest Johnson (New York: Harper & Row, 1955), 114: "The second level of religious symbols is the sacramental level, namely, the appearance of the holy in time and space, in everyday realities. Realities in nature and history are the bearers of the holy on this level. Events, things, persons can have symbolic power. *The danger in sacramental holiness is that the holy is identified with that which is the bearer of the holy.* Where this happens religion relapses into magic. I believe that the vigorous opposition of the Reformers to the transubstantiation theory was the belief that it was a regression into the magical identification of the Divine with

the bearer of the Divine. *When we speak of Jesus we have the same problem. He is the bearer of what in symbolic terms is called the Christ.* The same is true of the Church. The Church is a sacramental reality. It is sociological, historical as is every group, and at the same time, it is the 'Body of Christ.' *In all these cases, the confusion of the holy itself with the bearer of the holy is the beginning of the distortion of religion"* (emphasis added). This understanding is at the root of Tillich's problems with the doctrine of the incarnation, formulated baldly in an early essay, "A Reinterpretation of the Doctrine of the Incarnation," *Church Quarterly Review*, 147 (January-March, 1949): 133-48, and articulated in a more nuanced way in the second volume of his *Systematic Theology*, 92-96, 138-50.

[9]*Symbol*, 112.

[10]Tillich, *Systematic Theology* I, 237.

[11]*Symbol*, 197.

[12]Ibid.

[13]*Symbol*, 480, where Haight is speaking about how one penetrates to the point of trinitarian doctrine.

[14]Karl Rahner, S.J., "The Theology of the Symbol," in *Theological Investigations* 4 (New York: Seabury, 1966), 221-52 (*Schriften zur Theologie* 4 [Einsiedeln: Benziger, 1954] 275-311). Hereafter I cite first the English translation followed by the pagination of the German text in square brackets.

[15]Ibid.

[16]Ibid., 228 [283] (*wobei die Einheit und Verschiedenheit korrelate, im selben Maß wachsende, nicht sich gegenseitig bis zur widersprüchlichen Ausschließlichkeit herabmindernde Größen sind*).

[17]*Symbol*, 11.

[18]"The Cognitive Effect of Metaphor," *Listening* 25 (1990): 114-26, at 119. Consider the difference in the concept that "bungalow" would call to mind by the interaction of such notions: in India (a thatched or tiled one-story dwelling surrounded by a wide verandah), in Aberdeen, Scotland (a small granite cottage huddled between similar structures), or in New England (a single-story wood-framed home). Even among those who share a world of meanings, the understandings of such notions can vary somewhat from person to person, depending on factors such as background, education, and linguistic sophistication. Moreover, meanings can change over time if new associations are made between existing notions, or if a new notion is added to a field of meanings. In the gospels, when Jesus identifies the notion of Messiah with that of the Suffering Servant, the association significantly alters not only these notions but, as well, a host of other notions related to the idea of eschatological expectation (a field of meanings), if not the very fabric of Jewish faith (a still broader field of meanings).

[19]See *New Maps for Old*, 53-60, for a number of examples.

[20]Ibid., 52.

[21]For a discussion of Martin Buber's use of the term and an argument that God-talk involves such a "turning" (although described as grammatical, not metaphorical) see Nicholas Lash's *Easter in Ordinary: Reflections on Human Experience and the Knowledge of God* (South Bend, Ind.: Notre Dame University Press, 1988), 193 ff.

[22]See my articles "Analogy and the Metaphoric Process," *Theological Studies* 62 (2001): 571-96, and "Metaphor as Apt for Conversation: The Inherently Conversational Character of Theological Discourse," in *Relational Theology,* Leuven Encounters in Systematic Theology, III (Leuven: Leuven University Press/ Uitgeverij Peeters [forthcoming]).

[23]*Symbol,* 49.

[24]Ibid.

[25]Ibid., 168.

[26]Ibid., 176.

[27]Ibid., quoting Elizabeth A. Johnson, "Jesus, the Wisdom of God: A Biblical Basis for Non-Androcentric Christology," *Ephemerides Theologicae Lovanienses* 61 (1985): 261-94, at 261.

[28]*Symbol,* 171, citing James D. G. Dunn, *Christology in the Making: A New Testament Inquiry into the Origins of the Doctrine of the Incarnation* (Philadelphia: Westminster Press, 1980), 170 and 205-12.

[29]Ibid., citing Peter T. O'Brien, *The Epistle to the Philippians: A Commentary on the Greek Text* (Grand Rapids: Eerdmans, 1991), 216.

[30]Ibid., 173.

[31]Ibid., 172.

[32]Ibid., 13.

[33]Ibid., 112.

[34]Ibid., 437-38.

[35]Ibid., 173.

[36]Ibid., 432-33.

[37]*The God of Faith & Reason: Foundation of Christian Theology* (Washington, D.C.: The Catholic University Press, 1982, 1995), 48.

[38]Ibid., 36.

Response to Robert Masson:
The Clash of Christological Symbols

Roger Haight

Introduction

I welcome this chance to discuss christological issues, and I am most pleased that this is being done in dialogue with *Jesus Symbol of God*; for me this is invaluable. Further, I am grateful to Robert Masson for the high level of the interchange, and I hope the discussion will be creative.

I will make five points briefly that comment on Masson's paper and attempt to clarify what I am up to, both within the larger goal of addressing basic issues in christology.

Contrasting My View of Symbol with Rahner's

Masson's critique in some measure comes from a commitment to Rahner's thought on the matter of symbol. A major theme of Masson consists in a comparison between the conception or theology of symbol in Rahner and in my thinking. But I believe that someone living in a Rahnerian house could find much more agreement and family resemblance between the methods and concepts that I employ and those of Karl Rahner. Those looking for agreements would find many. One reviewer of *Jesus Symbol of God* locates it generally within a Rahnerian paradigm.[1] I hope that in the course of these comments it becomes clear that I have been deeply influenced by Rahner, whom I have internalized, even when at points I diverge from his positions. As a preface to comment on this point, however, I should say that in using all and any one of the many sources that have fed my positions in *Jesus Symbol of God* my general intention has not been to represent these authors in an historically accurate way. I have used the ideas and distinctions of others and then put them to work for me. This often results in expanding the meaning of the original source, sometimes producing something partially or significantly different.

Symbolic and Metaphoric Realism

To state the same thing more positively, I do not believe that as much distance separates my symbolic realism and Masson's metaphoric realism as Masson proposes in his critique. I say that largely on two counts: the first is that while much if not most of what he says about my use of symbol is accurate—for he proceeds with great care—still I do not agree with everything that he says about my understanding and use of symbol or of symbolic predication. The second point is that I resonate with most if not all of what he says about metaphoric realism, even when I might disagree with this or that use of it in the case of Jesus. What these add up to is that, should I have been schooled in metaphoric realism, I could have used it to make my case in a book entitled "Jesus Metaphor of God." I hope that Masson writes that book.

However, I do have a reservation: most of what Masson describes through "metaphoric realism" has to do with epistemology, judgment, and predication. Symbols as I analyze them are both conscious (epistemological) and concrete (beings, and in this sense ontological). This versatility allows analysis of both our language about God, including language about Jesus as medium for an encounter with God, and Jesus himself as a concrete symbol. Is there a place or the idea of a "concrete" metaphor that allows an analysis of the person of Jesus? I don't see why not: Jesus is often called the parable of God.

On My Conception of Symbol and Rahner's

I can define my relation to Karl Rahner on symbol briefly: first, I have been impressed by his famous article on the theology of symbol, but I have never accepted the structure of how he developed that essay beginning with a theology of the Trinity to show that being itself is symbolic in its being unity-in-plurality. I consider his procedure in this essay pedagogically unsound, as in a method moving from the unknown to the known. With an apologetic interest, I have always gravitated to the third part of that essay in which he reflects on the body as the symbol of the human person that yields to phenomeno-logical description more directly accessible to the reader.

Now one of the many things that Masson's essay taught me is that this starting point of Rahner represents a general structure of his think-ing on symbol, which moves from unity to plurality or differentiation. "For Rahner, symbol, in the most original and basic sense, is the oth-erness of a being itself through which the being is expressed" (Masson, p. 68). This theme plays out in a stress on unity of differences in Rahner (being is being-positing-itself-in-the-other) versus a stress on differ-ences in unity in my conception (dialectic between "is" and "is not"). There is some measure of truth to this, and it could have its conse-quences in preferences for a more Alexandrian in the sense of Cyrillian christology versus an Antiochene formula. Also, one sees at this point a difference between Rahner and myself relative to both symbol and christology: Rahner's theology of symbol in this essay entails a christology from above, whereas my christology is developed from below. My starting point leads first not to God as Word as symbolic of God's self, but to Jesus as symbol of God. I wonder whether this rep-resents the difference that Masson, in his own way, has uncovered between symbol in Rahner and as I have portrayed it: a difference that ultimately consists in two distinct strategies that proceed from very different imaginative frameworks serving as points of departure from above and from below.

But, at the same time, I also find genuine duality and altereity in Rahner's theology of symbol, which I understand as rooted in hylomorphism. That is to say, Rahner's theology of symbol can be understood within the Thomistic framework of the human spirit being the "form" of the "matter" of the human, where matter and spirit are really distinct and related as contraries: spirit is non-matter. This I take to be the root of real and even radical difference between consti-tutive elements of the structure of the real symbol that is the human person in Rahner. I hope that Masson can clarify this interpretation of Rahner's view of symbol as it is realized in the human person.

Finally, to conclude this point, I have some reservations about Masson's own conclusion that I cannot without more argument ap-peal to Rahner as warrant for my theology of symbol. Certainly there are differences of emphasis, especially since I have drawn Rahner's "real symbol" into the framework of a christology from below. But whereas Masson's generalized conclusion is in some respects true enough, it gives a wrong impression of too great a distance. I am too strongly influenced by Rahner, at least enough for an astute reviewer to call my position Rahnerian, for the implications of Masson's conclusion to be true.

Where Rahner's Influence Can Be Highlighted in My View of Symbol

There are several points at which I believe what I say is deeply in accord with Rahner, and I would like to highlight a few of them with less than adequate development.

First, the phenomenology of the self, where the body both "is" and "is not" the self. This is the prime analogate of a real or concrete symbol in my thinking, and I draw it from Rahner.[2] Interestingly, Masson's essay (Masson, p. 67) does not refer to my version of that phenomenology as it appears in *Dynamics of Theology*.[3]

Second, by the term "dialectic" I mean the interplay between "is" and "is not," whether in a real symbol or in a conceptual symbol, that is, in epistemology and predication. At times Masson gets this exactly right; at other times his interpretation of what I mean by dialectic seems to emphasize the difference between what are being held together, or the distance and "over-againstness" between symbol and symbolized. I draw my view from the prime analogate in which irreducible matter and form constitute a single human being or entity.

Third, I am deeply committed to Rahner's account of mystagogy describing the way concrete and conceptual symbols lead one into transcendence. This basic structure suffuses all the religious reference and directly spiritual language of *Jesus Symbol of God*. Religious symbols draw one into mystery.

Fourth, Thomas Aquinas provides a major text and conceptualization for my understanding of religious epistemology, that is, his statement of the *triplex via* (Aquinas, *ST*, I, 13, 2-3). I take it that the passage within symbolic knowledge of transcendence moves through an appreciation of something about God drawn from experiences of objects within this world, whose finite and created meaning within the field of this-worldly meanings has to be radically denied or negated, in order to open up its true meaning as applied to God within the horizon or field of an awareness of transcendence. I frankly found no dissonance between Masson's description of the epistemological process of metaphoric realism and the view of symbol that I propose.

The Question on the Table Today

Predication in the framework of metaphoric realism refers to statements that are uncalled for within a given field or sphere of meaning. In their realism these statements break open the field of meaning itself and alter many if not all of the meanings that exist within it. Masson has illustrated this well with his example of the statement that Jesus is the Christ. A couple of qualities of that very confession help to illustrate the question that is on the table today. One is that metaphoric realism is easier in the case of Jesus being messiah than in the case of Chalcedon and its attendant theology or theologies. For as far as I know, and I always hesitate in matters biblical, the idea of messiah did not imply a divine figure, but a chosen human being. Things get far more complicated in some interpretations of the application of Logos to Jesus, depending on how one construes the logical status, meaning, and referent of the term Logos. A second is that the realism of Jesus being messiah upset a Jewish field of meanings, but it became the status quo of the Christian field of meanings. In the current Christian field of meaning, Jesus' being messiah is so accepted that it has been turned into his name.

However, the question on the table in the increasingly globalized and postmodern culture of today, it seems to me, is whether, given our situation and culture, Christianity should rest content with more of the same, that is, our current modern and universalistic interpretation of Jesus (read Rahnerian), or whether we should accept the challenge of a new metaphoric or symbolic understanding of Jesus that breaks open the present Christian field of meaning, allowing it realistically to address this new world.

Notes

[1] Peter C. Hodgson, *Religious Studies Review* 27 (2001): 152.

[2] Also from John E. Smith, "The Disclosure of God and Positive Religion," *Experience and God* (New York: Oxford University Press, 1968), 68-98.

[3] Roger Haight, *Dynamics of Theology* (Maryknoll, N.Y.: Orbis Books, 2001), 136-39.

The Power of Divine Presence:
Toward a *Shekhinah* Christology

Gloria L. Schaab

The mystery of Christ is enveloped by both excess luminosity and historical darkness, and those who attempt to elucidate some aspect of this mystery "need to partner words with silence, truth with provisionality."[1] Because of the personal, historical, cultural, and theological limitations that each theologian brings to such attempts, all christologies are "transitory compositions that use contingent conceptual instruments"[2] by which to grasp the impenetrable and express the ineffable.[3] Nevertheless, a word, however halting, must be spoken, and a truth, however partial, must be risked, since the words of the Markan Jesus (8:29) confront each theologian with the challenge, "But who do you say that I am?"[4]

In response to this perennial question, this particular christological project of mine follows the feminist methodological process of critique, retrieval, and reconstruction. It seeks to provide a lens through which Jesus the Christ, divine and human, may be understood. Intended as a theological thought experiment, this venture has been pursued in response to three significant critiques of traditional christological models: the discounting or distortion of the Jewish heritage of Jesus; the issue of the significance of the maleness of Jesus for soteriology, anthropology, and ecclesiology; and the negative implications of atonement christologies that valorize suffering and victimization as salvific, redemptive, and exemplary in Christian life and belief. The paradigm advanced to address these diverse issues is termed "*Shekhinah* christology," based upon the traditionally female personification—and ultimate hypostatization—of the immanent presence of God with the oppressed and suffering people of Israel, commented upon in Jewish rabbinic and kabbalist literature.

Beginning with a cursory overview of the fundamental issues associated with each of the three critiques, this study proceeds with an extensive presentation of the tradition of the *Shekhinah* from rabbinic, kabbalist, and contemporary sources. These movements culminate in a process that seeks to correlate images, concepts, actions, and beliefs within the *Shekhinah* tradition with those employed in biblical and doctrinal interpretations concerning Jesus of Nazareth, proclaimed the Christ. The goal of this correlation is to suggest the possibility of an alternative christological paradigm, one that characterizes Jesus the Christ as the incarnation of the *Shekhinah* of God.

In doing so, this project encounters substantial biblical exegesis, research, and literature associated with the paradigm of Sophia christology, especially with regard to its appropriation of the Christian biblical witness. The scriptural imagery and concepts that this study places in dialogue with the *Shekhinah* tradition have generally been interpreted within the hermeneutical framework of the Hebrew and Hellenistic Wisdom traditions.[5] Nevertheless, while the Sophia interpretive framework has the capacity to bear the weight of Jesus' ministry as sage and prophet, it strains to account for his ministry to and identification with the oppressed, and for his passion and death on the cross. Hence, while acknowledging the extensive and influential scholarship in support of a Wisdom interpretation of this testimony, this study attempts to read the shared biblical witness through a different lens and to explore the possibility that the *Shekhinah* tradition may provide a more encompassing framework within which to understand the expanse of Jesus' mission and ministry. Therefore, its approach is exploratory, rather than exegetical; its intent is investigative, rather than authoritative.

Critiquing Christological Models

Jesus the Jew

In *A Guest in the House of Israel: Post-Holocaust Church Theology*, Clark M. Williamson details the detrimental effects that the Christian narrative of the life, death, and resurrection of Jesus has had for Jews throughout the Common Era.[6] Nevertheless, throughout much of its development, the Christian tradition in general and christology in particular seem to have ignored this reality. Failing to interpret Jesus within his historical context, the tradition had frequently portrayed the life and death of Jesus as an epic of ongoing conflict with the Jewish people and with Judaism itself, creating a "self-conscious Christian tradition . . . deliberately distanced . . . from the historical Jewish context in which Jesus lived and died."[7] According to Howard Clark Kee, Christian sources since the *Quelle* have repeatedly advanced conflict models of Jesus' teaching and actions.[8] In the interpretive development and redaction of the gospel narratives and Luke-Acts, Jesus' instruction explicitly confronts the teachings of Pharisaic Judaism (Luke 11:37-12:1; Matt. 23: 2-36); his actions are characterized as contradictions to Jewish ritual and custom (Matt. 11:18-19; Mark 2:18-3:3; Luke 5:29-30, 15:1-2); and responsibility for his death progressively shifts from the Romans (Mark 15:15-20; Matt. 27:26-31) to the Jewish people and their religious leaders (Luke 23:24, 26; John 19:16, 18; Acts 2:36, 4:8-11), who conspire with the Romans to eliminate him as a threat to their religious traditions and to the welfare of the nation as a whole. Furthermore, in the development of certain christological proposals, the resurrection became interpreted not only as Jesus' victory over death by the power of God, but also as his vindication over the Jewish rejection of his message and his claims.[9]

Significant voices raising the Jewish critique concerning christological constructions have arisen from feminist theological traditions, particularly in the scholarship of Rosemary Radford Ruether and Judith Plaskow.[10] Plaskow turns this critique toward feminist theologies themselves for separating Jesus from or contrasting Jesus with his Jewish context and heritage in their attempt to characterize Jesus' life and ministry as antithetical to the cultural and religious oppression of women prevalent in his historical context.[11] Such constructs attempt to distance Jesus from his patriarchal milieu in order to characterize his conduct and ministry as congruent with feminist sensibilities and goals.

Contemporary reconstructions of the Christ symbol reflect new understandings of Jesus in relation to the Judaism of his day and recognize Jesus' life, ministry, death, and resurrection as a revelation of the character of the God of Israel.[12] Such proposals point out the biblical testimony concerning Jesus' commitment to the "lost sheep of the house of Israel" and the witness of his early interpreters who identified him in terms of Judaic concepts and thought patterns, such as Messiah, Son of Man, Suffering Servant, Wisdom, and Son of God, which conveyed the significance of his life and teaching.[13] While many of these were transformed in content and meaning into christological

titles signifying his divinity, "to confess faith in Jesus Christ is to acknowledge the stubborn facticity, the unbudgeable particularity, of
the Jew Jesus in whom we believe . . . who takes form in the history of
the people Israel and in the scriptures of Israel."[14]

Jesus the Male

Despite attempts by feminist theologians to retrieve Jesus from his
patriarchal milieu, Elisabeth Schüssler Fiorenza nevertheless questions
"whether the historical man Jesus of Nazareth can be a role model for
contemporary women . . . [in] the struggle of women to free themselves from all male internalized norms and models."[15] Elizabeth A.
Johnson points out that since Christ's "deified" maleness has exem-
plified and reinforced the anthropological superiority and normativity
of the male and has been interpreted ecclesiastically as "essential to
his redeeming Christic functions and identity," the symbol of Christ
often "serves as a religious tool for marginalizing and excluding
women."[16] Thus, in the words of Jacquelyn Grant, "feminists ask what
can be said about a religious expression which makes its supreme deity totally represented in one male figure through whom everyone must
pass to be saved?"[17]

Certainly, there is no disputing the maleness of Jesus as a historical
reality, nor is there any need to consider his sexual particularity as
constitutive of the event of salvation accomplished through him.[18]
However, the critical issue of the erroneous deification of the maleness of Jesus, articulated in and perpetrated through the christological
tradition, clearly provokes a feminist critique.[19] This notion functions
to distort the *imago Dei* into an exclusively male concept and to exemplify, justify, and reinforce the dominance of the male over the
female in social, political, and ecclesial structures. Furthermore, it
buttresses the normativity of the male as representing the fullness of
human potential and restricts the full participation of women in ecclesial
ministry and leadership.

To address this apparent impasse, several reconstructive models
have been suggested. These include re-readings of the traditional texts
in ways that accentuate the liberative and compassionate praxis of
Jesus; allegorical interpretations of the power of the incarnation in
terms of love, relationship, and interdependence; and historical reconstructions that use biblical scholarship "to reduce the offensiveness of

the masculinity of Jesus" through interpretative paradigms such as the
Sophia tradition or the Christ of faith.[20] Nevertheless, if Jesus' humanity is circumscribed by his maleness and the Christ symbol is cor-
rupted through misrepresentation, contemporary christological reflections must discover and disclose images of the divine being that, of
their very nature, are resistant to being distorted by the patriarchal
imagination.

Jesus the Victim

While Anne Carr suggests that one can study the "great traditions"
of christology "without even encountering the question of women,"
the same could hardly be said concerning the question of suffering.[21]
Jesus' suffering and death, as well as his distinctive personal involvement with the suffering, the outcast, and the oppressed, are well documented throughout the Christian tradition. Jesus' experiences of and
responses to his own suffering and that of others have become paradigmatic for interpreting the meaning of Jesus' ministry and mission,
as well as for characterizing the Christian life modeled on his example.
This paradigm has been given expression in those christologies that
explain the suffering and crucifixion of Jesus as salvific, redemptive,
and essentially necessary in the divine plan of reconciling the world to
Godself.[22] Nevertheless, each of these theories of salvation has significant ramifications for the human response to suffering, the nature
of God, and the nature of suffering itself.[23]

While the classic image of the crucified Christ communicates the
message that suffering is redemptive and that suffering for others effects the salvation of the world, critiques from feminist, womanist,
liberation, and post-Holocaust theologies contend that this image glo-
rifies suffering, violence, and abuse and commends freely chosen suffering as an example to be emulated.[24] In their powerful essay, "God
So Loved the World?" Rebecca Parker and Joanne Carlson Brown
characterize the notion that Jesus suffered in accord with God's will
as an example of "divine child abuse" in which death is lauded as
salvific and the suffering child represents the hope of the world.[25]
Womanist theologian Delores Williams asserts that the event of the
cross legitimates the surrogacy experience of the black slave woman
by valorizing the notion of bearing others' burdens and insists that the
glorification of the cross is the glorification of sin.[26]

The image of the Crucified has also been characterized as the "scape-goat image," an idealization of the virtues of the victim in which self-sacrifice, humility, passivity, and suffering are accepted not only as the will of God, but also as qualities especially idealized for, ascribed to, and embodied by women.[27] Although liberation theologians have attempted to redeem the image of the cross as a viable and meaningful symbol of ultimate liberation for the oppressed peoples of the earth, Walter Rauschenbusch wrote in *A Theology for the Social Gospel*, "A conception of God which describes him as sanctioning the present order and utilizing it in order to sanctify its victims through their suffering, without striving for its overthrow, is repugnant to our moral sense."[28] From their perspective that "no one was saved by the death of Jesus," Parker and Brown ultimately articulate the essential truth of the Christian tradition—that the cross is a sign of tragedy where God's grief and love are revealed[29] and where "God sings *kaddish*" at the death of the beloved one.[30]

Retrieving the Traditions of the *Shekhinah*

According to Gershom Scholem, prominent twentieth-century scholar in the study of Jewish mysticism, "The *Shekhinah* . . . is a concept that has intimately accompanied the Jewish people for some two thousand years, through all phases of its turbulent and tragic existence . . . itself undergoing manifold developments and transformations."[31] The term *Shekhinah*[32] is derived from the Hebrew *shakan*, meaning *presence* or *act of dwelling*, and is expressed as a feminine-gendered substantive. Expressed in the Aramaic form *shekinta*, the appellation initially appeared between the first century B.C.E. and the first century C.E. in the *Targum Onkelos*, the interpretative Aramaic translation of the Hebrew Scriptures. In this translation, the term *Shekhinah* referred to an aspect of the deity perceived by humanity as an expression to avoid direct reference to God, or as an abstract concept in place of anthropomorphic language.[33] *Shekhinah* also appears in the Talmud, the Midrash, and other post-biblical rabbinic writings, as well as in the Kabbalah, the literature of the Jewish mystical tradition.[34] However, the term itself does not appear in biblical or non-rabbinic literature, despite creative attempts to infer its presence or reference.[35]

In the early rabbinic sources, the *Shekhinah* "connotes the personification and hypostatization of God's presence in the world," of God's immanence and immediacy in a specific place on earth.[36] The Talmud referred to the *Shekhinah* as a visible and audible manifestation as well as the omnipresence and activity of God in the world.[37] In the Midrash of the rabbis, the *Shekhinah* is recognized as an independent divine entity, female in form, who dwells with the chosen in times good or ill, who intercedes compassionately with God for humanity, and who is present even within the humblest circumstances and with the most insignificant of creatures.[38] In the earliest kabbalist sources, the *Shekhinah* attains a fuller sense and significance as a completely female hypostatization and becomes "simultaneously mother, bride, and daughter within the structure of the Godhead constitut[ing] a very meaningful step, with far-reaching consequences."[39]

While each interpretative framework communicated its specific notion of *Shekhinah* from a particular religious, theological, and philosophical position, each perspective cited above acknowledged *Shekhinah* as divine, as identified with God's very self, and as distinguished as an independent entity. Furthermore, *Shekhinah* is recognized as existent both transcendently within the Godhead and immanently within creation as a whole, and with the suffering in particular.

For the purposes of this christological study, four specific elements within and across the multiple strains of these traditions associated with the *Shekhinah* will be examined: her immanence as the divine presence within creation, her intimate alliance with the suffering and oppressed, her identification with the *Malchut* (kingdom) of God, and her characterization as a female hypostatization. By focusing upon these particular elements, this research intends to suggest an interpretative framework through which to image Jesus of Nazareth as the incarnation of the *Shekhinah* of God.

The Shekhinah *as the Immanence of the Transcendent God*

According to Ephraim Urbach, awareness of the *Shekhinah* arose as a consequence of the attempt to reconcile the duality of God's transcendent and immanent presence in relation to the world. While God was acknowledged as supreme and removed from human history, the Jewish people nonetheless experienced the nearness of God's providence and care.[40] While philosophers debated the relationship of the transcendence and immanence of the Divine, the witness of the people of Israel testified that this existence of God in the world was experienced not only as presence, but as intimacy and immediacy as well. This indwelling omnipresence of God was called by the name *Shekhinah* and was clearly understood as the link between the eternal and temporal worlds, one who had been sent by God as the very presence of the Divine.[41]

In rabbinic literature, *Shekhinah* was both an appellation interchangeable with God and a quality or possession of the Deity, given to the world solely because of Israel.[42] Images and metaphors linked with her appearance included radiant light, cloud, and wings. According to the tradition of the Hasidim, God produced a created light, the *kavod*, as "the first of all creation" from which resounds the voice and word of God to the prophets and holy ones.[43] This universal light is also associated with the glory of God resplendent in Israel, in the universe, and in the Temple, the "hidden radiance of the totality of the hidden divine life which dwells in every created, existing being."[44] During Israel's sojourn in the desert, the *Shekhinah* is correlated with the cloud that leads the chosen people by day, as well as the fire that guides them by night (Exod. 13:22f); she is the cloud of glory that descends on the Ark of the Covenant (Exod. 40:34-38). According to Abelson, the notion of the wings of the *Shekhinah* denotes both proselytism and protection. Those who are introduced to the Jewish faith are said to be brought under her wings, while these same wings represent God's sheltering care, covering the world as a mother bird shelters her young.[45]

Shortly before the appearance of Christianity, the *Shekhinah* began to develop as an independent entity and her spiritual presence took substance. According to a Talmudic tenet, the *Shekhinah* could be localized in a particular place and her movements among humanity become discernible. The *Shekhinah* speaks and acts, sings with joy and cries with grief, admonishes and encourages, becomes angry and appeased. She is said to have dwelt on the Mount of Olives for three and a half years waiting for Israel to repent and to have wept over the Temple, offering peace. "If two or more sit together and occupy themselves with words of Torah" or wherever ten or more are gathered, the *Shekhinah* abides in their midst.

In a truly radical development around the third century C.E., a midrash on Proverbs 22:29 concerning the stature of those who are skillful in their work tells of the *Shekhinah* standing before the Holy

One to argue for the just man Solomon. In a commentary on Leviticus 6:1-7 addressing those who commit a breach of faith against their neighbors, the *Shekhinah* is described as trying to influence God not to carry out retribution against Israel. These occasions mark a dialogical distinction between *Shekhinah* and the Holy One in which she finds her own voice in opposition to God. She is considered to have an opinion, a mind, a will, and a personality.[46]

Thus, the *Shekhinah* develops into a mediator between humanity and God, heaven and earth. In a kabbalist parable, the *Shekhinah* is symbolized as the king's daughter who is sent as an emissary from the divine realm to the lower world. Though separated from the king, she is close to him always, and even on earth retains the glory of her divine origin and essence. Through her embodiment, God enters the world. She alone is the medium through which God is accessible to human beings. Her mission is to aid Israel in fulfilling the Torah, in order that Israel may be reunited with God.[47]

While some commentators insist that sin and lack of faith cause the *Shekhinah* to depart, others contend that the *Shekhinah* of God dwells in Israel at all times and at all costs. In midrashim on Ezekiel 36 and Exodus 15:5, the rabbis assert that the *Shekhinah* remains with Israel even though the people are impure and reveals herself in places of filth and uncleanliness in order to redeem Israel. Nevertheless, all commentators agree that, though the *Shekhinah* may temporarily depart, she returns with repentance and, through acts of righteousness, the *Shekhinah* dwells on earth unceasingly.[48]

The Shekhinah *in Intimate Alliance with the Suffering and the Poor*

According to kabbalist master Ramchal (Rabbi Mosche Chaim Luzzato), God chooses to manifest God's *Shekhinah* to a greater degree in a particular place according to the "spiritual repairs" deemed necessary in that circumstance.[49] Undeniably, one such place in which the *Shekhinah* is considered consistently to dwell is among the suffering and the poor of Israel. Countless tracts from the rabbinic and kabbalist literature affirm that the *Shekhinah* shares the joys and the affliction of both the community and the individual person of Israel.[50] The *Shekhinah* is experienced as an ever-constant presence when Israel is in trouble, to the extent that the Divine feels the pain of the human.[51] "When a human being suffers, what does the *Shekhinah* say?

'My head is too heavy for me; my arm is too heavy for me.' And if God is so grieved over the blood of the wicked that is shed, how much more so over the blood of the righteous?"[52]

Thus, "by taking up residence amid the people of Israel, [the *Shekhinah*] has made Israel's destiny her own. She is responsible for Israel and Israel likewise for her. Only through her does Israel have access to God."[53] In the *Shekhinah,* the infinite God is linked with the destiny of a historical people in an earthly, limited space.[54] More than an isolated theophany, the *Shekhinah* literally walks in the midst of the people Israel, ever mindful of their sufferings, watching over them with love. She draws close to the sick and the dying to comfort them (TB Sabbath 12b) and helps those in need (Targum to Judges 6:13). She shows special concern for the repentant sinner (R. Akiba in Bet Ha Midrash III.29) and is attracted by their good deeds (TB Sanhedrin 103b-104a).[55] The *Shekhinah* is connected with expressions of love; she blesses bridegrooms, adorns brides (TB Sotah 17a), and turns the light of her face toward those who share their wealth with the poor.[56]

Most frequently, this personal presence of the *Shekhinah* is associated with the event of exile. As recorded in the Tractate Megillah, "Come and see how beloved are the Israelites before God; for wherever they went into exile, the *Shekhinah* followed them. . . . And when, in the future, Israel will be redeemed, the *Shekhinah* will then be with them."[57] This insight gives expression to two significant elements of this exilic perspective: the exile of the *Shekhinah* from God's very self and her consequent need for redemption and reunification. As articulated by Franz Rosenzweig in *The Star of Redemption*, the descent of the *Shekhinah* into exile, which is attributed to human sin, is considered to be a division in God's very self. In the decision of God to give the divine self away to the people of Israel, God cuts God off from Godself, emptying the divine self in self-surrender to the destiny of the chosen people.[58] In the *Shekhinah*, God is carried into captivity with God's people, sharing their misery and their wanderings. As the wounded one, *Shekhinah* not only weeps for the suffering of her people, crying out when someone undergoes punishment, but also suffers their persecutions with them, "like Israel's twin."[59] As a consequence, the *Shekhinah* herself is considered to be in need of redemption. "Since God's sufferings in exile were taken completely seriously, Israel's deliverance from Exile was logically bound to be seen as God's deliverance too. . . . In this intimate bond of common suffering, God and

Israel wait together for their deliverance."[60] As paradoxical and radical as this inference seems, it nonetheless serves to ground Israel's future hope, since "by 'selling himself' to Israel . . . and by suffering [Israel's] fate . . . [God] makes himself in need of redemption."[61] Therefore, if God's own self is in need of redemption, then "Israel knows it will be delivered, since God will deliver himself and his people with him. . . . The suffering of God is the means by which Israel is redeemed: God himself is 'the ransom' for Israel."[62]

The Shekhinah *and the Kingdom of God*

In the kabbalist Book of Bahir of the second century B.C.E. are recorded the divine emanations or powers called the *Sefirot* of the Tree of Life or *Adam Kadmon* (Primordial Man). Some commentators characterize these *Sefirot* as stages of the creative process through which God created the universe, while others recognize them as attributes of God.[63] Through them "the divine life pulses back and forth" in a network of channels that represent the flow of divine energy through creation.[64] For this study, two of these *Sefirot* are of interest: *Shekhinah* (Divine Presence) and *Malchut* (Kingdom).[65]

According to this tradition, the *Shekhinah* stands at the edge of creation, where she receives and collects the energies from the higher *Sefirot*. In this sense, the *Shekhinah* is characterized as the passive or receptive element in God, from whose receptivity creation emerges.[66] From the threshold of the earthly realm, the *Shekhinah* pours forth the divine energies within her to the world, while simultaneously directing these energies upward again toward the higher realm. Thus, the *Shekhinah* serves as the mediator between heaven and earth, sharing all that she has received from the Godhead with creation and returning all to the Godhead through her being. Furthermore, the *Shekhinah* is also known as *Malchut*, the Kingdom, which represents God's dominion and power in the world. Identified as the power of self-expression or the "world of speech," the *Malchut* both reveals its presence to earthly reality and guides that reality. Together, *Shekhinah/ Malchut* embodies the law and the conduct of the world, is associated with the oral Torah, and represents that part of the divine which is present to humanity and creation. Furthermore, this *Malchut* is the sphere of salvation, the place where creation began in God and where redemption and reunion of creation with God are accomplished.[67]

The Shekhinah *as a Female Hypostatization*

Throughout this exploration, the *Shekhinah* has been referenced as a female hypostatization of the one God, a reference that has been consistently affirmed throughout the variety of traditions and the centuries of development with regard to this divine being. In addition to the effect of grammatical gender, Gershom Scholem attributes this development to several influences associated with the kabbalist tradition. Scholem first cites the impact of gnosticism, with its bipolar conceptualization of the Divine. He suggests that the popularity of this notion may have signaled that a female hypostatization of the Divine "touched upon a fundamental and primal need" within the adherents of Judaism. Another source of this development, according to Scholem, may have been situated in the conceptualization of the *Tree of Life* in which the *Shekhinah* was characterized as a vessel of receptivity for the energies and creativities of other emanations. This notion carried with it attributes of passivity and receptivity, which, in a patriarchal environment, would have been stereotypically "feminine" traits. Finally, Scholem suggests that the female characterization may have arisen within some strains of the tradition that identified the *Shekhinah* with the community of Israel. Since the community was frequently referred to in female terms because of its covenant relationship with "her" male-gendered God, Israel's identification with the body of the *Shekhinah* resulted in the transfer of the female metaphor to the *Shekhinah*.[68]

From a feminist theological perspective, these initial influences hardly commend themselves as a basis upon which to appropriate this female symbolization for reconstructive use. With the exception of the notion that the tradition of the *Shekhinah* may have struck a profound chord within the adherents of Judaism throughout the centuries, the other proposals simply reinforce the patriarchal stereotypes of passivity, receptivity, and submission decisively associated with female gender roles. Nevertheless, it is noteworthy that the conceptualization and hypostatization of the *Shekhinah* steadfastly progressed throughout her history toward greater and fuller individualization. From an extension and possession of the Godhead, the *Shekhinah* rose to her feet to acquire and develop a voice, a power, and a purpose distinguishing her from a transcendent, distant God and setting her in intimate relationship with a suffering, marginalized people.

Toward a *Shekhinah* Christology

The insight of understanding Jesus through the tradition of the *Shekhinah* has been suggested in recent years by several theologians. Both Elizabeth A. Johnson and Michael E. Lodahl have associated the presence and action of the *Shekhinah* with that of the Spirit of God in Jesus. Lodahl, in particular, has progressed toward a *Shekhinah* christology, emphasizing the pneumatological evidence of the *Shekhinah* in the synoptic gospels.[69] In the essay *"Shekinah: The Home of the Homeless God,"* Jürgen Moltmann discusses points of correlation between a pneumatology of the *Shekhinah* and Christian incarnational theology. According to Moltmann, Jesus, like the *Shekhinah*, represents the indwelling of God in the world, with the fullness of deity residing in him.[70] In *The Trinity and the Kingdom*, Moltmann associates the *Shekhinah* with divine kenosis and pathos. As the anticipation of God's universal, eschatological indwelling, the *Shekhinah* is proleptic in her indwelling in Israel, her condescension to earth, and her representation of the glory to come. Present in Israel, the *Shekhinah* suffers its persecutions, its death, and its exile; thus, the suffering of Israel is embedded in the suffering of God. According to Moltmann, this is "the most moving potentiality" of the tradition of the *Shekhinah*—that it allows humanity to comprehend Israel's history of suffering as the history of the tortured *Shekhinah* of God.[71]

This association undergoes a significant development in an essay by Philip E. Devenish in which he draws the tradition of the *Shekhinah* into direct relation with the Incarnation, contending that "The *Shekhinah* functions for Jews as the incarnation functions for Christians."[72] Both Jesus and the *Shekhinah* encamp in the world, participate as co-sufferers with God's people, and involve Godself in the world with intimacy and immediacy.[73] Similarly, Peter Schäfer correlates the sending of the "Son" of God in Christianity with the sending of the "Daughter" of God in the Bahir. Although both dwell among humanity, the Son becomes flesh, while the Daughter does not, indicating to Schäfer that the Jewish Bahir "could press no further" to the idea of incarnation.[74]

The question that presents itself now is, "Can the *Christian* tradition press further?" While the traditional Jewish conception of God precludes a full hypostatization of the *Shekhinah* of God, can the *Shekhinah* find such expression within the tenets of Christianity? Can

Jesus the Christ be legitimately interpreted through the tradition of the *Shekhinah* of God?[75] This study recognizes that such a proposition is fraught with conditionality. It is fundamentally perilous to isolate a theological concept from one religious tradition to elucidate a construct from another. An appropriated concept seldom encompasses all the particularities it is intended to explain and frequently undergoes a process of selectivity consistent with one's project. While asserting the mutually illuminative potentials of Judaism and Christianity, this study, nonetheless, upholds the theological integrity of these two traditions. It does not intend to eclipse or ravage Jewish traditions, to demonstrate or advocate trinitarianism in the Jewish notion of monotheism, or to validate or promote Jesus' theological and soteriological claims based on Jewish belief. However, this project does seek to press forward within the Christian context to illuminate numerous points of conceptual, imagistic, and metaphorical contact between the traditions of the *Shekhinah* and of Jesus the Christ, and, thus, to propose a christological paradigm of Jesus as the *Shekhinah* of God.

Jesus-Shekhinah *as the Immanence of the Transcendent God*

Points of contact between the tradition of the *Shekhinah* and that of Jesus of Nazareth are found throughout the Christian testamental and doctrinal witness. While much of the witness involves Jesus' intimate association with and liberative actions toward the outcast, the marginalized, and the suffering, there exists a selection of images and metaphors that provide a symbol-system shared by both traditions. Perhaps the clearest representation of this symbol-system is found in the Gospel of John, beginning with the prologue and continuing through the images, affirmations, and theological claims attributed to Jesus in that tradition.

While the bridge across the chasm of the transcendence and immanence of God was provided, under Hellenistic influence, by Philo's notion of the *Logos*, in the Jewish rabbinic tradition it was mitigated through the concept of the *Shekhinah*. The opening proclamation of the Gospel of John (1:1-5, 14, 18) capsulizes the fundamental Jesus-*Shekhinah* tradition, which then unfolds through the remainder of the gospel. The prologue asserts that Jesus Christ, like the *Shekhinah*, shares the existence, eternality, and divinity of the transcendent God, and is, in fact, identified with God.[76] Jesus-*Shekhinah* participates in the creation of the universe, receiving and collecting the creative energies of the Source of all being, which are then poured forth into the universe through him. Furthermore, Jesus-*Shekhinah* serves as a mediator between heaven and earth, between God and humanity, since no one knows or approaches the Source of Being, but through Jesus-*Shekhinah* (John 14:6f, 9; 17:25f). Like the *Sefirot Shekhinah-Malchut*, Jesus is the locus of salvation, the one through whom life came into being, through whom all come to know God, and through whom all return to God. Moreover, like the *Logos*, Jesus-*Shekhinah* is associated with the power of divine speech, the self-communication of God to the world that is disclosive of the divine mystery.

The Jesus-*Shekhinah* traditions share several key images and metaphors. The *Shekhinah* is spoken of as a "created light," the "first of all creation," which is the *kavod*, the glory of God.[77] Likewise, Jesus-*Shekhinah* is the light of the world,[78] possessing "the glory of an only Son,"[79] which shines forth from his face like the splendor of God (2 Cor. 4:6). Jesus-*Shekhinah* is the one-who-is-sent as an emissary from the divine to the earthly realm, the son who is separated like the daughter of the king in the kabbalist parable, but who is nonetheless close to the Father always (cf. John 8:29) and retains his divine nature (cf. John 8:58). He too is the way to God and the truth about God (John 14:6), sent to restore the unity between God and humanity (cf. John 17:11). Like the presence of God in the Temple, Jesus-*Shekhinah* embodied would undergo destruction, only to inhabit the whole universe through his resurrection and exaltation (cf. John 2:19).

The Mission and Ministry of Jesus-Shekhinah *and the* Malchut *of God*

The tradition concerning Jesus-*Shekhinah*'s intimate and immediate presence with and action toward the suffering, the outcast, and the exiled people of Israel is well documented in the literature cited above. In the advent of Jesus-*Shekhinah*, the *Malchut* of the lower *Sefirot* becomes incarnate. Jesus-*Shekhinah* proclaimed and embodied the *Malchut* of God within the world and at hand in his very person. As the central theme of his life and ministry, Jesus-*Shekhinah* offered the people of Israel the possibility of eschatological salvation and liberation, expressed in the construct of the *Malchut* of God.

While the approaching reign of God was often characterized in

terms of signs and judgment, the Matthean Jesus-*Shekhinah* also indicated that the *Malchut* of God was within his listeners' experience.[80]
Manifold metaphors attributed to Jesus in the Gospels of Matthew
(13:24-52) and Mark (4:26-32) communicated and interpreted this offer
of salvation and liberation. Furthermore, the gospel writers presented
accounts of exorcisms (cf. Luke 11:14-23) and healings (cf. Matt. 10:7f)
as evidence of the inbreaking of the *Malchut* of God. Hence, through
the interpretative model of the *Malchut-Shekhinah*, it may be suggested that the reign of God was indeed in their midst in the person of
Jesus-*Shekhinah*, the *Malchut* of God (cf. Luke 17:20f).

Throughout the synoptic gospels, this presence of the reign of God
in Jesus-*Shekhinah* is continually expressed by his ministry to those
who were marginalized and exiled by illness,[81] by sinfulness, or by
social or religious standards.[82] It was not to the righteous but to those
in need that he came in compassion and forgiveness—healing, com-
forting, uplifting, and liberating the least and the lowly in the name of
Israel's God.[83] Through his dwelling among and advocacy for those
on the margins of civic and religious society, Jesus-*Shekhinah* made
their fate his own, experiencing their pain and sharing their oppression.[84] Jesus-*Shekhinah* wept over the city of Jerusalem and his people's
lack of faith (Luke 19:41) and yearned to gather them like a mother
hen gathers her brood under her wings (Matt. 23:37). Despite the sinfulness and hard-heartedness of some of those to whom he was sent,
Jesus-*Shekhinah*, as the incarnation of the faithful immanence of God,
promised to be present with them always "wherever two or three are
gathered" (Matt. 18:20).[85]

Pitching his tent in Israel at a time of oppression and insurrection,
Jesus' identification with and empowerment of the outcast and the
voiceless, the marginalized and the suffering, threatened the political,
religious, and social leadership of his day. Countless passages chronicle
the internal debates regarding the law and its disposition in which
Jesus-*Shekhinah* engaged the Pharisees of his day.[86] The gospel narratives indicate his followers' sense of the tensions and fears that led to
Jesus-*Shekhinah*'s arrest and conviction.[87] Nevertheless, Jesus-
Shekhinah did not abandon his people or his mission. He willingly
remained faithful to his people and to the One-who-sent-him, which
led to the ultimate exile of Jesus-*Shekhinah* on the cross.

Victim to the powers of evil, Jesus-*Shekhinah* himself was in bondage and in need of deliverance and redemption. Though one with God,

he could not save himself,[88] and, like his suffering people, Jesus-*Shekhinah* had to cling tenaciously to the promise to save of the God of Israel. In the light of this promise, his mission and ministry as the *Malchut* of God was not to end in death, but in resurrection through the unending life and unconditional love of God in and through whom Jesus-*Shekhinah* dwells with his people forever. The *Malchut* of God, which was proleptically mediated in Jesus-*Shekhinah,* flares forth—beyond despair, beyond defeat, beyond death, beyond boundaries—bringing liberation, salvation, and reconciliation through the power of unending life and unconditional love.

Analysis and Proposals

In *A Guest in the House of Israel*, Clark Williamson writes, "The revelatory event upon which all else turns in the Christian faith is that of Jesus Christ. It is an orienting event, from which we take our bearings."[89] Toward what does this christological proposal of Jesus as the *Shekhinah* of God orient the Christian? How does it affect one's bearings? How might this symbol function in Christian life and belief?[90]

To answer these questions, one may return to the critiques with which this thought-experiment began. The conception of Jesus as the *Shekhinah* of God situates Jesus squarely within the depth and breadth of the Jewish religious tradition, spanning biblical, rabbinic, and kabbalist perspectives. It provides a means by which to envision him within the Jewish experience of the immanent, intimate, and immediate presence of God in the history of a suffering, oppressed people, who, nonetheless, clung tenaciously to belief in the ultimate victory of God. Moreover, it suggests a religious context from which symbols, vocabulary, and insights concerning Jesus may have been drawn, which can serve to deepen understanding of the meaning and mission of Jesus to the people of Israel and thus to peoples beyond. In so doing, it provides a context for meaningful discourse and dialogue between the Jewish and Christian traditions.

Part of this understanding of Jesus-*Shekhinah*'s mission and ministry unequivocally involves Jesus' intimate involvement with the suffering and the poor. As the incarnation of the *Shekhinah* of God—the presence of the *Malchut* of God in the world—his mission and ministry to the afflicted and the oppressed embodied God's promise of compassionate presence as the prolepsis of salvific liberation. This understanding of the mission and ministry of Jesus-*Shekhinah* focuses Christian praxis toward compassionate presence and liberating action on behalf of the suffering and the oppressed, with the understanding that, wherever acts of justice and mercy are found, the *Malchut* of God is at hand.

Furthermore, the life, death, and resurrection of Jesus-*Shekhinah* serve to clarify Christian notions concerning the event of the cross. Although suffering and death may accompany intimate identification with and liberative praxis on behalf of the marginalized and oppressed, suffering and death are not redemptive in themselves. Rather, as the event of the resurrection symbolizes, suffering and death are enveloped and transformed through the vivifying and liberating presence and power of the God of Jesus-*Shekhinah*, whose unending life and unconditional love alone bring salvation.

In terms of the feminist theological critique, a christology of Jesus-*Shekhinah* undermines the patriarchal and ecclesiastical prejudices regarding the capacity of the female to image God and Christ. As the traditionally female hypostatization of the immanent and transcendent God, the *Shekhinah* is enfleshed in the humanity of Jesus of Nazareth, and two become one—"without confusion, without change, without division, without separation . . . the distinctive character of each nature being preserved."[91] A *Shekhinah* christology has consequences for both theology and ecclesiology. Theologically, the viable retrieval of the *Shekhinah* tradition in the christological dimension of the Trinity suggests the possibility of alternative trinitarian or pneumatological articulations based upon female models of divinity, similar to the Trinity of Sophia-God formulated by Elizabeth Johnson.[92] The construct of the *Shekhinah* has already proven to be amenable to pneumatology. However, rather than employing a single paradigm that strains to express the immensity of the Triune mystery, the person of Jesus-*Shekhinah* may be related to the persons of Spirit-Sophia, and She-Who-Is, unoriginate Source of all being, as a viable Trinitarian formulation. In terms of ecclesiology, the symbol of Jesus-*Shekhinah* functions inclusively, inviting all to full participation in ecclesial ministry and christic function, in the image of the One-Who-Is-Sent. Furthermore, it illuminates the mission and ministry of the church as that of *presence*, a presence that mediates the intimacy, immanence, and immediacy of Jesus-*Shekhinah* to the community of faith.

Shekhinah christology, therefore, is about divine *presence*—presence *with,* presence *for,* presence *to*—*indwelling* presence, *liberating* presence, *vivifying* presence, *saving* presence, *reconciling* presence, *healing* presence, *forgiving* presence, *redeeming* presence, *loving* presence—and *suffering* presence—immanent in any and all situations and gifted to any and all persons without distinction. Essentially, Jesus-*Shekhinah* did not incarnate the *presence of the unequivocal and unconditional power of God,* but the *power of the unequivocal and unconditional presence of God.* As immanence and gift, the power of the unequivocal and unconditional presence of God may be accepted, rejected, or ignored, but it is never withdrawn. Moreover, it is this fundamental reality to which the life, death, and resurrection of Jesus-*Shekhinah* witnesses concretely—there is no circumstance, no person, no event bereft of the presence of God in manifold and mysterious ways. While God's power of presence may not prevent all manner of evil, neither is it overcome by such evil. Rather, God moves inexorably through suffering and death toward the life, liberation, and transformation symbolized in the image of the *Malchut* of God. This is the good news of salvation and the hope for liberation inherent in the christology of Jesus-*Shekhinah.*

Notes

[1] Jon Sobrino, *Jesus the Liberator: A Historical-Theological View,* trans. Paul Burns and Francis McDonagh (Maryknoll, N.Y.: Orbis Books, 2001).

[2] C. Duquos, *Mesianismo de Jesús y discreción de Dios. Ensayo sobre los límites de la cristología,* in Sobrino, *Jesus the Liberator,* 2.

[3] My research, thought processes, and proposals are influenced by the fact that I am a white, North American, Catholic woman religious, steeped in the feminist theological tradition. I am committed to a constructive, kaleidoscopic model of theologizing that retrieves and collects the shards and fragments of various religious traditions, configures and reconfigures them in various ways, and produces a multiplicity of images that does reverence to the incomprehensibility and ineffability of God and Christ. See Gloria L. Schaab, SSJ, "Feminist Theological Methodologies: Toward a Kaleidoscopic Model," *Theological Studies* 62:2 (June 2001): 341-365.

[4] Sobrino, *Jesus the Liberator,* 5.

[5] See Susan Cole, Marion Ronan, and Hal Taussig, *Wisdom's Feast: Sophia in Study and Celebration* (Kansas City, Mo.: Sheed & Ward, 1996); Celia M. Deutsch, *Lady Wisdom, Jesus, and the Sages* (Valley Forge, Penn.: Trinity Press International, 1996); James D. G. Dunn, *Christology in the Making: A New Testament Inquiry into the Origins of the Doctrine of the Incarnation* (Philadelphia: Westminster, 1980); Elizabeth A. Johnson, "Jesus, the Wisdom of God: A Biblical

Basis for a Non-Androcentric Christology," *Ephemerides Theologicae Lovanienses* 61 (1985): 261-94, as well as Elizabeth A. Johnson, *She Who Is: The Image of God in Feminist Theological Discourse* (New York: Crossroad, 1993), 150-169; Elisabeth Schüssler Fiorenza, *Jesus: Miriam's Child, Sophia's Prophet: Critical Issues in Feminist Christology* (New York: Continuum, 1994); Robert L. Wilken, ed., *Aspects of Wisdom in Judaism and Early Christianity* (Notre Dame, Ind.: University of Notre Dame, 1975); and Ben Witherington III, *Jesus the Sage: The Pilgrimage of Wisdom* (Minneapolis: Fortress Press, 1994), to cite but a few.

[6]Clark M. Williamson, *A Guest in the House of Israel: Post-Holocaust Church Theology* (Louisville: Westminster/John Knox, 1993), 168-81.

[7]Paula Fredriksen, *From Jesus to Christ: The Origins of the New Testament Images of Jesus* (New Haven: Yale University, 1988), vii.

[8]Howard Clark Kee, *Jesus in History: An Approach to the Study of the Gospels* (San Diego: Harcourt Brace Jovanovich, 1977), 83.

[9]Williamson, *A Guest in the House of Israel*, 49, 168ff. See also A. Lukyn Williams, *Adversus Judaeos* (Cambridge: Cambridge University, 1935), and David Patrick Efroymson, "The Patristic Connection," in *Anti-Semitism and the Foundations of Christianity*, ed. Alan T. Davies (New York: Paulist Press, 1979), 98-117.

[10]Rosemary Radford Ruether, *Faith and Fratricide: The Theological Roots of Anti-Semitism* (New York: Seabury Press, 1974), and Judith Plaskow, "Feminist Anti-Judaism and the Christian God," *Journal of Feminist Studies in Religion* 7 (1991): 99-108.

[11]"Anti-Judaism still seems entrenched, however, in relation to the figure of Jesus, and in particular feminist attempts to articulate his uniqueness and significance . . . [which is] most easily established by contrasting him with his Jewish context." In Plaskow, "Feminist Anti-Judaism and the Christian God,"105-107, at 105.

[12]Marcus Braybrooke, "The Future of Jewish-Christian Dialogue," in *The Future of Jewish-Christian Dialogue*, ed. Daniel Cohn-Sherbok (Lewiston, N.Y.: Edwin Mellen Press, 1999), 25f.

[13]Daniel Cohn-Sherbok, "Background to Contemporary Jewish-Christian Dialogue," in *The Future of Jewish-Christian Dialogue*, 4f., and Elizabeth A. Johnson, *Consider Jesus: Waves of Renewal in Christology* (New York: Crossroad, 1993), 6, 42.

[14]Williamson, *A Guest in the House of Israel*, 192f.

[15]Elisabeth Schüssler Fiorenza, "Toward a Feminist Biblical Hermeneutic," in *The Challenge of Liberation Theology*, ed. Brian Mahan and L. Dale Richesin (Maryknoll, N.Y.: Orbis Books, 1981), 107.

[16]Johnson, *She Who Is*, 151.

[17]Jacquelyn Grant, *White Women's Christ, Black Women's Jesus: Feminist Christology and Womanist Response* (Atlanta: Scholars Press, 1969), 68.

[18]This perspective is disputed by some feminist theologians such as Mary Daly, who unequivocally asserts that because of the Christian fixation on the person of Jesus, the impact of his maleness on the notion of God and the event of salvation cannot be ignored, relativized, or redeemed. See Daly's *Beyond God the Father:*

Toward a Philosophy of Women's Liberation (Boston: Beacon Press, 1973), 71-73.

[19]Consider the teachings of Thomas Aquinas that asserted that the maleness of Jesus was not a historically contingent fact, but that, in fact, the male represented the fullness of the image of God, *Summa Theologiae*, I, q. 92, a. 1 and 2; III, supplement, q. 39, a. 1, cited in Anne E. Carr, *Transforming Grace: Christian Tradition and Women's Experience* (San Francisco: Harper & Row, 1988), 163); or the claim that, while other aspects of Jesus' personhood are "accidents" in the Aristotelian metaphysical sense, his maleness is of the "substance" of his humanity (Grant, *White Women's Christ, Black Women's Jesus*, 76). Furthermore, the Vatican document *Inter Insigniores*, concerning the ordination of women to the ministerial priesthood, states that the incarnation of the Word according to the male sex is "in harmony with the entirety of God's plan . . . Christ himself was and remains a man." See *Origins* 6 (February 3, 1977): 522.

[20]Kathryn Greene-McCreight, *Feminist Reconstructions of Christian Doctrines: Narrative Analysis and Appraisal* (New York: Oxford University Press, 2000), 77f.

[21]Carr, *Transforming Grace*, 161.

[22]Such atonement theories include the *Christus Victor* concept, which envisions the cross as a clash between the powers of good and evil. While Jesus' death appears to be the triumph of evil, the resurrection is the sign of God's greater power. The *satisfaction theory* postulates that Jesus died to pay the price or bear the burden for sin, dying in place of humanity to satisfy God's sense of justice. Finally, the *moral influence theory* predicates that an impediment to redemption exists within the human being, but Jesus' death overcomes that obstacle by revealing the vastness of God's mercy in the great love through which he died for human salvation. See Rebecca Parker and Joanne Carlson Brown, "God So Loved the World?" in *Violence against Women and Children: A Christian Sourcebook*, ed. Carol Adams (New York: Continuum, 1995), 39.

[23]Ibid.

[24]Greene-McCreight, *Feminist Reconstructions of Christian Doctrines*, 74, and Elisabeth Schüssler Fiorenza, "Ties that Bind," in *Violence against Women and Children*, ed. Adams, 50.

[25]Parker and Brown, "God So Loved the World?," 37.

[26]Delores Williams, "Black Woman's Surrogate Experience and the Christian Notion of Redemption," in *After Patriarchy: Feminist Transformations of the World Religions*, ed. William R. Eakin, Jay B. McDaniel, and Paula M. Cooey (Maryknoll, N.Y.: Orbis Books, 1991), 12f.

[27]Daly, *Beyond God the Father*, 77.

[28]See Jon Sobrino, *Christology at the Crossroads,* trans. John Drury (Maryknoll, N.Y.: Orbis Books, 1978) and Walter Rauschenbusch, *A Theology for the Social Gospel* (New York: Abingdon Press, 1917), 184.

[29]Parker and Brown, "God So Loved the World?," 57.

[30]Regina A. Coll, *Christianity and Feminism in Conversation* (Mystic, Conn.: Twenty-Third Publications, 1994), 54.

[31]Gershom Scholem, selections from *On the Mystical Shape of the Godhead: Basic Concepts of the Kabbalah* (http://dhushara.tripod.com/book/torah/cardoza/shape.htm, accessed December 1, 2001), 1.

[32]The appellation *Shekhinah* has a number of different spellings, including *Shekinah, Shekhina, Shechina,* and *Schechina.* Unless quoted from a specific source, the spelling used in this essay is *Shekhinah.*

[33]Raphael Patai, *The Hebrew Goddess,* 3rd ed. (1967, 1978; Detroit: Wayne State University Press, 1990), 98f.

[34]"Shekhina," *Encyclopedia Britannica* (http://www.britannica.com/eb/article?eu=68980, accessed December 1, 2001), 1; Patai, *The Hebrew Goddess,* 98; and Scholem, selections from *On the Mystical Shape of the Godhead,* 1.

[35]In rabbinic midrashim, the *Shekhinah* is associated with references to God's nearness and providence as expressed, for example, in Ps. 139: 7-10, Deut. 33:15, Is. 57:15, Ex. 3:2, 13:22, and 40: 34-38.

[36]Ephraim E. Urbach, *The Sages: Their Concepts and Beliefs,* trans. by Israel Abrahams (Cambridge, Mass.: Harvard University, 1987), 40.

[37]Gershom Scholem, *The Kabbalah and Its Symbolism,* trans. Ralph Manheim (New York: Schocken, 1996), 105.

[38]Patai, *The Hebrew Goddess,* 96.

[39]Scholem, selections from *On the Mystical Shape of the Godhead,* 11f.

[40]Urbach, *The Sages,* 38.

[41]Ibid., 43-48, and Chanoch Gebhard and Dovid Landesman, *As the Rabbis Taught: Studies in the Aggados of the Talmud—Tractate Megillah,* trans. Dovid Landesman (Northvale, N.J.: Jason Aronson Inc., 1966), 301.

[42]J. Abelson, *The Immanence of God in Rabbinic Literature* (1912; New York: Hermon, 1969), 122.

[43]Gershom Scholem, *Major Trends in Jewish Mysticism* (New York: Schocken Books, 1995), 111.

[44]Gershom Scholem, *On the Possibility of Jewish Mysticism in Our Time,* trans. Jonathan Chipman (New York: Schocken Books, 1991), 143.

[45]Abelson, *The Immanence of God in Rabbinic Literature,* 83-93.

[46]Ibid., 98f, 106, 143; Patai, *The Hebrew Goddess,* 100-110; and Urbach, *The Sages,* 42, 63.

[47]Peter Schäfer, "Daughter, Sister, Bride, and Mother: Images of the Femininity of God in the Early Kabbala," *Journal of the American Academy of Religion* 68:2 (June 2000): 228-233, and Sanford L. Drob, *Symbols of the Kabbalah: Philosophical and Psychological Perspectives* (Northvale, N.J.: Jason Aronson Inc., 2000), 366.

[48]Abelson, *The Immanence of God in Rabbinic Literature,* 135-139.

[49]Gebhard and Landesman, *As the Rabbis Taught,* 302.

[50]Max Kadushin, *The Rabbinic Mind* (New York: Jewish Theological Seminary of America, 1952), 227.

[51]Abelson, *The Immanence of God in Rabbinic Literature,* 104.

[52]Abraham Heschel, *God in Search of Man: A Philosophy of Judaism* (New York: Harper & Row, 1955), 21f.

[53]Schäfer, "Daughter, Sister, Bride, and Mother," 233.

[54]Jürgen Moltmann, "Shekinah: The Home of the Homeless God," in *Longing for Home,* ed. Leroy S. Rouner (South Bend, Ind.: University of Notre Dame Press, 1996), 174.

[55]Patai, *The Hebrew Goddess,* 103.

[56]Ibid., Abelson, *The Immanence of God in Rabbinic Literature,* 113, and Leah Novick, "The Schechinah," in *The Goddess Reawakening: The Feminine Principle Today,* ed. Shirley Nicholson (Wheaton, Ill.: Theosophical Publishing House, 1989), 206, 213.

[57]Tractate Megillah 29a, quoted in Abelson, *The Immanence of God in Rabbinic Literature,* 127.

[58]Franz Rosenzweig, *The Star of Redemption,* 2nd ed., trans. William Hallo (1930; New York: Holt, Rinehart & Winston, 1971), 192f, and Moltmann, "Shekinah," 174.

[59]Kadushin, *The Rabbinic Mind,* 224, and Moltmann, "Shekinah," 175.

[60]Scholem, *On the Mystical Shape of the Godhead,* 144.

[61]Rosenzweig, *The Star of Redemption,* 192f.

[62]Scholem, *On the Mystical Shape of the Godhead,* 144.

[63]Scholem, *On the Possibility of a Jewish Mysticism,* 206, and "The Divine Emanations: The Ten *Sefirot,*" *The Inner Dimension* (http://www.inner.org/sefirot/sefirot.htm, accessed December 2, 2001), 1.

[64]Scholem, *On the Possibility of a Jewish Mysticism,* 207f, and "The Divine Emanations," 3.

[65]Scholem, *On the Mystical Shape of the Godhead,* 174.

[66]For an intriguing discussion of a resonant notion of receptivity and activity as characteristic of the Second Person of the Trinity, see Margaret A. Farley, "New Patterns of Relationship: Beginnings of a Moral Revolution," *Theological Studies* 36 (1975): 627-646.

[67]Scholem, *On the Mystical Shape of the Godhead,* 145, 175f, and "*Malchut/Shekhinah*": *Mystic Judaism and the Ten Sefirot* (http://www.northcoast.com/`planzi/rst23, accessed December 2, 2001), 11.

[68]Scholem, selections from *On the Mystical Shape of the Godhead,* 11f. It has been suggested that the fundamental and primal need for the divine female has been manifested in the Catholic tradition through the phenomenon of popular and profound Marian devotion.

[69]See Johnson, *She Who Is,* 85f, and Michael E. Lodahl, *Shekhinah/Spirit: Divine Presence in Jewish and Christian Religion* (New York: Paulist Press, 1992), 151ff.

[70]Moltmann, "The Home of the Homeless God," 178ff.

[71]Jürgen Moltmann, *The Trinity and the Kingdom: The Doctrine of God,* trans. Margaret Kohl (Minneapolis: Fortress Press, 1993), 28-30, at 30.

[72]Philip E. Devenish, "Jews and Christians Searching for God," *America* 148:8 (February 26, 1983), 150-151, at 150.

[73]Ibid., 151.

[74]Schäfer, "Daughter, Sister, Bride, and Mother," 239.

[75]In *Christology in the Making,* Dunn poses a related question with regard to evidence in pre-Christian rabbinic Judaism of "intermediate beings" between God and humanity. He asks whether pre-Christian Judaism, especially in its Hellenistic phase, provided either language or conceptualizations concerning intermediaries or hypostases that led Christianity to identify Jesus with such divine beings. Responding emphatically in the negative, Dunn indicates that any such references— *Shekhinah* included—were circumlocutions for the divine and provided "expressions of God's immanence without compromising his transcendence" (p. 130). Rather than distinct from God, these beings, according to Dunn, were ways of asserting God's nearness, involvement, and concern for creation and its inhabitants (see 129-136, 176).

[76]To avoid the repetition of phrases such as "Jesus, like the *Shekhinah,*" I will use the appellation "Jesus-*Shekhinah*" to imply the shared tradition.

[77]In connection with the concept of the "created" light, it is interesting to note that theological debates concerning the created or uncreated nature of the *Shekhinah* took place that have a similarity with, for example, the Arian-Athanasian conflicts concerning the origin of the Son (cf. Maimonides and Nahmanides in Kadushin, *The Rabbinic Mind,* 222).

[78]Cf. John 3:19, 8:12, 9:5, 12:35f; Luke 1:79, 2:32, 17:24; Matt. 4:16.

[79]Cf. John 2:11, 17:22f; Luke 2:26, 24:26; Mark 13:26; Matt. 24:30, 25:31; Col. 3:4; 2 Cor. 3:18; 1 Peter 4:13f; Rev. 19:7, 21:22f.

[80]Cf. Matt. 24 and 25.

[81]Cf. Matt. 4:24, 8:16, 14:14; Mark 6:5f; Luke 4:40, 10:9.

[82]Cf. Matt. 5:3f, 25:1-46, 9:10f, 11:19; Mark 2:15-17; Luke 4:18, 6:20-26, 7:22, 14:13, 18:22.

[83]Cf. Matt. 9:36, 14:36, 15:32; Mark 6:34, 8:2; Luke 7:13.

[84]Cf. Matt. 10:40; Mark 9:37.

[85]This promise is a direct appropriation from rabbinic midrash on the *Shekhinah.* See above, n. 47.

[86]Cf. Matt. 9:11f, 12:2f, 15:12f, 19:3f; Luke 5:17f, 6:2f; John 9:13f.

[87]Cf. Mark 11:18, 14:1-2, 60; Luke 19:38-48, 23:1-14; John 11:47-50.

[88]Cf. Matt. 27:40 and parallels.

[89]Williamson, *A Guest in the House of Israel,* 25.

[90]Johnson, *She Who Is,* 38 and passim.

[91]"The Council of Chalcedon 451 A.D.," in *A Theology of Christ,* ed. Vincent Zamoyta (New York: Bruce, 1967), 69f.

[92]Johnson, *She Who Is,* 121-223.

The Spirit Christology of Piet Schoonenberg

Michael E. O'Keeffe

Anyone who has followed contemporary efforts to consider Jesus' relationship to God on the basis of pneumatology is probably familiar with Piet Schoonenberg, a Jesuit theologian born in 1911, educated in Maastricht, and active as a scholar and professor of systematic theology across Europe and throughout the United States until his death in 1999. But despite frequent references to his writings and several brief summaries, very little has been done systematically to examine Schoonenberg's Spirit christology, particularly as it came to mature expression in *De Geest, het Woord en de Zoon: Theologische overdenkingen over Geest-christologie, Logos-christologie en drieënheidsleer* (1991).[1]

This essay hopes to fill this gap. It is divided into five sections. The first explains Schoonenberg's biblical exegesis, which he defines as a "post-exegetical unified reading" of the New Testament. The second examines his insistence that Jesus Christ is fully human, a *person* like us in all things but sin, which he explains through two distinct theological models for re-appropriating the enhypostasis (the substance of the human in the divine nature). The first model centers on a "reciprocal enhypostasis" that stresses the mutual involvement of the divine and human persons. The second model concentrates on the union of two "personal" natures in one "divine-human" or "theandric" person.

The three remaining sections probe some of the implications of defining Jesus Christ as a human person and point to further possible directions for Spirit christology. Section three examines how Jesus became the Son through the incarnation of the Word and the inspiration of the Spirit. Section four concentrates on trinitarian implications of this claim, demonstrating how new interpretations of Jesus foster new interpretations of "the mystery of God himself."[2] Special consideration is given to Schoonenberg's claims that God "changes" in and through God's real relations to the world and that God "became" Father, Son, and Spirit through the Christ-event. The fifth and final section highlights several features that may be relevant in the development of Spirit christologies.

A "Post-Exegetical Reading" of the New Testament

Like most christologies today, Schoonenberg's christology begins with the biblical narratives and the recognition that the Bible does not reflect a monolithic assessment of Jesus, but is filled with competing images, metaphors, and titles that describe Jesus' identity and mission.[3] As a first step in Schoonenberg's recovery of a biblical Christ (as opposed to an exclusively Johannine or a Markan Christ), he highlights these differences, both between New Testament authors and within New Testament books:

> Up to now we have presented only one Spirit-christology in Mark
> and Luke; but both these evangelists also clearly use a Son-of-
> Man christology, which is not in opposition to a Spirit-christology;
> and Luke's gospel contains a Prophet-christology, which rests in
> harmony with a Spirit-christology. . . . [Moreover,] the Spirit-
> christology in Paul and John is mixed with other christologies.
> The Logos-christology of John's prologue stands in clear tension
> with the Spirit-christology in the same gospel. . . . It is not an easy
> task to distinguish the various christologies from one another.
> They influence each other and intersect with one another.[4]

After carefully examining these "different ways of viewing the one mystery of Jesus Christ," Schoonenberg seeks to bring about a resolution of perspectives, since these christologies are not contradictory but complementary.[5] He accomplishes this by proposing a "complementary perichoresis," a type of interpenetration, of texts, which enables Schoonenberg to surpass "both the picture of [the Jesus] of John and the stories of the synoptics."[6]

How this works is apparent in Schoonenberg's exploration of Jesus' relationship to God. Although all New Testament authors agree that Jesus stands in a unique relationship to the Father, their descriptions of that relationship do not agree.[7] Some texts describe Jesus as the Messiah, or as an eschatological prophet sent to carry out the plan of God. Others speak of Jesus' sonship as a consequence of the Spirit. John in particular focuses on Jesus as the Son who can be qualified as God.[8] Rather than opting for one of these approaches, Schoonenberg insists that we should draw upon the entire wisdom of the Bible and construct a unified understanding of Jesus, even if this entails abandoning the traditional favored status given to John in Catholic theology or the clarity of a single model like Spirit christology.[9] Nevertheless, in doing so, one does not abandon the important distinctions between biblical models, particularly the difference in "starting-points," which Schoonenberg defines as two-fold, namely, those that begin with a human being who, in the course of history, is recognized to be the Son of God; and those that begin with God and understand Jesus Christ as an "extension" or personal expression of the Father.[10] The first starting point is identified as an ascending christology, which begins "from below" with a human Jesus; the second as a descending christology, which begins "from above" with God.

As one might expect, Schoonenberg claims that the most important example of descending christology is the Logos christology, affirmed most clearly in the prologue of John's Gospel. In this model, "God's Word or 'Logos,' stands . . . at the beginning. He is with God and he is God (Jn 1:1), and this Logos becomes flesh (1:14), becomes Jesus of Nazareth."[11] The most important example of ascending christology is Spirit christology, which begins with the historical Jesus who, at some point in history, "became" the Son of God. Jesus' relationship with God is therefore historically constituted either at conception or at baptism or when Jesus was raised from the dead and, regardless of timing, attributed to the Spirit.[12] Because of this commitment to history and a starting point "from below," Schoonenberg claims that Spirit christology is better suited to articulate Jesus' relationship to God than is Logos christology.[13]

Schoonenberg's retrieval of a Spirit christology begins with the Gospel of Mark, which relies on Isaiah 42:1 and Psalm 2:7 to understand Jesus' relationship to God.[14] Mark represents the earliest form of Spirit christology because he uses a strictly ascending christology; that is, one that makes no mention of either Jesus' pre-existent sonship or Jesus' relationship to the Father at conception. Jesus became the Son of God through the Spirit's baptismal anointing:[15]

In Mark's own story Jesus does not appear as the Son of God at the beginning, but rather at the end of his earthly life. Any indication of a pre-existent sonship or a place as son of God in the Trinity is completely lacking. . . . God . . . makes Jesus his Son by giving him his Spirit. The words "you are my son" are effective—we could even call them sacramental—such that the sacramental sign (the "element of action") is the giving of the Spirit in this sacrament. Before Jesus arrives at the Jordan Mark mentions the prophecy of John about a baptism with the Holy Spirit. Now Jesus appears as one baptized with the Holy Spirit and the fruit of this baptism, which is greater than John's, is the sonship of God for Jesus.[16]

Schoonenberg argues that although several other New Testament books contain elements of a Spirit christology (for example, Acts 1:1, 2:33; Rom 1:3-1:4; Jn 1:29-34), the most developed Spirit christology is found in the Gospel of Luke, which advances the Gospel of Mark in two ways. First, Luke pushes the action of the Spirit to conception, insisting that "from the very beginning" Jesus was the Son.[17]

This christology says that at a definitive moment of his human existence Jesus became the Son of God, either at the beginning of his preaching or at the beginning of his life as the Risen One. This perspective became foreign to us; but it is precious because it shows us a history of Jesus, a history which is also [a history] of his divine sonship. This Adoption-christology, however, fails on one point. When this is not corrected, then we find ourselves slipping into adoptionism. The first generation of Christians experienced the resurrection of Jesus as a confirmation of his entire life and not only a part. That is why the Spirit and the divine sonship could not be totally absent in the earthly life before the baptism. Other christologies developed in order to express this, as we find in John. But even within Spirit-christology itself a completion was offered. The point at which the Spirit touched Jesus was presented and identified with the beginning of his human existence.[18]

Luke also strengthens the connection between Jesus and the Spirit, claiming that Jesus was continually "filled with the Holy Spirit" (4:1) and operated in "the power of the Spirit" (4:14; see also Luke 3:22, 10:21, 11:13 and Acts 4:14 and 10:38). Although both changes were necessary, Schoonenberg points out that Luke did not amend Mark where the question of the preexistence of Jesus is concerned. For both writers, Jesus' divine sonship remained historical, and therefore tied to the events of his life. Such a perspective, however, does not deny the divinity of Jesus. Spirit christology could function as an alternative to Logos christology, even though in Schoonenberg's later writings he uses Logos christology to "complete and enrich" his Spirit christology.[19] The central insights gained from the use of the Logos to illumine the identity of Jesus are the affirmation of Jesus' complete union with the Father and his share in the divine life. Without the insights of John, it would be possible to consider Jesus to be no more than the locus of God's Spirit and no more than an eschatological prophet commissioned by God to complete the plan of God. By drawing on Logos christology, Schoonenberg hopes to avoid a pitfall found in some Spirit christologies and to maintain a stronger commitment to the tradition, affirming Jesus' divinity expressed in classical christological formulations and creeds. He thus offers a Spirit-Logos hybrid rather than an exclusive Spirit christology, even though he continues to refer to his model as a "Spirit christology."[20]

This hybrid model, indicated by the title *Der Geist und Der Wort*, is a recent development. In *The Christ* (English translation, 1971) he did not propose a Spirit christology, although he did favor a "christology of presence" over Logos christology. Later, in "Spirit Christology and Logos Christology" (1977), his primary intent was to advance a Spirit christology over against a Logos christology, although in the end he conceded that a reconciliation between the two models was possible.[21]

Jesus Christ as a Human Person

The foundation of Schoonenberg's biblical Spirit christology or "Spirit-Logos" christology is the principle that everything said about Jesus Christ must be compatible with the claim that he was fully human. For example, Jesus must have experienced the same "growth, learning, seeking, conflicts, [and] temptations" we do. He could not have experienced the beatific vision from the beginning, since he grew in his understanding of God and in his intimacy with God.[22] Similarly, Jesus operated within the confines imposed by history and his humanity. He was given a specific "faith, a culture of prayer, a tradition, and a scripture."[23] His possibilities were finite,[24] and he was "dependent on the common concepts and outlooks of his contemporaries."[25] Many things in his life "could have been otherwise,"[26] and he could have sinned, even though he did not.[27] His eventual death was the result of his free choice to live in perfect "righteousness, holiness, obedience, service, [and] love," and was not a "fate" handed to him by his Father.[28] Comparable to the Spirit christology of G. W. H. Lampe, Schoonenberg claims that Jesus is our *archegos*, our "pioneer," precisely because he is the one who went before us on a journey we are all called to follow.[29] He cannot be different from us "in kind" because he is *homoousios* with us.[30]

Schoonenberg's most important defense of Jesus' humanity is his insistence that Jesus is a human person.[31] Three issues inform his claim. First, he criticizes the traditional approach to Jesus' personhood by claiming that it presupposes that Jesus Christ is a divine person and then relies upon a descending model to justify this claim. Since Schoonenberg regards the ascending model as more compatible with the entire New Testament and more capable of responding to contemporary concerns, he is critical of a position that requires a descending model.

Second, Schoonenberg insists the assertion that Jesus Christ is a divine person rests on the premise that God has always been triune. Schoonenberg challenges the eternity of the Son by claiming that it is incompatible with much of the New Testament, destructive to the full humanity of Jesus, and ultimately inconsistent with a Christian doctrine of God grounded in and limited by the economy of salvation. He does not reject the eternal relationship between the Father and the *Logos*, but questions the eternal relationship between the Father and the *Son*, since, for him, the Logos *became the Son* in and through the Christ-event. He also questions the traditional claim that God is eternally Father, Son, and Spirit on epistemological grounds. What we know of God, Schoonenberg insists, is limited to our experience of God:

There is no direct revelation to us of an eternal, and therefore prior to our history, existence either of divine decrees nor even of divine persons; nor is this known in itself, as if we had been made into participants of God's life before time. We speak of both things out of our insight alone, that it is the eternal God who is creatively present and communicates himself in our history. We recognize the existence of divine decrees or divine persons solely through a reflection upon the faith experience of God's presence in our time. We displace then that which God does and is in our history into his eternity.[32]

The eternity of God's Trinity, therefore, is a conclusion based on presuppositions involving God's relationality and God's immutability. These conclusions, Schoonenberg alleges, cannot legitimately function as presuppositions. Moreover, returning to the Bible as the basis for a doctrine of God in *Der Geist*, Schoonenberg insists that the scriptures do not consistently affirm Jesus' personal pre-existence. It is a possible claim, not a necessary one.[33] He also maintains that when Jesus' pre-existence is affirmed, two unavoidable distortions occur in our understanding of Jesus Christ. The most problematic is the obfuscation of Jesus' humanity. The divine person of the Logos becomes the "rival" to "the human being-person of Jesus," ultimately leading to the "de-personalization of Christ's humanity itself."[34] Earlier in *The Christ* he writes:

> What is contained in scripture, tradition, and the teaching magisterium on the divine and pre-existent person of the Son can never be in conflict with what is preached about Jesus Christ. Thus it cannot be in conflict with the most primary views on Christ, [namely,] . . . that he is one person and that he is a human person. What is said of the pre-existent divine person can never nullify this one and human person. We must then never conceive the divine person as added to the man Jesus in such a way that Christ would no longer be one, or no longer [be] man.[35]

Schoonenberg also claims that Jesus' pre-existence leads to the impairment of the Spirit's role. If Jesus is "God the Son" from eternity, he "cannot once again become this by the power of the Holy Spirit."[36] Hence the Spirit's anointing becomes inconsequential, something done for "our sakes" rather than something that happens to Jesus. To maintain the real work of the Logos and the Spirit, and to maintain the complete humanity of Jesus, Schoonenberg calls for distinctions between the pre-existent Logos and the incarnate Logos, and the Spirit before the Christ-event and the Spirit after this event. This "de-sharpening of the concept of person" as it is applies to the pre-incarnate Logos and Spirit renders the Logos and the Spirit "personifications" of the one God rather than "persons" in respect to God. Although more will be said about this in the discussion of Schoonenberg's trinitarian theology, it is important to note here that Schoonenberg justifies his re-interpretation of a personified Logos and Spirit by asserting that neither the Word nor the Spirit was regarded as "complete" or "full" hypostases in the Old Testament or throughout most of the New Testament.

Reflecting the views of exegetes like James D. G. Dunn, Schoonenberg claims that terms such as Word, Spirit, and Wisdom were personifications of God that addressed God's personal presence and activity in salvation history and not persons distinct from God.[37] Of the three, the most developed designation for God's activity in the Old Testament was Wisdom. The most important designation in the New Testament was Spirit. Both terms, however, expressed "the personified, complete presence of the transcendent God," not separate hypostases from the one God.[38] By drawing upon the entire Bible, Schoonenberg claims that Jesus Christ can be viewed as a human person who became the Son of God in history through a "personalizing" Word and a "personalizing" Spirit, both of which functioned as "extensions" of the one God.[39] If one grants this premise, then Jesus' sonship would apply only to his "earthly life" and to his life "after the resurrection." The preexistent Logos would not be "a Son."[40]

Finally, Schoonenberg insists that the denial of Jesus' human personhood rests on a faulty interpretation of the enhypostasis, which undermines "the personal reality of Jesus as human or his human reality as person" to such an extent that Jesus is not really human.[41] Since this interpretation would undermine "the entire testimony of the New Testament and [the intent of] Chalcedon," it must be recast.[42] Schoonenberg offers two models for doing so.[43] Especially in his earlier work, Schoonenberg speaks about the divine and the human natures involving a "reciprocal enhypostasis" such that the Logos is enhypostasized in the human person and the human person is enhypostasized in the divine person with neither person existing independently of the other.[44] Thus Jesus is a human person, but can be considered a divine person "in history," or "as incarnate" since "each presence of God in a creature includes the presence of that creature in God." Further, "the enhypostasis of the Word in Jesus . . . includes the enhypostasis of Jesus in the Word."[45] Although *homoousios* with God and with us, Jesus is not "two persons" since the divine person and the human person exist only in one another.[46] In addition, although the enhypostases is reciprocal, it is not symmetrical, since "the Word is not hypostatized through the humanity, but rather hypostatizes itself in that it becomes the hypostasis of the humanity of Jesus."[47] The reciprocal nature of the enhypostasis is made clear in this statement of Schoonenberg:

> [A]ll the human elements come to Jesus and he is therefore no less personal than we; on the contrary, he is more personal. If he is now, on the other hand, also a divine person, then no dialogue can be assumed between the divine and the human person within the one Christ such as between Christ and the Father. The divine person of the Word cannot be a "counterpart" to the man Jesus as the Father is. The Word is then person—and is the Son—not over against the man Jesus but in him, the Word is en-hypostatic in the man who is the Christ, the Son of the living God.[48]

Although Schoonenberg continues to utilize a "reciprocal enhypostasis" in *Der Geist*, he is aware that this model has raised concerns among his peers, particularly in respect to what some perceive as a less than clear affirmation of the divine personhood of Jesus Christ and some confusion in his treatment of the role of Jesus' humanity for the "becoming-person of the divine word."[49] Hence, an alternative model for understanding the enhypostasis is developed in *Der Geist* that focuses on the claim that in the reciprocal enhypostases the persons do not exist independently of the each other: there is no divine Son before the incarnation, nor a human person before being united in the Word. As indicated earlier, "If the Word is already a perfect person before the incarnation, then a new rivalry surfaces in relation to the human being-person of Jesus. Then the Word would be either a divine person, who brings into existence the human person of Jesus alongside itself, or it eliminates the human being-person in Jesus."[50] Since Schoonenberg finds this position untenable, he suggests that what actually took place in the incarnation was the union of a "personal" humanity and a "personal" divinity that came together to become one "person." Jesus is therefore the one "divine-human" or "theandric person" who remains fully human and fully divine:

> Jesus is a personal human being; he is human in a personal way and personal in a human way. We are [also] able to say of the divine Word in Christ that the Word is personal in a divine manner and divine in a personal manner. This divine-personal Word and the human-personal human being together form the single person, Jesus Christ, in a unity ("undivided and insepa-rable"). This person is not identical with the divine Word alone, nor with the human being Jesus alone, but rather with the God-human being. This person can then correctly be called a divine-human or a theandric person.[51]

The Becoming of the Son

In probing further the claim that Jesus Christ is a theandric person, Schoonenberg returns to the Bible and insists that Jesus became this one person, the Son of God, through the incarnation of the Word and the inspiration of the Spirit. The Christ-event is undeniably the work of "two" persons:

> In his complete human reality Jesus is carried by the Word and driven by the Spirit. Both make Jesus into the Son of God, so that both, Word- and Spirit-christology, are of equal value as an explanation of the divine sonship of Jesus.[52]

Schoonenberg defends this interpretation by a lengthy examination of John's prologue, where he claims that the "becoming of the Son" in John 1:4 ("the Word became flesh") includes an anointing by the Spirit that gradually occurred over Jesus' entire life.[53]

> The Word becomes on-going flesh in the story of Jesus, indeed, becomes flesh in an increasing measure. The incarnation of the Word can therefore join itself to the fulfillment, the "ascension (rising up)" of Jesus, as we find in Spirit-christology. The increasing incarnation can include a growing fulfillment by the Holy Spirit, whereby the incarnation and the in-spiration move themselves together to the high point of the Risen One, who has

become the life-providing Spirit. In this way both Logos- and Spirit-christology include each other.[54]

In Schoonenberg's Spirit christology, the Word is the "creative, foundational, [and] determining" activity of God in Jesus Christ; it "bears the existence of Jesus."[55] The Spirit "fills Jesus from within, anoints him for his prophetic-messianic office [and] drives him to the fulfillment of his mission."[56] The Logos "makes" Jesus the Son, but the Spirit ensures that his sonship moves beyond the Son, making Jesus Christ a Son "for us," and a Savior who makes his Father "our" Father.

> Thus do both Word and Spirit . . . make the human being-person of Jesus real according to two points of view: the existence itself and the turning to others, the possession of himself and the dissemination of himself, the identity and the emptying out. Jesus is able to appropriate the name which is above every other name for himself in the Word when he says, "I am"; he becomes in the Spirit the sacrifice which sanctifies all else, and the Spirit which makes alive (1 Cor 15:45). In the Word Jesus is the exact image of God's essence (Heb 1:3); in the Spirit he becomes the Christ, "all in all" (Col 3:11).[57]

Although the Spirit's work is directed outward, the Spirit is not ancillary:

> Just as there is a perichoresis of Word and humanity, so is there also a perichoresis of the Spirit and the humanity. . . . The Spirit not only fashions him into one of the prophets but also gives him, not only an anointing into an added sonship, but truly forms Jesus into the much-loved Son of God.[58]

The Becoming of a Triune God

To explicate the trinitarian implications of his claim that Jesus Christ became the Son through the Word and the Spirit, Schoonenberg once again returns to the Bible and makes three important claims about God.[59] First, God is a person who exists in person-to-person relationships. Such a claim is supported in the Old Testament when God reveals God's self as committed to Israel in a "personal covenant" that extends from creation to the end of time. God is a God "of people," a relational God, "the merciful and faithful One," and creation itself is qualified by its relation to God.[60] The same perspective continues in the New Testament when Jesus uses the term "Abba" to address God; when his followers refer to God as Lord, King, and Savior; and when the New Testament uses the *passivum divinum* to describe God's activity. In all these cases, what is being expressed is "the very foundation of God, his freedom, his interaction with our history, his anger and his mercy, his love."[61] Thus "the biblical faith directs itself towards God in a from-person-to-person relationship."[62] God is "the highest and deepest form of being" since personhood unites an "existing-in-oneself" with a "being-and-acting-outside-oneself."[63] Although "existing-in-oneself" means that God cannot be equated with God's relationships, God is so identified with creation that God's being can be defined as "a love for others" that "personalizes" others through that love.[64] Schoonenberg asserts:

> Today there is plenty to be found about "becoming a person." This occurs for us principally through other persons. Beloved persons, sisters and brothers, awaken in me my being-person and I then perhaps awaken it in others. In the final analysis, could I then not say the same thing about God our Father, Creator of heaven and earth? His entire work in our world, beginning with the first creation and extending right through to "God, all in all," is certainly directed towards the personal being of humanity, towards our being-person, in community, in our being as brothers and sisters.[65]

Schoonenberg's second claim is an extension of the first. Just as human persons personalize themselves "by entering into personal relationships with other persons," God "personalizes himself in acting for and in the human being."[66] God "becomes person on his journey to creation, his journey towards the 'all in all' of the final completion."[67] Although this "becoming personal" or becoming "more personal" is not fully developed by Schoonenberg, he does stress that when we address God's personhood and God's becoming as a person we need to respect the otherness of God. God is not personal in the same way we are personal. "To him is uniquely attributed the same being-person as with us, but in a totally other manner."[68] Similarly, God's becoming is not the same as our becoming, particularly the Father's, since the Father is the source of all becoming.[69]

Nevertheless, Schoonenberg argues that it is still legitimate to speak of God's becoming, and our doing so challenges traditional assumptions about God. If God becomes in Jesus, for example, God cannot be immutable as classical theology once taught:

> In the fullness of God's being God is unchangeable; [but] God changes himself through the relationships in which he enters with his creatures. God becomes more our God through the gift of himself. . . . God becomes more personal [literally, "more person"] in his self-initiated movement towards us. God becomes our God, our covenantal partner. God unfolds his "I" in that he says to his creature "you."[70]

Nor can we define transcendence as requiring immutability. God's transcendence applies to God's "never-abandoning love" that "seeks to overcome our rejection" through love, not to the fact that God is "above" or "beyond" being affected by us. Schoonenberg stresses:

> Aristotle was right when he named God the unmoved mover, for God moves that which exists outside of himself—indeed, he effects the existence of all—nor is he himself moved by anything outside of himself. But Aristotle and his disciples forget that God moves himself in that he enters into relations, indeed, that he communicates himself. It is true that God is immutable in substance, for he is not composite and knows no lessening or increasing of his divine being. However, in that he communicates himself, he changes himself in his relations, for he becomes more our God; he is on the way to be all in all; he becomes the Lord of all, the Almighty.[71]

Because God becomes through God's relations, Schoonenberg defines God's relations as "real." Without them, God would not be our God; God would not be the person we know God to be.[72] Not to affirm real relations would undermine "the good news that God is our Creator, that he loves us and enters into union with us, [and] that the Son of God is our fellow man and suffers through and for us."[73] God is also "time-related." We can speak about God "before the incarnation" and "since the incarnation," and we can ascribe joy and pain to God since God "experiences this history with us."[74] "God's relations to us also touch God in his depths."[75]

> That is why he moves and changes himself in his self-communi-
> cation, even if he remains unchanging in his substance. That is
> why he is not only eternal but also relates to our time, engaged in
> our history. That is why he is love which suffers, even though he
> remains eternal joy. It is in this sense that we may praise God for
> his history with us.[76]

Schoonenberg's final point concentrates on the change that the in-carnation introduced for God. As indicated earlier, the incarnation altered the way the Logos and the Spirit were in respect to the Father. The pre-incarnate Logos was the "personalizing" agent of the Father that "concretized" the Father's presence.[77] It was "God's expression of God's self, his promise to humanity, his call to and offer of community, but not yet, or not yet completely, a person."[78] Similarly, the Spirit was the "breath of life which inspired the prophets,"[79] and the "form" of the Father's "total turning towards us," "his perfect self-giving to us."[80] Like the Logos, it functioned as the "emanation," "emission," or "radiation" "of the [one] divine person,"[81] the "other hand" of the Father in the singular work of personalization.[82] The pre-Pentecostal Spirit, however, was not a self-standing hypostasis in respect to God the Father or in respect to God the Son. The Spirit did not yet exist in a person-to-person relationship. However, in and through the Christ-event, the personal Word and the personal Spirit became persons in the full sense of that word, existing in "interpersonal or dialogical relation[s]."[83]

In an effort to nuance this becoming personal, Schoonenberg concedes that the Logos and the Spirit were "persons" before the incarnation, in the sense that Richard of St. Victor used this term, namely, that prior to the Christ-event, they were "standing forth out of something," existing "as an outflow" from the Father. "They are then persons in their pre-existence as ex-sisting, coming forth out of the Father."[84] But they were not persons in respect to one another or to the Father. They were not "self-standing (in-self-standing) persons; personal beings standing opposite facing one another." He supports this view by appealing to John's prologue, which viewed the Logos as a person only as incarnate:

> [I]f we join John's prologue with the synoptic gospels, then it can be said that the Word *becomes* the Son. . . . This thought lies, perhaps, at the very root of John's prologue itself since it uses the expression "God" and "the Word" before verse fourteen and only afterwards speaks of "Father" and of the "only" or "begotten" (*monogenēs*). If we compare the prologue with the high priestly prayer, which acts somewhat as an epilogue, then the personalization [of the Word] in contrast to the Father clearly surfaces. The Word which goes out from God is now the answer to God; the one who came into the world now returns to the Father.[85]

The Word exists as Son in an interpersonal relationship.

Elsewhere in *Der Geist* Schoonenberg argues this position:

> Even for God, particularly for the Logos which is God, a new thing begins [in Jesus Christ]. This new reality is the being-human, by which the Logos stands among human beings on earth and remains a human being for all eternity. God's Word speaks as a human being, with human words and out of a human consciousness and amidst a human community of language and tradition. And he even speaks thus to God himself. The Word [*Wort*] has become response [*Antwort*]: the crown of the Johannine prologue is [therefore] the high-priestly prayer [for now the Word] . . . speaks to the Father in the prayer of a human being, whom it has become, and in the sacrifice of his human life. Moreover, God speaks to us through the incarnate Word in a love which was already suffering love previously but which is now a love right to death, a love in complete renunciation.[86]

In this picture, where is the Spirit? Jesus baptized "with Spirit," preached words that were "spirit and life," and performed actions through the Spirit, but, after Pentecost, the Spirit becomes the principal actor, a person who "teaches, reminds, testifies about Jesus, and overcomes the world."[87] For Schoonenberg, the Spirit "became a person" by "going out of Jesus or by being sent by him."[88]

> Jesus is so very much the receiver of the Spirit, and so very much personifies that to which the Spirit compels, that upon his

fulfillment the Spirit received from him in order to communicate him to us and in order to glorify him (Jn 16:14). God's Spirit is now simultaneously the Spirit of the Son. Thus is he person in a new way for us, the "other Paraclete" (Jn 14:16), and thus does he also face God to whom he now cries in us "Abba, Father" (Gal 4:6; Rom 8:15) and to whom he pleads with inexpressible sighings (Rom 8:26).[89]

The Spirit, although fully personal, is not a person in the same way as the Son is a person. The Logos became fully personal through the incarnation, while the Spirit did so through Pentecost. Only then does the Spirit become "the Paraclete, the spirit of Christ given to the Christian community."[90] The Spirit is also unique in respect to its "self-standing." Whereas the Logos became personal in a clear and concrete way in "the Son," the Spirit is personal only in respect to other persons—either in respect to the Son, since the Spirit represents "Christ's person," or in respect to us, since the Spirit is personal "by coming to us, [and by] dwelling in both the Christian community and its members."[91] In this way it might be fair to say that the Spirit is the "hypostasis of the Church," or a "community-person."[92] Although the "we" character of the Spirit prevents the Spirit from becoming a wholly independent, "self-standing" person, the Spirit is still fully personal and functions as the most important Person for our experience of God.[93]

With this change in the Logos and the Spirit, there is also a change in the Father. Just as they "are no longer merely extensions of God but also divine persons, the second and third person *vis-à-vis* God," so too, God the Father "has become the first person, the Father in the trinitarian sense of the word."[94] God now "becomes triune—or more triune, or more expressly triune—towards and in his creation."[95] The Father "personalizes himself," becoming the "Father in the fullest sense of the word, his Father and our Father, his God and our God," and "the 'spirator' of his divine Spirit."[96] "Thus do all three become in the Christ-event what they were not before while remaining at the same time what they are."[97] Only "in and since the Christ-event" can God be described as a communion of persons, existing in the "interpersonal" relationships of Father, Son, and Spirit.[98]

> God is always a God of the covenant, even before the Christ-event. . . . But in the Christ-event God places both his Word and his Spirit totally on the side of his people; in them God becomes

his own covenantal partner. . . . [T]he dialogue, which is always
a trialogue through the position of the idle person, is now in God
perfectly; God's trinity is the completion of the covenant within
God's own essence.[99]

Conclusion

With this final becoming of God as triune, Schoonenberg's
christology reaches its climax in the "mystery of God himself": Father, Son, and Spirit. In closing, it is important to highlight four features of Schoonenberg's Spirit christology that situate him in relation
to others in the field and indicate future directions for those engaged
in Spirit christology.

First, it is important to note how truly revolutionary Schoonenberg's
Spirit christology is. His incorporation of pneumatology is not a foot-
note to Logos christology but a serious effort to rethink Jesus Christ
and the God of Jesus Christ on the basis of the Spirit and the economy
of salvation. His work is grounded in biblical texts, attuned to the
problems that have beleaguered classical christology, and committed
to re-appropriating and re-expressing Christian doctrine for a modern
church.

Second, although Schoonenberg is pushing the boundaries with respect to many in the field, Schoonenberg is not jettisoning the tradition
or approaching the Bible as a collection of proof texts to justify his own
agenda. Schoonenberg's self-stated goal is to retrieve the entire Bible in
concert with the Catholic faith.[100] His commitment to a "post-exegetical
unified reading" of the New Testament demonstrates his willingness to
think beyond the limits of any one author or any one book, and his
efforts to introduce the methods and conclusions of modern biblical
studies stand as a testament to the continuing endeavor to reconnect
biblical studies with systematic theology and to the fecundity that arises
from this unification. Large sections of *The Christ* and *Der Geist, das
Wort und der Sohn* illustrate that Schoonenberg's constructive efforts
are in *dialogue* with the tradition, and that his efforts to correct, aug-
ment, re-appropriate, and re-express the church's tradition are an expression of his commitment to Jesus Christ. This is why Schoonenberg
works to retrieve Spirit christology *and* Logos christology, ascending
and descending perspectives, the views of John *and* those of the synoptics
in a model that is both grounded in the past *and* open to the future.

Third, Schoonenberg is deeply committed to a thorough examination of the issues his christology raises, particularly its implications for the doctrine of God. This is commendable, since many in the field avoid conflicts by refusing to probe the implications of their work. Schoonenberg takes the harder route. He brings christology, trinitarian theology, and pneumatology together in a creative "perichoresis" and, in the process, demonstrates how presuppositions involving God (such as divine immutability) impact our understanding of Jesus (he was always Son) and, conversely, how changes in christology offer new challenges to our understanding of God.

Finally, Schoonenberg's christology adheres to the limits imposed by a theology constructed from the economy of salvation. He refuses to begin "from above," with the presuppositions of trinitarian theology firmly in place, and instead proposes a theology of God based on the experience of God through the Son and in the Spirit. Because Schoonenberg begins "from below," all of his claims about Jesus Christ—namely, that through him the Logos has become the Son, or that in him we know who God is, or that because of him we are given a share in the divine life—are conclusions grounded in the economy of salvation. Schoonenberg's theology seeks to articulate the way Christians have experienced God, not the way they have traditionally thought about God, and perhaps that is the norm we ought to probe in light of his work.

Notes

[1]Piet Schoonenberg, *De Geest, het Woord en de Zoon: Theologische overdenkingen over Geest-christologie, Logos-christologie en drieënheidsleer* (Averbode: Altiora, 1991). The following essay will utilize the German translation, *Der Geist, Das Wort und der Sohn: Eine Geist-Christologie* (Regensburg: Friedrich Pustet, 1992), hereafter abbreviated *Der Geist*. Roger Haight, *Jesus Symbol of God* (Maryknoll, N.Y.: Orbis Books, 1999) is an example of those who make reference to Schoonenberg but do not concentrate on his work. For a recent commentary on Schoonenberg that does not include an examination of *Der Geist, Das Wort und der Sohn* see William J. LaDue, *Jesus among the Theologians: Contemporary Interpretations of Christ* (Harrisburg, Penn.: Trinity Press International, 2001), 97-103.

[2]Piet Schoonenberg, "A Sapiential Reading of John's Prologue: Some Reflections on the Views of Reginald Fuller and James Dunn," *Theology Digest* 33 (1986): 403.

[3]Piet Schoonenberg, *The Christ: A Study of the God-Man Relationship in the Whole of Creation and in Jesus Christ*, trans. Della Couling (New York: Herder &

Herder, 1971), 61, 114-115, hereafter abbreviated *The Christ*; and Piet Schoonenberg, "Spirit Christology and Logos Christology," *Bijdragen: Tijdschrift voor Filosofie en Theologie* 38 (1977): 350, hereafter abbreviated "Spirit Christology."

[4]Schoonenberg, *Der Geist*, 49. See also 55 and 96, and *The Christ*, 53-54, 114.

[5]Schoonenberg, *Der Geist*, 18.

[6]Ibid., 97-98.

[7]Ibid., 51.

[8]Schoonenberg claims that despite some texts that seem to equate Jesus with God, the New Testament respects the distinction between Jesus and the Father. Jesus is "*theos*," and even "our" God, but never "*ho theos*." See *Der Geist*, 52.

[9]Schoonenberg, *Der Geist*, 103-104. For Schoonenberg, the effort to revise classical christology in light of the New Testament's Spirit christology is valued precisely because it employs "the Bible's own theology" to understand Jesus Christ. See *Spirit Christology*, 360: "I find it intolerable that a main theme of Paul's, Luke's and even John's Christology remains either banished from our christological treatises or confined to some *scholion*. It has to be reconsidered. In one or another way Spirit-Christology must be re-introduced." See also *Der Geist*, 46-47; Piet Schoonenberg, "From a Two-Nature Christology to a Christology of Presence," in *Theological Folia of Villanova University: Speculative Studies*, vol. II, ed. J. Papin (Villanova, Penn.: Villanova University Press, 1975): 219-220, hereafter abbreviated "Christology of Presence"; and "Christ and the Spirit: An Essay in Spirit Christology," *Schola: A Pastoral Review of Sacred Heart School of Theology* 1 (1978): 34. In the last citation Schoonenberg addresses the value of uniting descending and ascending perspectives.

[10]Schoonenberg, *Der Geist*, 13. See also "Spirit Christology," 362-363.

[11]Schoonenberg, *Der Geist*, 55.

[12]Schoonenberg, "Spirit Christology," 353. Schoonenberg's definition of what constitutes a "Spirit christology" comes from *Der Geist*, 25: "By Spirit-christology I do not mean that christology which also speaks of the Holy Spirit; and certainly I do not mean that christology in which there is first talk of the Spirit and afterwards the identity of Jesus is explained out of a different source. No, Spirit-christology explains this identity completely in terms of the Spirit. Spirit-christology so defined differentiates itself from other christologies, especially those which begin with the pre-existence of Christ in God."

[13]Schoonenberg, *Der Geist*, 56-58, 71-72, 111-114. See also "Spirit Christology," 362, and *The Christ*, 177-178, 224. Schoonenberg's proposal reflects a consensus within contemporary theology that reasserts the value of an historical approach and highlights the difficulty of reconciling modern anthropology, biblical studies, soteriology, and the doctrine of God with classical christology. For an examination of his claims regarding the New Testament and the need for an ascending christology, see "God's Presence in Jesus: An Exchange of Viewpoints," *Theology Digest* 19 (1971): 29; "Christology of Presence," 222-225; and "Spirit Christology," 353-355 and 364-365. The last citation contains Schoonenberg's response to the Vatican's criticism of ascending christology in *Mysterium Filii Dei*, issued by the Congregation for the Doctrine of the Faith on 21 February, 1972.

[14]Schoonenberg claims that although Mark relied on Isaiah, Mark inverted Isaiah's order of events: whereas for Isaiah the chosen one is first the Son and then given the Spirit as the Son, for Mark Jesus is given the Spirit in order to become the Son. See *Der Geist*, 24.

[15]Schoonenberg, *Der Geist*, 23. Schoonenberg identifies additional traces of this model in 1 Cor. 15:45, 2 Cor. 3:17, Rom. 1:3-4, and Acts 2:33. The last two citations are important since for Schoonenberg they pre-date even Mark's Gospel and speak of Jesus becoming the Son at his resurrection. For additional comments see *Der Geist*, 12; "Spirit Christology," 351-353; and Schoonenberg, "Christ and the Spirit, 34-35.

[16]Schoonenberg, *Der Geist*, 20, 24.

[17]Ibid., 45-46. See also Schoonenberg, "Christ and the Spirit," 34, and "Spirit Christology," 362: "I want to emphasize Jesus' conception by the Holy Spirit, not in order to provoke debates on the historical or legendary character of the story, but to see here the point where Spirit-christology abandons the form of an ascending [christology], and takes on that of a descending christology. There is a danger that as we discuss the creedal text 'born of the virgin Mary' we forget the preceding words 'conceived of the Holy Spirit.' Nevertheless, here is expressed that Jesus is the fruit of the Holy Spirit from the beginning of his human history and hence in the totality of his human being. . . . I think, precisely here Spirit-christology proclaims Jesus not less divine than John does in his text: 'The Logos became flesh'."

[18]Schoonenberg, *Der Geist*, 26. See also pp. 56-58, 111-114, and "Christology of Presence," 224.

[19]That is evident if one returns to the New Testament's Logos christology rather than the post-New Testament "Logos-Son" christology. The former relies upon "biblical patterns of thought" while the latter represents "a different [theological] world" due to the introduction of Middle Platonism via Origen (see *The Christ*, 54-55). According to Schoonenberg, it was under the influence of Middle Platonism that the pre-existent Logos became a pre-existent Son, which in practice meant the displacement of the Spirit and the "ascending" perspective maintained by Spirit Christology. See *Der Geist*, 58-61, and *The Christ*, 54-65.

[20]To defend this change, which is most developed in *Der Geist*, Schoonenberg appeals to the New Testament, particularly its Wisdom christology and a number of early church fathers, especially Marius Victorinus.

[21]See Schoonenberg, "Spirit Christology," especially 365 and 374-375.

[22]Schoonenberg, *Der Geist*, 112. See also *The Christ*, 71-72.

[23]Schoonenberg, *The Christ*, 116.

[24]Ibid., 106.

[25]Ibid., 127.

[26]Ibid., 108.

[27]Ibid., 123-129, 141-145. See also *Der Geist*, 106-110.

[28]Schoonenberg, *Der Geist*, 140. Schoonenberg interprets the kenotic texts such as Philippians 2:6-11 as describing the self-emptying of a human person who rejects a human equality with God that would have given him "undisturbed joy and peace," and may have resulted in "power and majesty" in favor of self-sacrificing

love. Thus kenosis does not demand pre-existence. See *Der Geist*, 132-135, 143, and Piet Schoonenberg, " 'He Emptied Himself' Philippians 2:7,11," *Concilium* 11 (1966): 47-66.

[29]Schoonenberg cities Hebrews 12:2, which identifies Jesus as the "pioneer and perfector of our faith" in this regard. See his comments in *Der Geist*, 110; *The Christ*, 99-102, 145, 152; and "Christology of Presence," 239-241. See also G. W. H. Lampe, *God as Spirit* (Oxford: Clarendon Press, 1977).

[30]Schoonenberg, *The Christ*, 71-72, 97, and "Spirit Christology," 364.

[31]Schoonenberg, *Der Geist*, 153, 191, 200. See also *The Christ*, 73, 179, and "Spirit Christology," 366.

[32]Schoonenberg, *Der Geist*, 174. See also his "Trinity—The Consummated Covenant: Theses on the Doctrine of the Trinitarian God," *Studies in Religion* 5 (1975-1976): 11-16, and "The Doctrine of the Trinity: An Empty Dogma or a Fruitful Theologoumenon," *Louvain Studies* 16 (1991): 195-206.

[33]*Der Geist*, 58-59. According to Schoonenberg, there are three different New Testament models for understanding pre-existence: "The Word or the Logos which becomes flesh, the Son who was with the Father and is sent from there, and the Son of Man who descends from heaven." Only the last two affirm the personal pre-existence of the Son (e.g., John 6:38 and John 8:26). "The Logos with God in Jn 1:1 is not yet expressly designated as a pre-existent person, and certainly not in the sense that he would push aside the personal existence of Jesus as a human person." Hence Schoonenberg insists that the pre-Incarnate Logos is an extension or expression of the Father that "became" fully personal in the human history of Jesus Christ. See *Der Geist*, 102-103. See also "Spirit Christology," 353-356.

[34]Schoonenberg, *Der Geist*, 190.

[35]Schoonenberg, *The Christ*, 82. See also *Der Geist*, 65 and the following from 181: "Word and Spirit in God's substance and in God's self-communication are not personal in any manner which either divides the human reality of Jesus over both persons or robs it of the human being-person; for any such divided or human-impersonal Christ is not the Jesus of whom the New Testament speaks."

[36]Schoonenberg, *Der Geist*, 62.

[37]Ibid., 67-69. See James D. G. Dunn, *Christology in the Making: A New Testament Inquiry into the Origins of the Doctrine of the Incarnation* (London: SCM Press, 1980).

[38]Schoonenberg, *Der Geist*, 147. See also 146, 69-70, and "Christ and the Spirit," 32.

[39]Schoonenberg, *Der Geist,* 71-72, 74.

[40]Ibid., 185.

[41]Ibid., 102. See also 67, 74-75, and "Christology of Presence," 231. Schoonenberg rejects the Neo-Chalcedonian interpretation of the enhypostasis, namely the anhypostasis, because it denies Jesus' human personhood. In "Christology of Presence" he claimed that to accept the anhypostasis would mean that Jesus did not exist "in the only way that humans can exist—as an individual person." His humanity "has no personal being that is its own," but exists as "the instrument or tool, or even the puppet, of the eternal Word" (224). He attributes

the movement from the enhypostasis to the anhypostasis as a consequence of the church's struggle with Arius and changes in the Western approach to the doctrine of the Trinity, beginning with Augustine.

In *Der Geist* Schoonenberg offers a bit more nuance. On pp. 153-154, n. 9, Schoonenberg claims that there are two ways to understand the *anhypostasis:* Protestant scholars tend to view the *anhypostais* as a way to express the claim that "the human nature of Christ has no human, personal being of its own outside its hypostatic unity with the divine Word," or "before the incarnation," while Catholic theologians tend to interpret the anhypostasis in such a way that Christ's human personhood is denied even "within the hypostatic unity" or "since the incarnation" (153). Schoonenberg accepts the first interpretation as valid, but not the second. For additional insights, particularly his understanding of the impact of Augustine's trinitarian theology on christology, see "God's Presence in Jesus: An Exchange of Viewpoints," 33-34; *The Christ*, 58-72; and "The Doctrine of the Trinity," 195-198.

[42]Schoonenberg, *Der Geist*, 191.

[43]In addition to a reinterpreted enhypostasis, Schoonenberg also explored the relationship between God and Jesus Christ under a model based on God's *pleroma* or fullness (Col. 1:18, 2:9) in *The Christ*. There, Jesus was understood to be the unique Son of God because in him the fullness of God's presence, or the "paramount presence of God" dwelled. Thus the Father (rather than the Logos, or the Logos in conjunction with the Spirit) dwells in Jesus Christ "in such a way that his human element is itself salvific for all creation." Jesus is not a divine person, but a human person filled with "God's total presence" (192, 123). Schoonenberg also explored several models in "Christology of Presence" (232-234), but these earlier efforts are not taken up in *Der Geist*.

[44]Schoonenberg, *Der Geist*, 153.

[45]Schoonenberg, "Spirit Christology," 364-365.

[46]Schoonenberg, *Der Geist*, 153-154.

[47]Ibid., 154.

[48]Schoonenberg, *The Christ*, 179.

[49]Schoonenberg, *Der Geist*, 154, n. 10. Schoonenberg goes on to claim that in his earlier work *The Christ,* when he asserted that "the human nature is . . . not enhypostatic in the divine person, but rather the divine nature is en-hypostatic in the human person," what he was seeking to do was not "turn Chalcedon into ruins, but to reverse the model of thought," beginning with a fully human Jesus rather than the Second Person of the Trinity. The "humanity itself is passive in the most radical way, for it did not exist at all before the incarnation and it is called into existence through the acceptance of the Word itself." See p. 153, n. 8 and pp. 186-187.

[50]Schoonenberg, *Der Geist*, 190.

[51]Ibid., 200-201.

[52]Ibid., 152-153.

[53]Ibid., 95. Schoonenberg claims that the prologue of John's Gospel is correctly understood as an "Easter message" since the incarnation was not a static, one-time event identified with the moment of conception, but an ongoing process

completed with the resurrection and glorification of Jesus Christ. See *Der Geist*, 114.

⁵⁴Ibid., 80.

⁵⁵Ibid., 152.

⁵⁶Ibid.

⁵⁷Ibid., 203-204. See also 149-150.

⁵⁸Ibid., 203-204.

⁵⁹Schoonenberg's movement from christology to trinitarian theology needs to be emphasized, particularly when comparing him with theologians like Marcus Borg and Lampe, who do not develop a doctrine of God, and theologians like Walter Kasper, who advocates a modified Logos christology but with clear trinitarian presuppositions in place. *Contra* Lampe and Borg, Schoonenberg insists that one cannot address the presence of God in the Son unless one explores who this God is and how this God relates to us; *contra* Kasper, Schoonenberg emphasizes the christological foundation of trinitarian theology rather than the "trinitarian logic" that stands behind christology. For him, trinitarian theology is an "extension of christology." One cannot begin with the "mystery of God himself" since that mystery is only made available to us through the economy of salvation. Any claims about God and God's life with us must be "rooted" in and evaluated by the experience of God that takes place in the Son and through the Spirit. See "A Sapiential Reading of John's Prologue," especially 403, 415-416.

⁶⁰Schoonenberg, *Der Geist*, 162-164, 172-173. See also *The Christ*, 22.

⁶¹Schoonenberg, *Der Geist*, 166.

⁶²Ibid.

⁶³Ibid., 167.

⁶⁴Ibid., 169, 172.

⁶⁵Ibid., 217. Schoonenberg's emphasis on "personalization" as the outcome of God's interaction with us is particular to his later writings. Before the 1980s, he focused on a number of other ways to express the positive outcome of God's interaction with us, particularly the claim that God "humanizes us" by "divinizing us" and the claim that God "perfects us" by being involved with us. See *The Christ*, 7-8, 33-47, and 73-74.

⁶⁶Schoonenberg, *Der Geist*, 172.

⁶⁷Ibid., 177, 183.

⁶⁸Ibid., 167.

⁶⁹Ibid., 116-123, 188-189. See also *The Christ*, 86; "God as Relating and (Be)coming: A Meta-Thomistic Consideration," *Listening* 14 (1979): 265-278; and "Process of History in God?," *Louvain Studies* 4 (1972-1973): 303-319.

⁷⁰Schoonenberg, *Der Geist*, 176-177. See also *The Christ*, 82-84, and "Spirit Christology," 370-371.

⁷¹Schoonenberg, *Der Geist*, 119. See also 120, 137, 142-143, and *The Christ*, 84-86.

⁷²Schoonenberg, *Der Geist,* 119.

⁷³Schoonenberg, *The Christ*, 84.

⁷⁴Schoonenberg, *Der Geist*, 123-124, 129-130. Although Schoonenberg ac-

knowledges the importance of process theology and its views on God's becoming, he insists that his theology is not dependent upon process philosophy (such as that of Alfred North Whitehead). See *Der Geist*, 115; "God as Relating and (Be)Coming," 265-278; and "Process or History in God?," 303-319. In the last essay he concentrates on the limits of process theology, particularly its reluctance to acknowledge the unknowability of God and for implying God is dependent since God is "enriched" or "fulfilled" through God's relations.

[75]Schoonenberg, *Der Geist*, 121. See also 137-140.

[76]Ibid., 126.

[77]Ibid., 215, 271.

[78]Ibid., 195, 200.

[79]Ibid., 38-40. See also 129-130, 196, 206, and "Spirit Christology," 367.

[80]Schoonenberg, *Der Geist*, 216, 186.

[81]Ibid., 215.

[82]Ibid., 197-198.

[83]Ibid., 191.

[84]Ibid., 199.

[85]Ibid., 185-186. See also 198-200, 203, and 218.

[86]Ibid., 127-128. Schoonenberg admits that although there are passages in the New Testament that can be interpreted to view the pre-incarnate Logos as a divine *person*, they can be interpreted to emphasize the *change* that took place in the Christ-event, such that only since the incarnation is the Logos "a distinct person, not only among human persons but also in his distinction from the Father." See also "A Sapiential Reading of John's Prologue," 412-416.

[87]Schoonenberg, *Der Geist*, 206.

[88]Schoonenberg, "Christ and the Spirit," 45-46. See also *Der Geist*, 205, and *The Christ*, 182.

[89]Schoonenberg, *Der Geist*, 129. See also 41-42, 128, 205-206.

[90]Schoonenberg, "Spirit Christology," 368.

[91]Piet Schoonenberg, "A Letter from Piet Schoonenberg," *Theology Digest* 23 (1975): 225.

[92]Schoonenberg, "Christ and the Spirit," 46. See also "Spirit Christology," 368-369, and *Der Geist*, 186, 205, and 217.

[93]Schoonenberg, *Der Geist*, 156. See also "Spirit Christology," 352-353, 374.

[94]Schoonenberg, "Spirit Christology," 368.

[95]Schoonenberg, *The Christ*, 185. See also *Der Geist*, 186-191, 217.

[96]Schoonenberg, *Der Geist*, 129, 188.

[97]Ibid., 188-189.

[98]Ibid., 191-193, 210. In his "Trinity—The Consummated Covenant," 114-115, Schoonenberg expresses his effort to unite "what is true in both trinitarian modalism and personalism. The modalistic view of the Trinity is serviceable inasmuch as it presents the Logos and the Spirit not merely as roles but as modes of self-communication and presence of God or as his 'extensions' or 'expansions' towards the world. Before Christ, the Logos and the Spirit can be seen *merely as such modes;* in Christ, however, the Logos as Son faces the Father and the modalistic Trinity of

God becomes *a Trinity of persons* by God's full self-communication in the mystery of Christ" (emphasis mine).

[99]Schoonenberg, *Der Geist*, 211. Although Schoonenberg's earlier work tended to dismiss the possibility of knowing whether God was triune apart from creation (see, for example, *The Christ*, 82-83, and "Trinity—The Consummated Covenant"), in *Der Geist* he seems to answer that question in the negative. Since God became Father, Son, and Spirit in history, God was not triune apart from history. See especially *Der Geist*, 194-195 and 214.

[100]Schoonenberg, "Spirit Christology," 360.

Derrida's Use of Scripture

Jacquelyn Porter

Some recent essays of Jacques Derrida, such as those collected in the volume entitled *On Cosmopolitanism and Forgiveness*,[1] illustrate the religious relevance and ethical import of his controversial thought. As John Caputo and others have noted, Derrida has increasingly drawn upon his own Jewish background in works with a practical ethical dimension, admitting the influence of a residue of terms, practices, and concepts framed within the context of promise and messianic hope.[2] He himself professes no faith, but acknowledges the complex influences of his background as a Jew born in Algeria and educated through classical philosophical and religious texts of the Western tradition. Thus his work appeals to many religious thinkers who find that he has spoken afresh of classical religious texts as well as of the realization of justice in a global context.

At the same time, Derrida's turn toward the religious raises critical questions for the religions. His use of biblical concepts spotlights their significance but also lifts them out of their setting in the lived experience of religious communities and their traditions. Those within the religious traditions may well ask if indeed he is evacuating the religions of what makes them religions. Believers may well be concerned that deconstruction traces a perilous path for faith.

While recognizing the depth and complexity of the questions that Derrida's approach raises for religion, this paper has a more limited scope. It aims to examine his turn toward the religious by focusing upon the two recent essays that comprise the volume *On Cosmopolitanism and Forgiveness*. I want to consider specifically his use of scripture in these essays, in particular the tension he posits between the unconditionality of certain biblical concepts and their translation into a more philosophical and juridical Western language. This essay seeks to situate his analysis of the concepts of hospitality and forgiveness within the framework of alterity, the messianic, and the future yet to come. Finally, and more specifically, I am concerned with the questions that this understanding raises for Christianity, which speaks of Jesus Christ as mediator, as incarnate Messiah, and Word of God.

Derrida's work demonstrates convincingly that religious thought must acknowledge the need for its own purification, an ascesis that would lead to greater emphasis upon the ethical. He shows that "the religious" may be contaminated by religion's search for its own identity, which in turn relegates "the other" to its borders. Yet this essay argues that religion in its dispossession must not divest itself of what makes it a religion, and what a broader approach to scripture might encompass. After some critical observations I will point to some ways in which Christian thinkers working from within the tradition are taking into account deconstruction's import and challenge.

The Movement toward Alterity

While our focus is upon particular examples of Derrida's use of scripture, it may be helpful here to place that turn toward scripture in the framework of the critique of philosophies of presence and identity that runs throughout his extensive work.

Derrida's reading of texts often identifies in them a preference for the *same* over the *other*, which ultimately results in violence. These categories, familiar to thinkers since Plato, suggest for Derrida a tension too often resolved in Western thought by a reduction of the other to the same, which assimilates the other to itself. Bruce Benson has described this tendency as a systemizing that "tends to impose a *logos* or structure on the world, or to put the world into a kind of schema that looks like me, so that the alterity of the other is thereby reabsorbed into my own identity as thinker or possessor."[3] This imposition upon the other, this totalization, is inherently violent, reducing the particularity and difference of the other in the very exercise of autonomous reason. Whether Derrida speaks of the sovereign acts of persons or nation-states, he calls into question that self-sufficient, sovereign thought that either ignores the other or attempts to absorb the other to itself.

In order to subvert this tendency, Derrida frequently reinterprets classic and religious texts, exposing their pretensions by calling into question the very ground or foundation of their language. Kevin Hart has noted that Derrida challenges a fundamental assumption of classical philosophy, the notion that presence always precedes representation.[4] Derrida exposes a "vulnerability of the sign" that is inherent in its openness to translation and repetition. The sign can always be repeated outside of its context, so that even though a first repetition aims to preserve the sign's identity, a second puts the original meaning at risk. The sign's meaning is always open to change, so that alterity can be said to be a structural feature of the sign.[5] For Derrida this means that signs have not "fallen from presence" but that presence cannot fulfill its promise of being able to act as a ground.

Deconstruction, a term that has many meanings in Derrida's work, can be described as an analysis that dismantles the text in order to open it up and disclose therein a more profound tendency toward alterity. Rather than allowing the reader to find there an origin or ground through which to enhance the self, it provokes an ambivalence that Derrida hopes will lead the reader toward inventive and responsible action.

Though difficult to define, the term deconstruction is often associated with an analysis that attends to what texts leave out, what they assume or relegate to their margins. As Bruce Benson notes, deconstruction takes texts apart to expose what is already going on in them: "If anything, it is something that happens to texts and systems and ideas, and even us."[6] This encounter with contradictions, tension and ambiguity may paralyze thought but it also prevents premature and self-serving closure. The reader comes into contact with the text's alterity.

In contrast to philosophies of presence that tend to enclose the reader in the self-legitimizations of the same, the scriptures, especially those writings centered around Abraham, are framed by the structure of the promise and of an impossible hope in what is yet to be. In this sense, scripture privileges alterity. Thus while Derrida most often comments on philosophical and literary texts, he has also increasingly examined ethical issues in relation to scripture. He makes use of scripture to bring to realization that which cannot be said in the prevailing order, what is yet to be spoken, what cannot be reduced to the familiar and the *same*. We turn now to his method of appropriating scripture and the implications of that approach.

Hospitality and Forgiveness

In response to requests by particular groups that he address specific and troubling world problems, Derrida wrote the two essays on
hospitality and forgiveness. Although the essays "On Cosmopolitanism" and "Forgiveness" were published in a single volume, they first
appeared separately. "On Cosmopolitanism" was originally presented
as a lecture before the International Parliament of Writers in 1996.
This forum dealt with issues raised concerning asylum both for writers under threat of persecution and for those termed *sans-papiers,* thousands of Algerians without immigration papers who had fled to France
from African nations. The so-called Pasqua laws—named for Charles
Pasqua, the French Interior Minister who introduced them—set strict
limits on immigration and established conditions that made many immigrants illegal. While the children of these immigrants could not be
expelled, their parents were not allowed to receive papers. In 1996 a
group of these refugees participated in protests that demanded mediation, and hearings were held that exposed the racism behind the immigration policy. These events, which required a just and pragmatic resolution, served as a catalyst for Derrida's reflections on hospitality.
The second essay, "On Forgiveness," first appeared in a newspaper
interview. It examines forgiveness in light of global calls for amnesty
and reconciliation. The relevance of these topics and the promise of
new life that Derrida brings to tired discussions of them have attracted
the attention of many religious thinkers.

Derrida's strategy in these essays is similar to that which he has
used to analyze other familiar concepts, such as community. Through
a long history of usage these terms have lost their original religious
associations and have come to be taken in a more secular sense. Derrida,
however, aims to expose an inner tension within these concepts. He
hopes to break them down and open them to alterity.

In speaking of hospitality to the conference of writers, he recalled
that in previous meetings the members had called for the opening of
cities of refuge around the world, "each as independent from the other
and from the state as possible, but, nevertheless, allied to each other
according to forms of solidarity yet to be invented."[7] The notion of
cities of refuge is a familiar one for Europeans, associated with the
memory of the medieval history of sanctuary given, for example, to

such figures as Dante at Ravenna.[8] Yet Derrida would push the analysis further. He strives to relate the notion of the cities of refuge to the more ambivalent and all-encompassing imperative of hospitality.

The notion of hospitality, the opening of one's home to the other, is central to Derrida's ethics. He claims that hospitality is culture itself and not simply one ethic among others. "Insofar as it has to do with the *ethos*, that is, the residence, one's home, the familiar place of dwelling, inasmuch as it is a manner of being there, the manner in which we relate to ourselves and to others, *ethics is hospitality*."[9] At the same time, this way of being at home with oneself supposes a reception or inclusion of the other that one seeks to appropriate, control, and master according to different modalities of violence. The tension between the same and the other makes itself felt in an aporia. What appears to be an unconditional *law* of hospitality is in fact vulnerable throughout history to distortion. There is a history of hospitality, an always possible perversion of "*the* Great Law of Hospitality," which can appear unconditional.[10]

We may ask where Derrida derives this notion of *the* law of hospitality that precedes our juridical language of hospitality. In this very condensed essay, Derrida alludes to scripture, referring to the biblical establishment of six Levitical cities of refuge according to the Law (Num. 35:7-15). He does not elaborate here on what he considers to be the significance of the narrative of Abraham, who heard the promise and acted in uncompromising obedience. His readers would assume this association. Caputo and others have discussed in depth the messianic motif that characterizes much of his work and is associated with the Abrahamic tradition.[11] Derrida is drawn to this tradition not so much because of the faith and leadership of the person but because of the unconditionality of the command and the obedience that it reflects. Moreover, Judaism, Christianity, and Islam, three religions frequently in conflict with one another, trace their roots back to this common ancestor so that they illustrate how the messianic can be distorted when realized in what Derrida calls "messianisms."[12] For Derrida the notion of hospitality recalls a framework of promise that envelops scripture, an overarching expectation of justice yet to come that is reinforced by teachings of the prophets. At the same time, in the practical sphere, it has been transformed by the history of its concrete realizations.

Derrida identifies this compromise particularly with Greek stoicism

(adapted through Cicero) and with Paul and claims that it is their understanding of cosmopolitanism as well as that of the secular tradition
that he is calling into question. He cites in this regard a Pauline passage: "And so, therefore, you are no longer foreigners abroad (*xenoi,
hospites*), you are fellow-citizens of the state, you belong to the House
of God" (Eph. 2:19-20). In Derrida's view, this kind of tolerance—
this cosmopolitanism—implies the assimilation of the foreigner.
Whether the act of hospitality is personal or political, it discloses a
sovereignty that imposes itself upon the right of the other to be welcome as other. By alluding to the biblical notion of the unconditional,
Derrida discloses a tension within the concept of hospitality, an ambivalence beneath the urbane, and sophisticated tolerance in which
the West takes pride. The need for asylum today cannot be met by
such humanistic *bonhomie*.

At the heart of any state's offer of asylum is its confident sovereignty, a power to dominate that is potentially violent. In the personal
sphere as well, Derrida observes, the offer of hospitality implies a
power to dominate that reinforces the sense of identity. Hospitality
implies a *host* with a certain control of the home who may give or
deny hospitality. The host's generous welcome of the guest duels with
protectiveness toward self and family, so that the question inevitably
rises: "But when will they leave?" On the political and personal level
the offer of hospitality is in reality an uncomfortable one.

In the light of this analysis, Derrida does not minimize the difficulty of realistic action. On the one hand there is a need for political
solutions—without which, he admits, "*the* unconditional law of hospitality would be in danger of remaining a pious and irresponsible
desire."[13] What is needed, he claims, is "knowing how to transform
and improve the law." Recognition of ambivalence in fact gives no
knowledge of what that transformation would be. Rather, it gives rise
to action and experimentation. The creation of cities of refuge is something that cannot wait. The situation calls for an "*urgent response*"
and a "*new order of law and a democracy to be put to the test.*"[14]
Derrida thus retrieves the biblical notion of the unconditionality of
hospitality in service to a vision of a new world order.

In his essay on "Forgiveness" Derrida discloses a similar aporia.
His notion of forgiveness (*pardon*) is situated within a rich discussion
of "gift" (*le don*).[15] In a world governed by the laws of economic exchange nothing is given except in response to what has been received;

in other words, gifts are given only with conditions attached. Yet, with the exercise of forgiveness, there is a memory of what seems impossible, namely, an unconditional gift. Thus every concrete effort to forgive is haunted by an aporia. Questions range from the personal, such as how the living can forgive in the name of a dead victim, to how the state should organize tribunals to judge "crimes against humanity."

For many, the very notion of "crimes against humanity" is derived from a biblical understanding. Derrida claims that it is not enough to speak of forgiveness in terms of the one who forgives, whether it be a "noble soul" or a sovereign state. This power to forgive, this sovereignty, is rebuked by the silence of the victim, by that "absolute victimization which deprives the victim of life, or the right to speak." Thus Derrida dreams of a forgiveness that would be "without power: unconditional but without sovereignty."[16] It is necessary to dissociate unconditionality from sovereignty, or the forgiveness negotiated by persons and states will be purely pragmatic, lacking in universality.

As with hospitality, forgiveness cannot be translated into a program. It requires a negotiation that takes into account both poles of the unconditional and the conditional. And again, as with hospitality, Derrida's reflections take on a note of urgency, but offer no guidelines. He retains a confidence and a hope that this task may yet be realized: "be it as a dream for thought, this madness is perhaps not so mad."[17]

In sum, Derrida makes use of the biblical concept of unconditionality in order to disclose the ambivalence inherent within terms that in the course of history have been translated and transformed. He uncovers a formal structure in which unconditional imperatives are transformed as they flow into Westernized and often juridical language. Yet in becoming "globalatinized" these concepts become in fact less truly unconditional and universal.[18] In positing the unconditional, Derrida offers no exegesis of texts. Rather, he evokes a universal imperative by allusion to a timeless *Law,* posing a contrast that shows how the concept has become perverted. The experience of ambivalence has a positive dimension in that it may lead to invention and a more responsible ethic. "I also imagine the experience of cities of refuge as giving rise to a place (*lieu*) for reflection," he writes, "for reflection on the questions of asylum and hospitality—for a new order of law and a democracy to come to be put to the test (experimentation)."[19]

This deconstruction of a modern concept by referring to its biblical roots does not necessarily imply for Derrida a return to that faith in which the promise was first received. Rather, he wants to lay bare the formal structure of a movement. At the same time that concept, lifted out of its original context, retains a power. Its tension with the present opens it to something new. Derrida implicitly discourages any return to an origin or presence, to biblical faith, to its prayers, rituals, beliefs, or institutions. He retains an interest in biblical texts, primarily as a means of speaking of the unconditional and of recalling a messianic structure.

The Messianic Hope

In a world in which Judaism, Christianity, and Islam seem often to be at war with one another and at a time when the religions seem torn by a need for reconciliation from within, these reflections on hospitality and forgiveness raise serious questions. Yet we may ask how Derrida can be confident that awareness will lead to effective action rather than incapacity. As a man raised within Judaism but educated in a tradition dominated by the Western heritage, he retains a memory of biblical notions and of their complex transmission. Will those without this experience share the same sense of the unconditional and of the structure of messianic hope? To what extent does the significance of the formal structure that he presents depend upon a biblical understanding that has been passed on as more than a formal notion and kept alive through centuries of a living faith?

Derrida's retrieval of the biblical notions of hospitality is set within a broader framework that Caputo has described as "an overarching aspiration, which on a certain analysis can be called a religious or prophetic aspiration . . . a movement of transcendence."[20] Caputo attributes this movement to the promptings of something that cannot be seen, "the provocation of what is to come, *B venir,* against the complacency of the present . . . in order to prevent it from closing in upon itself, from collapsing into self-identity."[21] This movement of transcendence is thought in relation to the religious. Yet the religious must not cling to any past, not even to the forms of scriptures. For Derrida, openness to the other precludes any home or dwelling place for faith. The movement of transcendence corresponds to the messianic hope of biblical faith but must not be identified with that faith.

While it may be useful, then, to recall the relation of Judaism, Christianity, and Islam to Abraham and the commonality of an Abrahamic tradition, these religions must admit that at the core of each there is a universal structure: "If the messianic appeal belongs properly to a universal structure, to that irreducible movement of the historical opening to the future, therefore to experience itself and to its language (expectation, promise, commitment), how is one to speak within the figures of Abrahamic messianism?" Derrida distinguishes here between messianism and the messianic. "Was not Abrahamic messianism but an exemplary pre-figuration, the pre-name *(prénom)* given against the possibility that we are attempting to name here? But then why keep the name, or at least the adjective (we prefer to say messianic rather than messianism, so as to designate a structure of experience rather than a religion) there where no figure of the arrivant, even as he or she is heralded, should be pre-determined, pre-figured, or even pre-named?"[22]

Thus, in valorizing the messianic Derrida distinguishes it from any concrete realization of the past and remains wary that any embodiment or form will impede the movement toward what is yet to come. The rituals, dogmas, and symbols of the religions appear inevitably idolatrous. How much more problematic, then, is prayer to an incarnate Messiah and speech about Jesus the Christ? Not only do these incarnations restrict hope, as Derrida sees it; in their confidence in being grounded in an originary presence, they cannot let the other be other. What appears to be a movement of transcendence too often masks a movement toward totalization that ends in violence.

Derrida's turn to the religious has appealed to many religious thinkers. Faith has always been aware of the danger of representation and admits a history of contamination. His use of biblical texts raises the question of whether it is now time to separate the religious from the religions, to accept the inevitable in freedom. As Caputo observes, "The question of deconstruction and religion comes down to the question of deconstruction as religion, as the repetition of religion without religion, as the messianic without messianism . . ."[23]

In the tradition of Kant and others, Derrida appears to make use of scripture in order to support a new and secular humanism. Concepts such as hospitality, forgiveness, and justice that had once been integrated within religion when God was named are now to be given a thoroughly humanistic context. The religious is to function without the encumbrance of the religions, the structures of prayer, belonging, ritual, and dogma that have held the religions together in the past. The messianic, he insists, implies a waiting without any horizon of expectation. It is a "desert-like messianism (without content and without identifiable Messiah)."[24]

Questions

As we have seen, Derrida appeals to the biblical origins of concepts to uncover their internal logic.[25] The notion of unconditional hospitality, for example, functions similarly to a transcendental and stands in tension with its meaning in everyday speech. To retrieve these biblical concepts as unconditional and universal, Derrida simply posits them as such and assumes in the reader a religious memory. Although he has commented more extensively on scriptural texts in other works, he does not concern himself with the setting in which these concepts are found, the relation of texts to one another, or the history of their transmission. The persons of the Bible, their relationships to one another, the communities of faith that they inspired are all relegated to the past so that the biblical concept may be isolated and abstracted. The positive contribution of his deconstruction is that it opens up what had seemed impossible, that we might forgive the unforgivable or live with foreigners in our homes without demanding that they become like us.

For this reason, a dialogue with Derrida's thought suggests the need for an ascesis of the religions. He argues convincingly for a greater focus upon the messianic and for a passion for justice that will be inventive. As Derrida himself has described it, "Ascesis strips the messianic hope of all biblical forms, and even all determinable figures of waiting or expectation; it thus denudes itself in view of responding to that which must be absolute hospitality. . . ."[26] Yet the religions, even in accepting a need for dispossession, must rightly question of what they are dispossessing themselves. Must they denude themselves of what has allowed them to transmit and give an account of their hope?

In his use of scripture in these essays, Derrida ignores the relation of the Word to the community that received it, the settings of the texts, and their history of transmission. He is concerned with isolating a universal. However, the scriptures have their own integrity. Is there not a kind of presentism manifest in disregarding that integrity and the otherness of the past? Derrida's abstraction of biblical concepts from their context ignores the complex ways in which notions such as hospitality are dealt within varied texts. A tribal and inadequate notion of hospitality, for example, is called into question by the story of the Outrage of Gibeah (Judg. 10), in which the concubine/wife is sacrificed in a parody of tribal belonging. In various ways communities have sought to deal with this diversity, sometimes suppressing it for their own ends.

Yet, the texts have been kept alive and transmitted in the interpretations of communities that sought to relate them to their lived experience. The notion of the unconditional, of a hope in what is yet to come, has been passed on not simply because it could be discerned in texts but because it was related to the lived experience of communities of interpretation. These interpretations have not always led to an idolatrous fixation upon the past or upon presence. Before abandoning its liturgies and structures of belonging, religion may well ask how these structures function in relation to the promise, an ethics of responsibility in a future yet to be realized.

Derrida's formal description of messianic hope abstracts it from the forms and figures through which it has been mediated. John Caputo has argued that in questioning every finite realization of the infinite, Derrida resists determinations "not because he is against body, flesh, but because he fears giving finite forms an infinite warrant."[27] This critique poses a particular challenge to Christianity's affirmation of the incarnation. Yet Christian theological affirmations about Christ are complex, reflecting today a critical engagement with historical research on Jesus as eschatological prophet. The themes of recent reflection on christology show that theologians and Derrida have some common concerns. They are asking how to express more adequately the relation of the finite and the infinite, how to recover the relation of Jesus to the Hebrew and prophetic tradition, how to interpret Jesus' death and resurrection in a way that discloses its critical force.

The religions have always been troubled with the problem of mediation. They have always risked confounding the ineffable with its representation, and yet they have always needed to make use of representation to reach out toward God. They have needed to name their God even in recognizing the limits of these names. The question may well be how to submit these mediations to critique while making positive use of them. Richard Kearney describes the messianic as a "no place *(non-lieu)* of . . . incessant waiting and welcome, preceding and exceeding every historical revelation of a specific messiah. . . ." In the need to keep all options open, Kearney claims, something is also lost, for scripture has also a role in preparing for recognition of the other, for responding to something other than the self. In this respect, deconstruction "is like waiting for Godot, not just in two acts but forever."[28] Such a thought does not seem to allow for the divine initiative, for the eschatological as what is to come from the "Other."

Religion in such a context is stripped of the rites, rituals, beliefs, and institutional context through which the relation to the other is mediated in a community of faith. The religious is extricated from the liturgical setting in which scripture has been heard, from the world of life experience and communal reflection. Thus disengaged, will the Abrahamic tradition retain its power to enhance present consciousness? Does it not risk becoming a dead tradition, a memory destined to be forgotten?

To the extent that Derrida's analysis illuminates the workings of language, it would seem that religious thinkers and theologians must remain critically engaged with his project. His interpretations of religious texts, mindful of what is written in their margins, have demonstrated and renewed interest in their power. His turn toward the religious may indeed provide a better language and setting for negotiating a new world order. Yet, believers must also ask if his approach to scripture does not restrict religion's nature and possibilities. This ideal of the religious may prematurely sacrifice the religions to a desert death.

New Directions

The French philosopher Stanislas Breton once observed in an interview that "the Christian doctrine of dispossession can be translated into modern socio-political terms as a critique of power." He notes that it challenges the status quo and sustains "a categorical imperative for human justice and liberation," although it cannot to be reduced to it. Christianity and Marxism both point toward a Utopian future, but "Christianity transcends the limits of historical materialism in the name of a prophetic eschatology (i.e., the Coming of the Kingdom)."[29] In Christianity and in the other religions there are resources that address the concern for justice and may serve to keep the hope alive.

We do not seek here to derogate the faith that would liberate itself from religion because of what it sees as fidelity to the religious. Rather, we ask for a greater openness toward the unrealized possibilities of the religions. There are signs that thinkers who are responsive to the issues raised by Derrida can engage Derrida's critique from a position within a religious tradition. The scope of this essay does not allow for a detailed exploration of these responses. We will simply point toward some of the directions that these thinkers have traced, suggesting the potential within their thought.

Stanislas Breton, for example, has emphasized the critical function of the cross within the scriptures. In *The Word and the Cross*,[30] he relates passages from Corinthians and Philippians to one another and brings the Pauline understanding of the cross into dialogue with that of the Gospel of John. His approach to scripture, while philosophical rather than exegetical, reflects the capacity of texts to critique one another and challenge the communities that interpret them. Breton is not a follower of Derrida, but as a colleague of Derrida's at the *École Normale Supérieure* in Paris he participated in the same revolutions of thought and shares some of his colleague's concerns. Much of his own philosophy was articulated in a climate dominated by Derrida and philosophers of dissonance. Yet he has continued to insist on doing philosophy from within a religious tradition and taken up such questions as how philosophy can speak today of scripture as word of God.

Central to Breton's hermeneutic is his presentation of the cross, which he describes as a sign appearing within the biblical language as the untranslatable *logos staurou*,[31] an expression whose impossibility suggests its power. This sign is a Sign of Contradiction that interrupts the prevailing world view and signals toward what is beyond being, language, and will. The cross does not inform, as Breton understands it, but transforms. It orients the Christian community toward an ethical engagement for the sake of the other in a kenotic rejection of all sovereignty, an engagement that has the power to transform personal and communal consciousness.[32] Breton recognizes that the cross, in being lifted up, has also been abandoned to a history of interpretation. It shares the vulnerability of symbols to perversion but also, as Sign of Contradiction, provides the community with a purifying resource. Thus the cross also stands in judgment upon the very history in which it has been forgotten and misconstrued. Breton's work argues in behalf of faith's capacity for dispossession and critical distance within the religions, thus affirming their capacity to create anew.

This attention to the cross allows Breton to speak of Christianity as unique and distinct while affirming its universality. Aware of Eastern as well as Abrahamic understandings of God, he tends to speak of the divine in its emptiness and nothingness as having the power to become all things. Within a historically situated community, faith makes use of words and symbols from the tradition to reach out to God, but submits its language and works to the cross, which stands in judgment of any tendency to say too much.

In emphasizing the cross, Breton recognizes the significance of the Jesus of history while reminding us that we must no longer seek Christ in the tomb. The christological question for Breton is how the Word is to become flesh in us. At the same time, in emphasizing that the cross is "nothing of that which is," he reaffirms a radical distinction between finite and infinite. The path of the religious must be an austere one; although it requires dispossession, it does not admit the dissolution of all boundaries. Faith operates not outside of religion but as a critical principle within all of the religions. Breton thus attempts to take into account the claims of philosophies of dissonance, demonstrating a certain deconstructive tendency within scripture itself, while allowing also for signs and symbols of affirmation.

Another example is Richard Kearney's discussion of "the God of the Possible." Kearney identifies a problem in any religious language that describes God as beyond being and desire. He claims that in such speech something is lost concerning the God of love, the God of *caritas* and *kenosis* "who takes on definite names, shapes and actions at specific points in time."[33] In *The God Who May Be,* Kearney uses a phenomenological method to reconsider the narratives of the burning bush, the transfiguration, and the resurrection, and attempts to re-think the function of signs and symbols. Reflecting the influence of Paul Ricoeur, Kearney holds that such signs do not point backwards to a totalizing presence but rather disclose how transcendence may be recognized. The Messiah makes himself known in the breaking of the bread and through this specific epiphany "reveals to the disciples their own desire."[34] Recognition of the other is joined to a liberating experience of the self and aided by signs of recognition: "How could we ever recognize a God stripped of every horizon of memory and anticipation?" he asks. "How could we give a content to a faith devoid of stories and covenants, promises, alliances, and good works, or fully trust a God devoid of names. . . ? If the powers of human vision are so mortified by the impossible God of deconstruction . . . then must not our encounter with the coming of the other find itself not only blind but empty?"[35]

Kearney seeks philosophically to conceive of God in terms of "*posse* (the possibility of being) rather than *esse* (the actuality of being as fait accompli)," as a God who allows possibility in our world from out of the future.[36] A sense of urgency comes from the awareness that things may or may not be and that their outcome in a sense depends on us. In this way he attempts to underscore the human capacity to accept or refuse a divine initiative, so that God "may be" or not.

I cite Kearney's work here because he suggests that the signs and names of scripture can point toward the future as well as the past. They can liberate the self in the welcome of the other and the Other.

My final example is the work of David Power, and in particular his discussion of the appropriation of scriptural texts within a liturgical context. We have noted that Derrida makes use of scripture by bringing its concepts into play with contemporary usage, thereby drawing the contemporary reader to experience a sense of urgency. Yet for the religions of the book the challenge of scripture lies also in its capacity to address the hearer of the word. The Christian, for example, not only reads scripture but listens to the word within a community that receives it in a liturgical context. Power has taken up this particular issue and has examined the relation of the liturgical context to postmodern theories of language. His works *Sacrament: The Language of God's Giving* and *The Word of the Lord* explore the ways in which the biblical text is brought into the exchange of Christian communities through preaching, teaching, and liturgical use.[37]

Power investigates the way in which these texts are related to the life and celebration of a community with all its pre-understandings, interests, and expectations. In emphasizing this lively transmission of scripture, he argues that "no text of the Judeo Christian tradition can be called *sacred* in the sense that it is untouchable or has a once and for all determined meaning. Texts receive life from their place in oral transmission."[38] In other words, the notion that the sense and impact of a text is fixed for all time is an illusion. With that in mind readers and hearers of the word can respond to the text with greater attention and will to act. Power argues that this openness to the text is not the product of human self-awareness. It resounds differently among different persons and different communities.

These thinkers are cited here as examples of those doing theological reflection who share many of Derrida's concerns but continue to write from within a religious tradition. Although they speak of a biblical imperative of justice, their use of scripture shows an interest in its diversity, even with its inner tensions and aporias, even in its claims to be the Word of God. Each of these thinkers respects the way in which the scriptures address the lived experience of persons and communities. They thus leave room for the possibility that the believer may be addressed by the Other, in various ways but also in the context of ecclesial liturgical dialogue. Without christocentrism, they offer ways of thinking anew in our times of Jesus Christ.

Conclusion

While the question of Derrida's own religion remains unanswered, he appears to encourage the retrieval of certain values that were found in religious traditions. At the same time he wants to avoid the violence that he relates to the totalizing tendencies of these religions. His own experience as a Jew born in Algeria and teaching in Paris has perhaps sharpened his awareness of the way in which the messianic has been betrayed by concrete messianisms. He exposes a tendency in the religions toward self-perpetuation that can privilege its own prayers, dogmas, and rituals over the universal imperative of justice. The affirmation of identity seems so linked to either indifference or violence that he would prefer to speak of a religious "heritage" that can best serve human progress when detached from any particular faith.

I have argued, however, that this vision, nonetheless, may strip religion of what makes it authentically religious. An approach to scripture as the Word of God heard in its diversity in an ecclesial setting suggests that those within religious traditions may share Derrida's concerns but may indeed take another path. As communities of interpretation, these traditions possess within themselves an imperative toward dispossession. That dispossession needs to be understood in terms of a humble use of its structures of belonging. It may strive to offer hospitality and forgiveness more profoundly, pursuing an eschatological imperative without being reduced to it.

Derrida wants to retrieve certain values that were found in religious traditions while avoiding the violence that has been expressed by the religions, especially Judaism, Christianity, and Islam. The unconditionality of biblical concepts seems best expressed for him when the religious is liberated toward justice. Identity seems to him to be tied inevitably to violence, and so he must resort to the religious as a "heritage" that best serves human progress when detached from any particular faith. Yet, there is a loss in such an evacuation of religion. It is a question of human persons who follow the imperative of justice, and persons cannot be abstracted from the particularities of their perspectives. What is needed is more profound awareness of that particularity so that they can then respond to the particularity of the other.

Yet the rigor of Derrida's analysis must continue to haunt the religions. When viewed in terms of hospitality and forgiveness, they have often seemed unmindful of their gifts. Without an ascesis from within, they may become hardened in their totalizing tendencies or lose their incisive force. This essay has argued that the religions, by attending to scripture in more comprehensive ways, may recover a voice that will sustain the richness of the heritage. For Christianity this may mean speaking in new ways of the Word of God, Jesus Christ.

Notes

[1] Jacques Derrida, *On Cosmopolitanism and Forgiveness*, trans. Mark Dooley and Michael Hughes, ed. Simon Critchley and Richard Kearney (London and New York: Routledge, 2001).

[2] See, for example, John D. Caputo, *The Prayers and Tears of Jacques Derrida* (Bloomington: Indiana University Press, 1997); Gideon Ofrat, *The Jewish Derrida*, trans. Peretz Kidron (Syracuse: Syracuse University Press, 2001).

[3] See Bruce Ellis Benson, *Graven Ideologies: Nietzsche, Derrida and Marion on Modern Idolatry* (Downers Grove, Ill.: InterVarsity Press, 2002), 113-114.

[4] Kevin Hart, *The Trespass of the Sign: Deconstruction, Theology and Philosophy* (New York: Fordham University Press, 2000).

[5] Ibid., 2.

[6] Benson, *Graven Ideologies,* 126.

[7] Derrida, *On Cosmopolitanism and Forgiveness*, 4.

[8] Derrida refers particularly here to the meditations of Emmanuel Levinas on "The Cities of Refuge" *(les villes-refugées)* in *L'au-delB du verset: Lectures et discours talmudiques* (Paris: Editions de Minuit, 1982), 5.

[9] Derrida, *On Cosmopolitanism and Forgiveness*, 16-17.

[10] Ibid., 18.

[11]See, for example, Caputo, *Prayers and Tears,* 117-18, 269-70, and Ofrat, *The Jewish Derrida,* 38.

[12]For a discussion of the relationship between "the messianic" and messianisms, see Caputo, *Prayers and Tears,* 134-43.

[13]Derrida, *On Cosmopolitanism and Forgiveness*, 22-23.

[14]Ibid., 22.

[15]He presented an expanded version of his thoughts on this topic at the conference "Religion and Postmodernism 2: Questioning God" held at Villanova University in 1999. See "To Forgive: The Unforgivable and the Inprescriptible," in *Questioning God,* ed. John D. Caputo, Mark Dooley, and Michael J. Scanlon (Bloomington and Indianapolis: Indiana University Press, 2001), 21-51.

[16]Derrida, *On Cosmopolitanism and Forgiveness*, 59.

[17]Ibid., 59-60.

[18]Ibid., 32.

[19]Ibid., 23.

[20]Caputo, *Prayers and Tears*, xix.

[21]Ibid., xx.

[22]Jacques Derrida, *Specters of Marx*, trans. Peggy Kamuf (New York/London: Routledge, 1994), 167-68.

[23]Caputo, *Prayers and Tears*, 195.

[24]Derrida, *Specters of Marx*, 40

[25]Derrida, *On Cosmopolitanism and Forgiveness*, 11-12.

[26]Derrida, *Specters of Marx*, 167-69.

[27]Caputo, *Prayers and Tears,* 243.

[28]Richard Kearney, *The God Who May Be: A Hermeneutics of Religion* (Bloomington and Indianapolis: Indiana University Press, 2001), 73.

[29]From an interview with Richard Kearney, "Being, God and the Poetics of Relation," in Kearney, *States of Mind: Dialogues with Contemporary Thinkers* (New York: New York University Press, 1995), 254.

[30]Stanislas Breton, *The Word and the Cross,* trans. Jacquelyn Porter, ed. John D. Caputo (New York: Fordham University Press, 2002*).*

[31]See ibid., 1.

[32]For a discussion of *kenosis,* see ibid., 83-99.

[33]Kearney, *The God Who May Be,* 74.

[34]Ibid., 75.

[35]Ibid., 76.

[36]Ibid., 4.

[37]David N. Power, *Sacrament: The Language of God's Giving* (New York: Crossroad, 1999); idem., *The Word of the Lord: Liturgy's Use of Scripture* (Maryknoll, N.Y.: Orbis Books, 2001).

[38]Power, *The Word of the Lord*, 45.

Jesus Turns the Wheel of Dharma: Emerging Christologies of Contemporary Buddhism

Peter A. Huff

Groundbreaking works published in recent years have introduced many Western readers to the "Asian faces of Jesus," new and alternative christologies emerging from some of the most creative quarters of contemporary Asian Christian theology.[1] An equally important phenomenon in contemporary religious thought is the appearance of other innovative Asian christologies, particularly those developed by teachers active in the Buddhist tradition. This essay concentrates on two such attempts at a Buddhist christology. Specifically it provides an exposition and critical examination of the readings of Jesus offered in popular venues by two major figures in worldwide Buddhism: Tibetan leader Tenzin Gyatso, the fourteenth Dalai Lama, and Vietnamese Zen master Thich Nhat Hanh. More than simply Buddhist appreciations of Jesus or imitations of Christian christologies, even Asian ones, these experiments in what tentatively can be called "non-Christian christology"[2] demonstrate the degree to which Jesus has been appropriated as a symbol and (at times) a source for popular Buddhist spirituality.

Both the Dalai Lama (b. 1935) and Nhat Hanh (b. 1926) are among a handful of Buddhist leaders with near-universal name recognition. Arguably, they have even achieved global celebrity status. Their books and tapes are best-selling commodities in many North American and European bookshops and their public speaking engagements routinely draw substantial crowds. Over the years the Dalai Lama's headquarters in Dharamsala, India, has become a regular stop on the spiritual tourism circuit, largely though not exclusively due to the attention of Hollywood. Similarly, though with less media hype, Nhat Hanh's Plum

Village, a monastic-style community in the south of France that functions as both his home and an international retreat center, has greeted an increasing number of visitors and would-be disciples every year since its founding in the early 1980s.[3]

More importantly, the lives of these two men have been shaped by similar experiences of monastic and philosophical training as well as political oppression, military conflict, and cultural exile. For decades each has dedicated his career to the promotion of intercultural understanding, international peace, and spiritual maturity in contemporary life. In recent years each has also given attention to the figure of Jesus. While a number of other Buddhists, especially Western-born converts from Christianity, have written on Jesus from a variety of Buddhist perspectives,[4] the Dalai Lama and Nhat Hanh represent the most prominent living Asian-born Buddhist leaders who have attempted to render positive and intelligible portraits of Jesus in terms meaningful to a general audience of Buddhists and Christians. Though some Western scholars of Asian religions might dismiss them as mere popularizers, discounting their books as superficial treatments of complex Buddhist doctrine and their efforts to translate Jesus into a Buddhist idiom as trivializations of the interfaith imperative, the Dalai Lama and Nhat Hanh deserve serious academic attention, if for no other reason than precisely because they are so popular.

When it comes to the task of interpreting Jesus, each man goes about the task in his own way and according to his own lights. The Dalai Lama's approach to Jesus, shaped by his axiomatic principle of religious toleration, intuitively grasps the universal relevance of Jesus but remains largely impressionistic and ultimately tangential to his native Buddhist spirituality. By contrast, Nhat Hanh's treatment of Jesus, informed by his hallmark concept of "interbeing" (defined below), constitutes a fundamental incorporation of Jesus into the mythic structure and spiritual outlook of his non-dogmatic Buddhist practice. As they endeavor to see Jesus with a Buddhist face, both readings of Jesus provide suggestive models for further reflection on the issue of non-Christian christologies and the direction of interreligious dialogue.

Jesus the Bodhisattva

For the first third of his life, the Dalai Lama knew little of Christianity or Jesus. In fact, for centuries the fortress-like Potala, the winter palace of all Dalai Lamas overlooking the "forbidden" city of Lhasa, functioned in the Western mind as the supreme symbol of cultural isolation. Aside from a tiny Muslim population and a handful of Europeans, no more than a small minority of Tibetans have ever had anything approaching a meaningful acquaintance with traditions about Jesus. The current Dalai Lama has cultivated significant contact with Christianity only since the beginning of his exile in India. From the 1960s to the present, he has forged positive relationships with important Christian leaders, including key figures in the World Council of Churches and individuals such as Thomas Merton, Mother Teresa, Pope Paul VI, Pope John Paul II, and Archbishop of Canterbury Robert Runcie.[5]

In the course of his collaboration with Christians on issues such as the environment, interfaith relations, and freedom for the Tibetan people, the Dalai Lama has emphasized the complementary nature of Buddhism and Christianity. His views of Jesus, occasional in nature rather than systematic, have emerged out of this context of dialogue and activism. The invitation to lead the tenth annual John Main Seminar on the topic of the life and teachings of Jesus provided the Dalai Lama with a unique opportunity to articulate his evolving perception of Jesus in a more comprehensive fashion.

Organized by the World Community for Christian Meditation, the seminar is named in honor of John Main (1926-1982), a London-born Benedictine monk who played a pioneering role in stimulating the post-World War II revival of contemplative prayer in Christian circles, especially the sort of "centering prayer" practices currently associated with figures such as fellow Benedictine Laurence Freeman and the Trappist Thomas Keating. Previously the seminar has featured prominent thinkers and writers such as philosopher Charles Taylor, Benedictine monk Bede Griffiths, pastoral theologian Jean Vanier, and Jesuit scholar William Johnston on subjects related to nonconceptual prayer and mysticism. The Dalai Lama's participation in the 1994 seminar, held on the campus of Middlesex University in London, marked an important moment in the history of the seminar and, more broadly, of christological reflection. Never before had such a well-known religious figure outside of the Christian community led the seminar, and never before had a Buddhist leader in so public a forum articulated his understanding of Jesus for an audience composed largely of Christians.

The format of the seminar called for a series of meditation sessions, formal presentations, and panel discussions organized around eight passages from the New Testament Gospels: two from the Sermon on the Mount (Matt. 5:1-10, 38-48); the narrative of Jesus with his family and a selection of parables from Mark (Mark 3:31-35; 4:26-43); the Lukan accounts of the commissioning of the Twelve and the Transfiguration (Luke 9:1-6, 28-36); a summary of Johannine teaching on belief and judgment (John 12:44-50); and John's narrative of Mary Magdalene's encounter with the Risen Christ (John 20:10-18). The Dalai Lama's commentary on these texts, recorded in the book *The Good Heart* (1996) and the four-volume video series by the same title, demonstrates the extent to which he has applied a non-sectarian Buddhist hermeneutic to the figure of Jesus.

Throughout his talks the Dalai Lama frames his remarks with reminders of the non-authoritative nature of his interpretations, calling his commentary "quite 'sketchy' and rather extemporaneous."[6] He also makes a point of stressing the dangers of ignoring the differences that separate religions. In this regard, he employs a traditional Tibetan expression to warn against overemphasizing parallels between religions in the hope of manufacturing an artificial "composite" religion: "Don't try to put a yak's head on a sheep's body."[7] Reminiscent of an earlier concern that observers would misconstrue his openness in interfaith matters as an attempt to "steal Christ for Buddhism,"[8] this cautionary theme regarding syncretism permeates *The Good Heart*. The Dalai Lama lends no support to any effort that would cite spiritual cross-fertilization as legitimation for any kind of Christian Buddhism or Buddhist Christianity. His comments betray a marked uneasiness with what some scholars and religious practitioners currently describe as "religious dual citizenship" or "hyphenated religious identity."[9]

In a similar vein, his reflections revisit standard debating points in the Buddhist-Christian dialogue: the problem of a personal creator God, the notion of a permanent self, and the issue of resurrection as opposed to rebirth. The Dalai Lama also rejects any remnant of the colonial Christ in his distinction between mission and conversion. Mission, he says, fosters reciprocity and the mutual sharing of wisdom, while conversion, the violent imposition of beliefs upon another, breeds only inequality and injustice.[10]

Despite these reservations, the Dalai Lama's view of Jesus is on the whole positive. Like other Asian interpreters of Jesus since the nineteenth-century neo-Hindu propagandist Vivekananda, he respects the non-violence, tolerance, and asceticism he finds in the Gospel stories. Mainly, though, he responds to Jesus as if to a mythic ideal. Unconcerned by questions of Jesus' specific historical situation and seemingly oblivious to issues of modern textual criticism, he collapses the Jesus figures of the canonical Gospels and the divine savior of Christian belief and piety into a single synthetic reality. Consequently, his christology assumes a largely docetic or gnostic character. It concentrates on Jesus as supernatural spiritual teacher with no identifiable ethnic, social, or religious identity and no concrete historicity. His Jesus is neither eschatological nor apocalyptic. In contemporary academic categories, his is a "christology from above," approximating the "purely primordial Jesus" that Thomas J. J. Altizer associates with gnostic strains in ancient and modern Christianities.[11]

The heart of the Dalai Lama's commentary is anchored in two motifs drawn from the mythic and philosophical dimensions of Mahayana Buddhism. First, he connects Jesus with the path of the bodhisattva, the awakened or to-be-awakened being, according to classic Buddhist teaching, that strives for perfection through selfless service to others in the realm of *samsara*. Cast in the light of Shantideva's seventh-century treatises on the bodhisattva way, the Dalai Lama's Jesus exhibits many of the hallmarks of the savior figures who inhabit the vast Mahayana pantheon. By virtue of his compassion, equanimity, and especially his practice of what is called "skillful means" (*upaya*), the pedagogical sensitivity to diverse conditions of spiritual receptivity among humans, Jesus joins the ranks of the heroic beings who ferry others across the stream. "For me," the Dalai Lama says, "Jesus Christ is . . . a fully enlightened being or a bodhisattva of a very high spiritual realization."[12]

The second mythic category utilized by the Dalai Lama is the "three-body" doctrine or *trikaya*, the complex teaching of the three-fold body of the Buddha. According to this theory, developed by the Yogacarin school of Buddhist thought in the fourth century, both the earthly (apparition) body of the historical Buddha and his transfigured (enjoyment) body in the "pure lands" are finite, subtle projections of the elusive *dharma*-body or *dharmakaya* (ultimate reality or universal Buddha-nature).[13] For over a hundred years, modern Buddhist apologists in conversation with Western audiences have attempted to connect the *dharmakaya* doctrine to foundational elements in the Western worldview.

In *Sermons of a Buddhist* (1913), the Japanese Zen master Soyen Shaku, famous for his participation in the 1893 Parliament of the World's Religions and his status as D. T. Suzuki's teacher, spoke of *dharmakaya* as "equivalent to" the idea of universal moral law and the "Christian conception of Godhead," especially the Johannine view of God.[14] Likewise, nearly half a century later, Christmas Humphreys, founder of the London Buddhist Society, linked *dharmakaya* with the idea of "God the Father of Christianity."[15] More recently, though in a more nuanced fashion, Japanese philosopher Masao Abe has also explored parallels between Christian models of God and *dharmakaya*;[16] and British Buddhologist Peter Harvey has referred to *dharmakaya* as "somewhat akin to the concept of God in other religions."[17]

The Dalai Lama follows this normative practice, introducing the category of *dharmakaya* to give Buddhist traction to basic Christian beliefs regarding Trinity, incarnation, and resurrection. The "physical, historical manifestations of enlightened beings [like Christ]," he says, are "spontaneous emergences from the timeless, ultimate state of the *dharmakaya*, or Truth Body of a buddha."[18]

In the end, the Dalai Lama's commentary supports a rather rudimentary Buddhist christology, noteworthy not only for its generosity but also for its provisional and improvisational qualities. By the standards of Whalen Lai and Michael von Bruck's research in the history of Buddhist-Christian dialogue,[19] it appears to be a fairly conventional modern Buddhist portrait of Jesus, emphasizing the moderate asceticism and tolerance of Jesus and citing parallels between the historical Buddha and the Christ of the Gospels and Christian myth. Willing to lend Christianity the metaphysical apparatus he apparently thinks it lacks, the Dalai Lama engages in the christological venture evidently out of bodhisattva-like charity, not for its own sake. The result is a non-Christian christology, remarkable not so much for its philosophical depth as for its proficiency in successfully transposing Jesus into a distinctively Buddhist key. The Dalai Lama's Jesus has a Buddhist face but, like the apparition-body of Shakyamuni Buddha, it is ultimately ephemeral.

Jesus the Spiritual Ancestor

While the Dalai Lama grew up in relative seclusion from Christianity and Jesus traditions, Thich Nhat Hanh has spent most of his life in close contact with Christianity and Christianity's Christs. His initial impressions of the Christian tradition, however, were overwhelmingly negative. Knowing only the imperialistic, colonial Christianity that contributed to the exploitation of his native Vietnam, Nhat Hanh found little to admire in the missionary religion focused on Jesus. "In such an atmosphere of discrimination and injustice," he admits, "it was difficult for me to discover the beauty of Jesus' teachings."[20]

By the time Thomas Merton wrote his famous letter/essay entitled "Nhat Hanh Is My Brother" (1966),[21] the Zen monk's perceptions of Christianity and Jesus had dramatically changed. His meetings with Merton, Martin Luther King, Jr., and other socially conscious Christians of the 1960s, especially anti-war Christians associated with the Fellowship of Reconciliation, transformed his understanding of Christianity and the Jesus of Christian devotion. At the same time, Nhat Hanh's revolutionary approach to peace activism during and after the Vietnam War, reorienting traditional features of the Zen monastic heritage toward what he dubbed "engaged Buddhism,"[22] forced many Westerners to reexamine their attitudes about Buddhism's alleged quietism and other-worldliness.

In exile from his homeland since 1966, Nhat Hanh has made the West the center for his work in social activism, retreat direction, and interreligious dialogue. His leadership of the Buddhist Peace Delegation during the Vietnam War and his humanitarian efforts on behalf of the Vietnamese "boat people" after the war brought him to the attention of many North American Christians. His creation of the Order of Interbeing in the West and two monastic communities in the United States established a privileged place for him in mainstream American Buddhist culture. Currently his market share of the rapidly expanding Buddhist publishing industry rivals that of other successful Buddhist writers such as Steven Batchelor, Sylvia Boorstein, and Robert Thurman.[23] Though popular opinion has not elevated him to the "Gandhi-like status" enjoyed by the Dalai Lama, according to Richard Hughes Seager, he "has a stature in the American Buddhist community comparable only to that of the Dalai Lama."[24] Robert King, one of his few serious academic interpreters, portrays Nhat Hanh as a pioneer of a "new spiritual paradigm," an "engaged spirituality" integrating action and contemplation into a seamless response to the challenges of an age of globalization.[25]

Nhat Hanh's commitment to enriching Buddhist-Christian relations has done much to contribute to this level of eminence. In the 1970s, he collaborated with Jesuit activist Daniel Berrigan on a series of Buddhist-Christian conversations called *The Raft Is Not the Shore*.[26] Twenty years later he published two other books charting the evolution of his thinking about Jesus: *Living Buddha, Living Christ* (1995), described by Robert King as "a major contribution to the Buddhist-Christian dialogue," and *Going Home: Jesus and Buddha as Brothers* (1999), a collection of Christmas "dharma talks" delivered at Plum Village during the 1990s.[27] Devotional, aphoristic works designed for the general reader seeking a contemplative lifestyle, these books provide a bifocal portrait of a Jesus with a Buddhist face. While it shares some of the gnostic qualities of the Dalai Lama's understanding, Nhat Hanh's christology is distinctive for the way it is integrated into his Buddhist spirituality.

Upon first glance, Nhat Hanh appears to erect the same protective hedge about his christological explorations as does the Dalai Lama. He encourages his readers, especially disenchanted Western Christians seeking refuge in Eastern spiritualities, to "go back to their own traditions and get rerooted."[28] At the same time, though, he seems guilty of the syncretism that the Dalai Lama hopes to avoid. The altar in his hermitage in France features an image of Christ alongside traditional Buddha and bodhisattva images; his books and talks make liberal use of Christian creeds and prayers; and he is well known for his open participation in Christian rites and sacraments.[29] To some observers these elements of his spiritual practice might look like so many yak heads on sheep bodies.

This tension between the integrity of each religion and the creative interchange between religions lies at the heart of Nhat Hanh's theory of the relationship among world religions and ultimately informs his thinking about Jesus. "If you are rooted in your own culture," he says, "you may have a chance to touch deeply and become rooted in another culture as well."[30] Bede Griffiths, well known for his efforts in the Hindu-Christian dialogue, developed a similar argument in his book *Christ in India*. "As we come to the inner depth of our own tradition," he wrote, "we find ourselves drawing near to the depths of the other traditions, and it is in that interior depth that the final meeting [between religions] has to take place."[31] In other words, these interpreters suggest, religions converge at the center.

Griffiths's disciple Wayne Teasdale and others now call the experience of this convergence "inter-spirituality."[32] Although Nhat Hanh does not employ that term, it corresponds nicely with his signature category of "interbeing." Based on the ancient Buddhist concept of Dependent Origination or Conditioned Arising (*paticca-samuppada*), the principle that speaks of the fundamental conditionality or interdependence of all things, Nhat Hanh's interbeing idea points to the radically non-absolute, interconnected character of all elements constituting experience, including religions, cultures, and worldviews. He writes: "Just as a flower is made only of non-flower elements [clouds, rain, sunlight, minerals, time, and earth], Buddhism is made only of non-Buddhist elements, including Christian ones, and Christianity is made of non-Christian elements, including Buddhist ones."[33] Contact with any tradition, then, means contact with something else, too. To speak of inter-spirituality is simply a way to describe the empirically available facts of reality.

Nhat Hanh sets his portrait of Jesus against the horizon of inter-spirituality and interbeing. With many Buddhists, he admires the pacifist Jesus of the Sermon on the Mount but departs from fellow Zen writers who criticize Jesus' dualistic notion of "enemy." Haunted by his memory of the self-immolation of the monk Quang Duc and his own disciple Nhat Chi Mai during the Vietnam War, he also goes against the Zen grain and recognizes the importance of the cross in the Jesus story. D. T. Suzuki once said that whenever he saw a figure of the crucified Christ he could not "help thinking of the gap that lies deep between Christianity and Buddhism."[34] By contrast, Nhat Hanh connects the wartime self-sacrifice of Buddhist monks and nuns with the Christian myth of atonement through redemptive suffering: "When you are motivated by love and the willingness to help others attain understanding, even self-immolation can be a compassionate act. When Jesus allowed Himself to be crucified, He was acting in the same way, motivated by the desire to wake people up . . . and to save people."[35]

Despite these links to standard themes of Christian christology, Nhat Hanh's christology concentrates on neither the literary Jesus of the Gospels nor the historical Jesus of modern scholarly reconstruction. *Buddhist-Christian Studies* co-editor Terry Muck has claimed that Nhat Hanh emphasizes "the activist side of Jesus' ministry,"[36] but there is little evidence in Nhat Hanh's works to support this thesis. Rather, Nhat Hanh's Jesus or "Christ" (he uses the terms interchangeably) emerges from his experience of inter-spirituality with Christian practitioners and from his insights into the interbeing of Buddha and Jesus, who by definition are not alien from each other. Closer to the non-apocalyptic "living Jesus" of the Gospel of Thomas than to the Jesus of orthodox canon or creed or the Jesus of contemporary historical scholarship, the body of Nhat Hanh's Christ—his *dharmakaya*, as he puts it—is the living presence of a timeless wisdom, neither Christian nor Buddhist, available in the context of genuine spiritual practice. As he writes in *Going Home*, "We want to discover Jesus' Dharmakaya. 'Kaya' means body. We are not really interested in the body made of flesh. We are interested in his Body that is made of the Holy Spirit. We are interested in knowing his Body as teaching, because that is very crucial to us."[37]

Nhat Hanh's christology, however, is not gnostic in a negative sense. Metaphors of relationality govern his thought from beginning to end. Just as taking refuge in the Buddha and the Dharma entails taking refuge in the Sangha, the experience of the Body of Christ implies incorporation into a web of mutuality. Capitalizing on Jesus' Oriental credentials, as have other modern Asian interpreters since Vivekananda, Nhat Hanh transfers Jesus the "only Son" from Christian myth and Hellenistic metaphysics to the dense East Asian filial network of domestic kinship and Zen lineage. While the Dalai Lama elevates him to the heaven of the bodhisattvas, Nhat Hanh ultimately places Jesus among the relatives around the hearth, squarely in what Soka Gakkai leader Daisaku Ikeda has called the East Asian "ethos of symbiosis."[38] "I have adopted Jesus Christ as one of my spiritual ancestors," Nhat Hanh writes.[39] In *Living Buddha, Living Christ*, he sums up his experience this way: "Before I met Christianity, my only spiritual ancestor was the Buddha. But when I met beautiful men and women who are Christians, I came to know Jesus as a great teacher. Since that day, Jesus Christ has become one of my spiritual ancestors."[40] Embracing the Christian Merton as brother, Nhat Hanh has adopted the rest of his family, too.

Conclusion

The new Buddhist christologies set forth by the Dalai Lama and Thich Nhat Hanh make an important contribution to the cross-cultural and cross-confessional task of interpreting the life, teachings, and person of the universal man Jesus. Together they signal an unprecedented christological "moment" in contemporary Buddhism. While the Dalai Lama does not go far beyond translating Jesus into Buddhist terms, Nhat Hanh's christology represents a more venturesome attempt to transplant Jesus into Buddhist soil. Each takes the equivalent of a "christology-from-above" approach, privileging a "primordial Christ." Neither puts much stock in the Jewishness of Jesus or the scholarly debates regarding his historical situation. Both imaginative exercises, despite their limitations, carry important implications for the future of christology, the future place of Jesus in interreligious dialogue, and the future meaning of Jesus in Buddhism's evolving view of the world.

Defined broadly as "the discussion of the religious significance of Jesus Christ,"[41] christology has long played an integral role in Christian theology. There have always been numerous christologies animating Christianity, and these rival christologies, as Altizer has pointed out, have helped to make Jesus the Christian tradition's "profoundly dichotomous center."[42] At the same time, Christian christology has traditionally been performed with at least moderate awareness of the world's religious diversity. In the modern period, Christian intellectuals orchestrated a more direct encounter between christology and their religiously pluralistic environment—so much so, that during the last century a significant number of Christians began to transfer insights from other religious traditions into their post-colonial reflections on the person and work of Jesus.

The new attempts at contemporary Buddhist christology examined in this essay reinforce this process and underscore its importance. Huston Smith, scholar of world religions and son of Methodist missionaries to China, once claimed that it was only in a Vedanta Society meeting, while listening to a Christmas Eve message on "Jesus Christ, the Light of the World," that he truly experienced the reality of Christ's incarnation. "That the Swami regarded Jesus as one of a number of incarnations," he wrote, "was altogether secondary to the fact that he believed—believed absolutely—that God literally became a man that first Christmas night."[43] In that experience Smith came to realize what is becoming increasingly clear in a variety of ways to many people today: religious practitioners outside of the Christian tradition are seriously engaging in critical reflection on the meaning and significance of Jesus. Apparently Jesus not only has many faces, but some of the most provocative portraits, bearing little resemblance to the classic icon of Western Christianity, have been produced by visionary artists outside the Christian intellectual community, East and West.

Of course, since the seventh century, when Islam began to proclaim Jesus as the virgin-born "word from God" and Messiah (Surah 4:171), Christianity has never enjoyed exclusive claim to the enterprise of christology. But the interest of such high-profile Buddhist leaders in the figure of Jesus gives the non-Christian christological impulse a new lease on life. It serves to remind anyone captivated by the figure of Jesus that Christianity has no proprietary rights over Jesus. Simply the appearance of such compelling non-Christian Asian christologies confirms what historian Jaroslav Pelikan wrote in the final chapter of his magisterial *Jesus Through the Centuries*: "Jesus of Nazareth may have been a provincial, but Jesus Christ is the Man Who Belongs to the World."[44] While Nietzsche once declared that Jesus defies all *"ecclesiastical"* prejudice, "stands outside of all religion, all cult concepts, all history,"[45] the new Buddhist christologies portray Jesus as standing within multiple traditions, as something of a cosmic exemplar of contemporary hyphenated religious identity. Future christological work that takes account of these remarkable achievements will no longer be able to afford an exclusive concentration on Christian concerns and questions. Energy and insights from quarters far from Christianity will have a hand in setting a new worldwide christological agenda. Jesus will remain at the heart of christology, but as the christological circumference continues to expand, christology will no longer see itself as centered in Christianity.

Just as the new emerging Buddhist christologies push the boundaries of christological endeavor, they also raise questions about the place of Jesus in the context of interfaith encounter. In the 1980s, Harvey Cox leveled a critique against Christian participants in interreligious dialogue who stressed the universal vision of their tradition at the expense of its unique, particular vision. The result of this practice, he said, was an unfortunate "loss of the personal voice" in Christian contributions to interfaith discussion and a theologically misleading "soft-pedaling of the figure of Jesus." What non-Christian partners in dialogue truly desire, he argued, is not hypersensitive theological prudence on the part of Christians but honest testimony from them regarding the significance of Jesus in their faith and the relevance of Jesus to the larger interfaith mission. Drawing from his extensive experience in interreligious conversation, Cox came to the realization that Christianity's distinctive "Jesus factor" is precisely the subject that non-Christian participants "often seem most interested in and most eager to get to."[46]

Cox's incisive critique of the wider ecumenism represented a long-overdue call for the restored presence of a Christ-centered Christianity in global dialogue. In his plea for a rediscovery of Christianity's robust christological voice, however, he failed to conceive of the possibility that Christians' conversation partners would be anything but passive listeners when it came to Jesus. With each tradition controlling the discussion of its particular vision, Christians, it was assumed, would have sole authority over the topic of Jesus.

The christological experiments of the Dalai Lama and Nhat Hanh challenge that assumption. They suggest that the future of dialogue may be quite different from what Cox imagined. Since some Buddhists are at least willing—at most eager—to interpret Jesus from the perspective of a Buddhist paradigm, Buddhist initiatives in christology are in an unusual position to spark a reconfiguration in the patterns and protocol of interreligious dialogue. With their popular reflections on Jesus, the Dalai Lama and Nhat Hanh have effectively moved Jesus' locus from the particular dimension of Christianity to the universal dimension shared by all religious traditions, from the peculiar dialect of Christian faith to the shared discourse of pluralistic dialogue. Such a christological shift, as potentially transformative as any experienced during Christianity's early centuries, could arguably engender not only new visions of Jesus but radically new visions of the nature of dialogue, too. A Jesus even only partially integrated into Buddhist mythic structures and spirituality has the potential to alter the ethos of symbiosis currently characterizing the international dialogue community.

The effect of the new christologies on Buddhism itself is far more difficult to assess and virtually impossible to predict. All that can be safely said for the present is that key leaders of the contemporary Buddhist community have, in the words of John Macquarrie, asked "the question of Jesus Christ" and have evidently found it worth asking.[47] About a century ago, Albert Schweitzer concluded his distinctive response to the question of Jesus Christ, his landmark *Quest of the Historical Jesus*, with the poignant image of the "mangled body of the one immeasurably great Man" hanging upon the "wheel of the world" that he helped to set in motion and that tragically crushed him.[48] Like many of the Christs that have been proposed since the publication of that classic in 1906, Schweitzer's Jesus was a stranger and an enigma to modern readers. The christologies currently emerging from two of modern Buddhism's most respected teachers also yield intriguing images of an unknown Jesus putting his hand to the wheel of the world. Though they register serious reservations about the uniqueness of that great man, contemporary Buddhists like the Dalai Lama and Thich Nhat Hanh are now beginning to recognize the man's wheel as the Wheel of Dharma.

Notes

[1] See R. S. Sugirtharajah, ed., *Asian Faces of Jesus* (Maryknoll, N.Y.: Orbis Books, 1993), and Peter C. Phan, "Jesus the Christ with an Asian Face," *Theological Studies* 57 (1996): 399-430.

[2] The term "non-Christian," limited because of its attempt to describe people and ideas in terms of what they are not, is used here simply for convenience.

[3] See Richard Hughes Seager, *Buddhism in America* (New York: Columbia University Press, 1999), chaps. 7, 8, and 12.

[4] See Rita M. Gross and Terry C. Muck, eds., *Buddhists Talk about Jesus, Christians Talk about the Buddha* (New York: Continuum, 2000).

[5] The Dalai Lama, *Freedom in Exile: The Autobiography of the Dalai Lama* (New York: HarperCollins, 1990), 189-190, 201-202.

[6] The Dalai Lama, *The Good Heart: A Buddhist Perspective on the Teachings of Jesus* (Boston: Wisdom Publications, 1996), 129.

[7] Ibid., 105.

[8] The Dalai Lama quoted in Whalen Lai and Michael von Bruck, *Christianity and Buddhism: A Multi-Cultural History of Their Dialogue*, trans. Phyllis Jestice (Maryknoll, N.Y.: Orbis Books, 2001), 20.

[9] Ibid., 2, 184, 191. See Catherine Cornille, ed., *Many Mansions? Multiple Religious Belonging and Christian Identity* (Maryknoll, N.Y.: Orbis Books, 2002).

[10] The Dalai Lama, *The Good Heart*, 97.

[11] Thomas J. J. Altizer, *The Contemporary Jesus* (Albany: State University of New York Press, 1997), 31.

[12] The Dalai Lama, *The Good Heart*, 83.

[13] See Richard H. Robinson and Willard L. Johnson, *The Buddhist Religion: A Historical Introduction*, 4th ed. (Belmont, Calif.: Wadsworth, 1997), 91-96.

[14] Soyen Shaku, *Zen for Americans*, trans. D. T. Suzuki (1913; New York: Barnes & Noble Books, 1993), 47-48.

[15] Christmas Humphreys, *Buddhism: An Introduction and Guide* (London: Penguin Books, 1951), 154.

[16] Masao Abe, "Kenotic God and Dynamic Sunyata" and "A Rejoinder" in *The Emptying God: A Buddhist-Jewish-Christian Conversation*, ed. John B. Cobb, Jr., and Christopher Ives (Maryknoll, N.Y.: Orbis Books, 1990), 3-65, 157-200.

[17] Peter Harvey, *An Introduction to Buddhism: Teachings, History and Practices* (Cambridge: Cambridge University Press, 1990), 127.

[18]The Dalai Lama, *The Good Heart*, 60.

[19]See Lai and von Bruck, *Christianity and Buddhism*, especially chaps. 1-4.

[20]Thich Nhat Hanh, *Living Buddha, Living Christ* (New York: Riverhead Books, 1995), 5. See Robert Ellsberg, ed., *Thich Nhat Hanh: Essential Writings* (Maryknoll, N.Y.: Orbis Books, 2001).

[21]Thomas Merton, *Faith and Violence* (Notre Dame: University of Notre Dame Press, 1968), 106-108.

[22]See Leo D. Lefebure, *The Buddha and the Christ: Explorations in Buddhist and Christian Dialogue* (Maryknoll, N.Y.: Orbis Books, 1993), 145-166. See also Christopher S. Queen and Sallie B. King, eds., *Engaged Buddhism: Liberation Movements in Asia* (Albany: State University of New York Press, 1996), and Christopher Queen, ed., *Engaged Buddhism in the West* (Boston: Wisdom Publications, 1999).

[23]Diana L. Eck, *A New Religious America: How a "Christian Country" Has Now Become the World's Most Religiously Diverse Nation* (San Francisco: HarperSanFrancisco, 2001), 181.

[24]Seager, *Buddhism in America*, 179.

[25]Robert H. King, *Thomas Merton and Thich Nhat Hanh: Engaged Spirituality in an Age of Globalization* (New York: Continuum, 2001), 35 ff.

[26]Thich Nhat Hanh and Daniel Berrigan, *The Raft Is Not the Shore: Conversations toward a Buddhist/Christian Awareness* (1975; Maryknoll, N.Y.: Orbis Books, 2000).

[27]Thich Nhat Hanh, *Going Home: Jesus and Buddha as Brothers* (New York: Riverhead Books, 1999). King, *Thomas Merton and Thich Nhat Hanh*, 98.

[28]Nhat Hanh, *Living Buddha, Living Christ*, 89.

[29]Ibid., 2, 6, 100; Nhat Hanh, *Going Home*, 195.

[30]Nhat Hanh, *Going Home*, 181.

[31]Bede Griffiths, *Christ in India: Essays towards a Hindu-Christian Dialogue* (Springfield, Ill.: Templegate, 1984), 222-223.

[32]See Wayne Teasdale, *The Mystic Heart: Discovering a Universal Spirituality in the World's Religions* (Novato, Calif.: New World Library, 1999).

[33]Nhat Hanh, *Living Buddha, Living Christ*, 11. See also Thich Nhat Hanh, *Interbeing: Fourteen Guidelines for Engaged Buddhism*, 3rd ed. (Berkeley, Calif.: Parallax Press, 1998).

[34]D. T. Suzuki, *Mysticism: Christian and Buddhist* (London: Mandala, 1979), 94.

[35]Nhat Hanh, *Living Buddha, Living Christ*, 81.

[36]Terry C. Muck, "Buddhist Books on Jesus," in *Buddhists Talk about Jesus, Christians Talk about the Buddha*, 146.

[37]Nhat Hanh, *Going Home*, 139-140.

[38]Daisaku Ikeda, *For the Sake of Peace: Seven Paths to Global Harmony, A Buddhist Perspective* (Santa Monica, Calif.: Middleway Press, 2001), 77.

[39]Nhat Hanh, *Going Home*, 195.

[40]Nhat Hanh, *Living Buddha, Living Christ*, 99-100.

[41]John Hick, *The Metaphor of God Incarnate: Christology in a Pluralistic Age* (Louisville: Westminster/John Knox Press, 1993), 1.

[42]Altizer, *The Contemporary Jesus*, xiv.

[43]Huston Smith, "Jesus and the World's Religions," in *Jesus at 2000*, ed. Marcus Borg (Boulder, Col.: Westview Press, 1998), 111-112.

[44]Jaroslav Pelikan, *Jesus Through the Centuries: His Place in the History of Culture* (New Haven: Yale University Press, 1985), 221.

[45]Friedrich Nietzsche, *The Antichrist*, 32, in *The Portable Nietzsche*, ed. and trans. Walter Kaufmann (New York: Penguin Books, 1976), 605. See Altizer, *The Contemporary Jesus*, 139-159.

[46]Harvey Cox, *Many Mansions: A Christian's Encounter with Other Faiths* (Boston: Beacon Press, 1988), 5, 8.

[47]John Macquarrie, *Jesus Christ in Modern Thought* (Philadelphia: Trinity Press International, 1991), 26.

[48]Albert Schweitzer, *The Quest of the Historical Jesus*, trans. W. Montgomery (New York: Macmillan, 1968), 370-371.

Part III

PRACTICE

To Live at the Disposal of the Cross: Mystical-Political Discipleship as Christological Locus

M. Shawn Copeland

Out of his very self, that is, out of his body, [Jesus Christ] has made a stairway, so as to raise us up from the way of suffering and set us at rest!
—Catherine of Siena

We are climbing Jacob's ladder,
Every round goes higher, higher,
Soldiers of the Cross.
—African American Spiritual

Introduction

Standing in the laundry room of her apartment building, the theologian fidgets as the rinse cycle of the washing machine slows to an end. She bends to clear away a thick wad of lint from the dryer; absently, she looks out of the window. In the parking lot below, a black woman picks through the building's refuse dumpster. Mesmerized, the black woman doing laundry cannot but watch: the woman below works systematically, opening and inspecting small white bags, setting some aside and discarding others. It is difficult from the eighth floor to see precisely what the black woman below selects, but the black woman above wonders if the woman has found the remains of her half-eaten roasted chicken or salad or bread or cheese.

Uncomfortable, angry, and sad, I turn away and put my things in the dryer. I take the elevator to my apartment. I sit down at the computer where I am struggling to complete an essay on discipleship and the cross of Christ. I am unnerved: writing on such a theme, after such looking, provokes recognition and dis-ease. The woman in the parking lot below is no one other than Christ. Such glimpses of him beg for a theology of the cross, a theology of discipleship that makes both his presence and a praxis of concrete solidarity and compassion more visible in our time. What sort of christological reflection is needed in our situation? What can it mean to tell the woman who searches my garbage that God in Jesus is also alienated, a stranger, a despised "other"? Can memory of his passion and death unmask our pretense to personal and communal innocence, to social and religious neutrality before structural evil and suffering? What sort of christological reflection can do justice to Jesus of Nazareth, to his radical freedom and profound consciousness of God and neighbor, to his desire for life, to his acceptance of the cross? What sort of christological reflection can address adequately the meaning of the cross to children, women, and men brutalized by social suffering?

In this brief essay, I want to explore these questions by sketching discipleship as a *locus* or starting point from which to understand Jesus of Nazareth as the absolute meaning of life for the world. This topic, discipleship as a christological locus, can make no claim to novelty; it forms a conspicuous strand in Christian tradition. Scholars suggest that the word disciple (*talmîd*) appears rarely in the Hebrew Scriptures, but its usage was part of the fabric of the ancient world. However, in the gospel narratives, Jesus of Nazareth invests the relationship of teacher (*rabbi*) and disciple (*mathētēs*) with new and remarkable meaning. For, rather than appeal solely to the acquired knowledge and presumptive authority, conventional prerogatives of the rabbi, Jesus invites and nurtures in his disciples faith in *who* he is and in the "good news" he is sent to proclaim. Yet, Jesus tests their faith: to follow the "way" he teaches requires that Jesus' disciples take up a new and different "way" of being *in* and *for* the world. Thus, they face a commanding and paradoxical challenge: "If any want to become my followers, let them deny themselves and take up their cross and follow me. For those who want to save their life will lose it, and those who lose their life for my sake, and for the sake of the gospel, will save it. For what will it profit them to gain the whole world and forfeit their life?" (Mark 8:34-36; Luke 9:23-25; cf. John 6:35-51).

For our purposes, the Lukan account of the story of the life, death, and resurrection of Jesus of Nazareth will provide the basic

performative meaning of discipleship. Biblical exegetes have identified the theme of discipleship almost exclusively with the Markan
gospel. To borrow a term from Ched Myers, scholars have read this
gospel as a kind of "catechism" on discipleship.[1] But, since the whole
of the New Testament stands as an invitation to radical discipleship,
the Lukan account need not be excluded from reflection on this theme.
Further, Luke's account of the story of Jesus strategically adverts to
and incorporates Torah texts that foreground the tradition and customs of "jubilee," that is, the complex of cyclical practices concerned
with restorative justice, reparation and release, healing and re-creation
(Lev. 25). These references, coupled with parables in which Jesus
describes the reign of God, underscore the importance of justice in the
Lukan narrative.

At the same time, feminist scholars have called into question the
treatment of women in Luke-Acts, for while the writer shows an interest in women, it is an ambiguous interest.[2] Clarice Martin writes that
the Lukan writer demonstrates "redactional and apologetic tendencies
[that] actually restrict women's prophetic ministry in some instances,
reinforcing women's conformity to conventional, culturally prescribed
roles of passivity, submission, silence, and marginality."[3] Turid Karlsen
Seim concurs, yet alerts us to the possibility that the Lukan gospel
may carry a "double message . . . [with] an ironic twist." While the
very structure of the narrative may enable male domination and co-
optation of women, nonetheless, it "preserves extraordinary traditions
about the women from Galilee . . . [who] were indeed capable and
qualified, but the men suspected and rejected them. The male consolidation of power occurs against a story in which the men have shown
weakness and failure rather than strength."[4]

In order to tell the story of Jesus, Luke must tell the story of the
women from Galilee. Silenced by male power, they "continue to
speak." Moreover, the women and their roles in the story of the life,
death, and resurrection of Jesus of Nazareth constitute a "dangerous
remembrance."[5] Through faith, commitment, and service, these women
teach us what it means to be a disciple of Jesus.

Scholars date the writing of Luke-Acts in the final decades of the
first century, and Sharon Ringe argues that Luke wrote for a community of mixed economic and social standing. Textual evidence suggests that Luke sought to address strained relations between the poor
and the non-poor. But, as Ringe states, he "pulled his punches": Luke

speaks *about* the poor, but he speaks *to* the rich; he emphasizes charity, but not change in repressive political and economic arrangements.[6] Certainly, for us Christians living in nations of wealth and power, the privileged of the "first world," Luke's gospel presents a challenge: How can we live as disciples of Jesus? Will we speak truth to power or pull our punches?

To live as Jesus' disciple means to live at the disposal of the cross—exposed, vulnerable, open to the wisdom and power and love of God. A lived response to Jesus' call requires a praxis of solidarity and compassion as well as surrender to the startling embrace of Divine Love. Christian discipleship as a lived mystical-political way forms the locus for the fundamental grasp of who Jesus of Nazareth is and what following and believing in him means.

This thesis will be elaborated in four sections. The first section, "The Way of Jesus," sketches his ministry and the demands he places on those who would follow him. The second section, "The Cross," draws on the work of Martin Hengel to retrieve the horror and disgust felt by the men and women of the ancient world toward crucifixion. I want to suggest some of the shock they would have experienced at Jesus' summons to "take up your cross and follow me." This discussion prepares the background for the next section, "The Cross as a Condition of Discipleship." For the women and men drawn to his prophetic praxis, Jesus offered a new and compelling "way" of being for God's people that included, even demanded, the cross. The fourth section, "The Way Jesus Is," offers a meditation on the crucified Jesus as the way through the Spirit to union with the Father. This section draws on insights gleaned from reflection on the mystical experiences of Catherine of Siena and of enslaved Africans in the United States. There is, I suggest, a resonance in these experiences that disclose what being caught up in love of God means. They capture what it means to understand that the power of God in the cross is the power to live and to love—even in the teeth of violence and death.

The Way of Jesus

In the Lukan account, the ministry, that is, the teaching, preaching, and healing through which Jesus of Nazareth met his death on the cross, began in a small synagogue in his home town. Jesus takes the scroll from the attendant and reads: "The Spirit of the Lord is upon me, because he has anointed me to preach good news to the poor. He has sent me to proclaim release to the captives and recovering of sight to the blind, to let the oppressed go free, to proclaim the year of the Lord's favor. . . . Today this scripture has been fulfilled in your hearing" (Luke 4:18-19, 21; Isa. 61:1-2; 58:6).

The narrator portrays the congregation as reacting with pleasure and pride: "All spoke well of him and were amazed at the gracious words that came from his mouth. They said, 'Is not this Joseph's son?' (Luke 4:22). But Jesus' evocation of Elijah (Luke 4:25-26) stings the conscience, and neither the cautious nor the cynical can tolerate the concluding coda—an irruption of messianic time that hints at the meaning of who Jesus is. Appreciative amazement pitches into anger and attempted violence: "They got up, drove him out of the town, and led him to the brow of the hill . . . so that they might hurl him off the cliff" (Luke 4:29).

Almost from the outset of the Lukan narrative, Jesus is identified with the prophecy. His ministry signs the in-breaking of the reign of God: he is sent to those who are wounded and impaired; who are possessed by demons; who are poor, broken-hearted, and despised; who are imprisoned by occupation or disfigurement and, thereby, rendered incapable of ritual purity. These children, women, and men are without choice, without hope, and without a future. Jesus announces to these "least" the comfort and judgment of the reign of God. He pledges that God is *for* them and *with* them.

Jesus eats and drinks with women and men of questionable character—tax collectors, prostitutes, outcasts, and public sinners. When questioned about his associates, he replies, "Those who are well have no need of a physician, but those who are sick; I have come to call not the righteous, but sinners to repentance" (Luke 5:31-32). Women— Mary Magdalene, Joanna, the wife of Herod's steward, Susanna, Mary the mother of James (Luke 8:1-3)—form part of the band of disciples who travel with Jesus to various cities and villages and share in his ministry. Jesus does not shy away from talk and debate with women; he heals them, forgives them, and takes them and their experiences seriously. When a woman named Mary sits at his feet as a disciple, Jesus affirms her agency over against narrow and constricting roles set for women by culture and society (Luke 10:38-42). Finally, the proclamation of the resurrection itself is entrusted to women; their remembrance of the very words of Jesus grounds their witness (Luke 24:9-10).

Through his audacious proclamation of the reign of God and his astonishing healing power, Jesus attracts crowds and, eventually, disciples. The men and women who would follow him (Luke 8:2-3) are challenged to sever all ties with the past (Luke 5:11), to address God intimately in prayer, to fast without ostentation, to practice self-examen (Luke 11:1-4; 6:42), and to allow no familial obligation, no cultural custom, no ritual observance to turn them to another way (Luke 14:26-27; 9:57-62; 12:22-23).

Through word and deed, Jesus taught his disciples to center themselves *in* and *on* the God whom he knew and loved with all his heart, all his soul, all his strength, and all his mind (Luke 10:25-27; 11:1-13). He enjoined them to love others—particularly the poor, outcast, and despised children, women, and men—concretely and without reservation, to act on behalf of these "little ones" for restoration to God and to community (Luke 10:29-37).

The proclamation of the reign of a God "merciful and slow to anger" (Jon. 4:2) formed the core of Jesus' preaching. In parables and sermons, he drew a vivid portrait of life lived under the reign of this God. What would this new life be like? Like the watchfulness of a farmer at harvest, like the consolation of acceptance, like a lavish and festive feast for those who can neither return the honor nor provide a comparable meal, like the joy at rescuing a stray lamb in the parched wilderness, like the relief at recovering lost funds, like the unshakable love of a broken-hearted parent for a wayward child, like the fruitfulness of the mustard seed and the capaciousness of its tree, like the force of leaven (Luke 8:4-18, 44-48; 14:12-14; 15:4-10, 11-16; 13:18-21). Jesus envisioned life lived under the reign of this God as a realization of truth and love, holiness and grace, justice and peace. Moreover, this God staked the gift of that reign *in us* and *in* present existential reality (Luke 17:21). Finally, Jesus taught his followers to pray that the reign of God might come—and to pray for its coming in the way in which God wills it. The disciples are to pray for that reign of justice and peace which, while not yet realized, is seeded in the here-and-now, the point of change where the old order yields to God's dream (Luke 11:2-4).

Jesus cultivated in his disciples a desire, a yearning, an expectation for the coming of God's reign. He led them through the "narrow gate" to glimpse the secrets of living for God (Luke 13:24), to discern just what was required of those who would enter the way (Luke 12:22-

48), to grasp the purity of heart and action its realization needed (Luke 12:49-53; 16:13; 14:26). Jesus granted his disciples a share in his healing power; the miracles they worked were a sign for him that the reign of God was breaking through.

But the ministry of Jesus is a dangerous ministry. Discipleship costs. The praxis of compassionate solidarity that he inaugurated on behalf of the reign of God disrupted social customs, religious practices, and conventions of authority and power. Without hesitation, Jesus made the cross an undeniable condition for discipleship (Luke 9:23, 14:27). By his own death on the cross, Jesus incarnated the solidarity of God with abject and despised human persons. The disciples who heard and responded to his word and the deed of his life came, even if haltingly, gradually, fitfully, to dedicate their lives and their living to the concerns, commitments, and compassion of the God of Jesus. In this way, they placed their lives at the disposal of the cross.

The Cross

From the beginning of his ministry, Jesus taught a "way" of life that not only offered a distinctive "understanding [of] the fulfillment of Israel's hope," but substantively "radicalized [his religious] tradition."[7] In his prophetic "performance" of parable, sign, and deed, Jesus broke open "the prevailing worldview and replace[d] it with one that was closely related, but significantly adjusted at every point."[8] But it is his crucifixion, his brutal death on the cross (Luke 23:33, John 19:18), that set "the way" apart from other religious movements in the ancient world.

The cross was the mark of shame, the sign of the criminal, and the slave. Martin Hengel delineates this point in his monograph *Crucifixion in the Ancient World and the Folly of the Message of the Cross.*[9] To accept the message of the cross, first-century Jews would have had to overcome deep-seated religious, cultural, and political sensibilities toward the very act of crucifixion, while, at the same time, they would have had to grapple with a new notion of the meaning of messiah. Recall the injunction in the Torah: "for anyone hung on a tree is under God's curse" (Deut. 21:23).

In the Hebrew Scriptures, the promise of a messiah is bound up with the covenant established by God with the chosen people. Yet, as N. T. Wright argues, during the Judaism of Jesus' day, there was no single or uniform conception of the messiah. The various messianic movements shared no common notion of the messiah and exhibited "considerable freedom and flexibility" toward the "idea of Israel's coming king."[10] However, these movements shared the expectation that with the arrival of the messiah Israel's divinely ordained destiny would be realized: the Roman occupation, colonization, and defilement of sacred land would end and a new age would begin.

The conflicting aspirations of long-subjugated women and men were projected onto the notion of messiah. He would lead the final victorious battle against the enemies of Israel. Not only would he bring about the political liberation of the people and the transformation of their historical situation, the messiah would transform history itself. The messianic age would bring an end to suffering, alienation, and exile. God's chosen people would be gathered-in to their ancestral home. A *crucified messiah*, a messiah who would die dishonored as a criminal, was unthinkable. A crucified messiah was not, could not be the *true* messiah. Paul's message of the cross (1 Cor. 1:22-24) was offensive, monstrous; it could not be tolerated. A crucified messiah would have to be rejected on the grounds of fidelity to religious orthodoxy.

Gentile groups also would have been scandalized by the notion of a crucified God. For these women and men, religious revulsion at the cross was joined to intellectual objections. Potential converts, particularly sophisticated Romans and Greeks, held the notion of a crucified God and of any who would follow such a God in contempt.[11] In the *City of God*, Augustine preserves an oracle of the Greek god Apollo as recorded by the philosopher Porphyry nearly two hundred years earlier. A man petitions the oracle about how to dissuade his wife from Christian belief. The god replies: " 'Let her go [continue] as she pleases, persisting in her vain delusions, singing in lamentation for a god who died in delusions, who was condemned by right-thinking judges, and killed in hideous fashion by the worst of deaths, a death bound with iron.' "[12] Belief in a crucified God was deemed madness, mania.[13]

Given the disgust that both Jews and Gentiles felt toward crucifixion, Paul's proclamation of the cross, as Hengel explains, "ran counter not only to Roman political thinking, but to the whole ethos of religion in ancient times. . . ."[14] The contemporary Christian remains equally perplexed. There is little in modern or postmodern life to assist us in comprehending the shame that crucifixion denoted in the ancient world. The supreme Roman penalty, crucifixion was a military and political punishment primarily used against insurrectionists, murders, and robbers, and reserved in nearly all instances for men and women of the lower classes, slaves, and subjugated peoples.

Crucifixion was intended to intimidate by example and subdue by spectacle; it was high state theatrical violence. Crucifixion called for the public display of a naked victim in some prominent place—at a crossroads, in an amphitheater, on high ground. Often the condemned was flogged, then made to carry a cross-beam through the streets to the place of execution. The victim's hands and feet were bound or nailed to the wood. If, after this torment, the victim were still alive, he could expect to die by suffocation: unable to support the weight of the body with torn hands, the upper body pressed down, and slowly crushed the diaphragm. Further dishonor and insult accompanied death: the crucified body was left to wild beasts and rot or, sometimes, as Tacitus reports, "when daylight faded, [they] were burned to serve as lamps by night."[15] Jesus was spared this last indignity, although the very manner of his death confounded the claim of divinity. By his death on the cross, Jesus demonstrated the cost of discipleship, even as the cross hallowed in him the capacity for radical resurrection-life.

Whatever resurrection means, the disciples "saw" the risen Jesus. If the sight of him left them dazed, they remained gripped by an unshakable certainty that the Jesus of Nazareth who had been crucified was, by the power of the God of Israel, raised from the dead. The body in which Jesus is raised does not belong to this world; his resurrected body is a new and different reality and signals a new and different mode of living. Not to be confused with resuscitation, resurrection breaks radically with material reality as we experience it. Yet, the appearances on the road to Emmaus (Luke 24:13-32) and in Jerusalem (Luke 24:33-43) are characterized by an insistent corporeality. Jesus eats with the disciples, invites them to examine his hands and feet, to touch him, to feel flesh and bone. "Touch me and see!" (Luke 24:39). The recognition of the heart is grasped by the senses and confirmed by the mind.

Resurrection is an event for Jesus; something radical has happened to him. Resurrection is also an event for the disciples. Jesus' post-resurrection appearances awaken in them the embers of a bold witness that the gift of the Spirit will fan into flame. Even as resurrection characterizes the destiny of Jesus, it is not a private destiny intended for him alone; it is the beginning of the absolute transformation of all creation. Resurrection breaks through, formally and materially, the cosmic, psychic, and moral disorder brought about by the reign of sin. Resurrection signals eschatological healing and binds a marred and broken creation back to the heart of God.

The appearances of the Risen Lord to the disciples are gratuitous and, as such, remind us that the resurrection is not primarily about the sight of Jesus, but rather about *insight* into his mission. Real, transformative encounters with the Risen Lord, these appearances refine for the disciples (and for us) just what it costs to live the way of Jesus, to confess him as the absolute meaning of life for the world. At the same time, the death of Jesus discloses God's own struggle against the powers and principalities of this world and manifests God's desire to emancipate those ensnared in psychic or religious or cultural or social bondage. The crucified Jesus is the sign of the cost of identification with poor, outcast, abject, and despised women and men in the struggle for life. He incarnates the freedom and destiny of discipleship.

The Cross as a Condition of Discipleship

With this background, perhaps, we now may be able to grasp the astonishment of the disciples and the people gathered around Jesus when he said, "If any want to become my followers, let them deny themselves and take up their cross and follow me" (Mark 8:34). Given the humiliation associated with crucifixion, these words could scarcely have been inviting. Surely, more than once, these ordinary women and men of the ancient world had witnessed the barbaric rite of crucifixion: the brutalized man dragging the cross-beam through the streets, the staggering arrival at the place of execution, the torture and mutilation, and, finally, impalement.[16] The summons to such imitation ("take up your cross") surely provoked incredulity and bewilderment; they wanted no part of it. Perhaps, more than once, these ordinary women and men had joined a mob watching the spectacle—feeding on the terror, amazed by their own relief: it is finished. Now, listening to the rabbi from Nazareth ("take up your cross and follow me"), these ordinary people are, at once, attracted and repulsed.

In the third Gospel, the Lukan Jesus puts the cross as a condition for discipleship quite starkly:

"Whoever does not carry the cross and follow me cannot be my disciple. For which of you, intending to build a tower, does not first sit down and estimate the cost, to see whether he has enough to complete it? Otherwise, when he has laid a foundation and is not able to finish, all who see it will begin to ridicule him, saying, 'This fellow began to build and was not able to finish.' Or what king, going out to wage war against another king, will not sit down first and consider whether he is able with ten thousand to oppose the one who comes against him with twenty thousand? If he cannot, then, while the other is still far away, he sends a delegation and asks for the terms of peace. So therefore, none of you can become my disciple if you do not give up all your possessions." (Luke 14:27-33)

Jesus demands that his disciples go the distance, walk the entire "way." His illustrations here are simple, but striking. He teaches a lesson designed to drive home the necessity of self-examen, sacrifice, personal resolve, and love. The prosperous builder and the successful military strategist meet their goals through painstaking attention to detail, thorough planning, and meticulous assessment. The outcomes of such exacting preparation earn admiration. The lesson the disciples must absorb is sharpened by contrast: "the children of this age are more shrewd in dealing with their own generation than are the children of light" (Luke 16:8).

Jesus entrusts to them (and to us) a venture of absolute importance— his own mission, that is, announcing and preparing a context for the coming reign of God. If a builder or military strategist can succeed, certainly his disciples can muster similar dedication, sacrifice, and personal resolve. But the reign of God is no utopian project, it is a very different kind of reality. Over time and in time, the disciples (we as well) learn that they (and we) can and must prepare a context for its advent, but it is most fundamentally God's gratuitous gift. Moreover, this absolute endeavor calls not merely for planning, self-examen, sacrifice, and personal resolve but for love unmeasured, unstinting, overflowing, fearless, passionate. Thus his mission on behalf of the reign of God required of Jesus something bold: that he stake his whole life and very personhood on being absolutely directed toward God in love without measure.

The Way Jesus Is

The foremost lesson of Christian discipleship is that Jesus is the way, and the way Jesus is is the way of the cross. While walking that way is, at once, the same, it is also distinctive for each woman and man who would follow him; it will include privation, intense longing, an acute awareness of emptiness and failure, confusion and loss. Following the way of Jesus, the disciple is exposed, humbled, and opened to the wisdom and power of the Spirit. Just as the cross hallowed in Jesus a capacity for resurrection-life, so too it hallows in the disciple a kind of infinite desire and capacity for life in and with God.[17]

Catherine of Siena knew more than a little about the way of Jesus. In the *Dialogue*, she tells us that in order to draw us into God's extravagant love, Christ makes a bridge and a staircase of his very crucified body.[18] So eager is God for our love, for union with us, that the Son is sent to demonstrate that love through the sacrifice of his own life on the cross for love of us.[19] Catherine writes:

> The first stair is the feet, which symbolize the affections. For just as the feet carry the body, the affections carry the soul. My Son's nailed feet are a stair by which you can climb to his side, where you will see revealed his innermost heart. . . . Then the soul, seeing how tremendously she is loved, is herself filled to overflowing with love. So having climbed the second stair, she reaches the third. This is his mouth, where she finds peace. . . .[20]

The disciple scales the tree of life, moving upward in love and virtue, seeking the fruit of union. At each phase of the ascent, the disciple is drawn on by great desire to know and love as Jesus knew and loved. Just as a mother nurses her child, so too Christ nourishes the disciple: "Through the flesh of Christ crucified, we suck the milk of divine sweetness."[21]

Like the roots of the tree, the nailed feet secure the disciple in the initial stage of the climb. At the first stair the disciple confronts and comes to know self in order to know and love Christ. In a letter to cloistered women religious, Catherine comments on the significance of reaching the heart of the crucified Jesus in the second stage of the climb. His great heart, she writes, is "open and utterly spent for us."[22]

Immersed in the heart of Christ, the disciple is nourished for a praxis of solidarity and compassion. At the final stage of the climb, the disciple reaches the mouth of Christ and "learns to savour souls . . . [to] become a true shepherd ready to lay down [her or his] life" for [the little ones].[23] The disciple is *for* others. Yet, the disciple flames with desire for the very God who with unimaginable love has looked upon us and fallen in love with us.[24]

"Jacob's Ladder," the familiar African American spiritual, has a strong metaphorical resonance with Catherine's image of the body of the crucified Christ as a staircase. The spiritual conflates and fuses the story of Jacob's vision (Gen. 28:10-17) with the cross of Jesus.

> We are climbing Jacob's ladder, / We are climbing Jacob's ladder,
> We are climbing Jacob's ladder, / Soldiers of the cross.
>
> Every round goes higher, higher, / Every round goes higher, higher,
> Every round goes higher, higher, / Soldiers of the cross.
>
> Sinner, do you love my Jesus? / Sinner, do you love my Jesus?
> Sinner, do you love my Jesus? / Soldiers of the cross.
>
> If you love Him, why not serve him? / If you love Him, why not serve him?
> If you love Him, why not serve him? / Soldiers of the cross.[25]

As simple as the spiritual is, it is more than simplistic repetition, call and response; it engages singer, listener, and disciple in a meditative dialogue about growth in the life of the spirit, knowledge of God, and discipleship.

In Genesis, Jacob, fearful and yearning, dreams of a ladder that reaches upward from earth into the heavens and upon which angels ascend and descend. Jacob is gifted with both a *disclosure* of God's identity ("I am the Lord, the God of Abraham your father and the God of Isaac" [Gen. 28:13]) and a *promise* ("I am with you and will keep you wherever you go . . . I will not leave you until I have done what I have promised you" [Gen. 28:15]). The first and second stanzas of the spiritual offer a thematic statement of the ladder's direction toward God and its end in God. But unlike Jacob, those of us who would be disciples are awake; we sin even as we seek. We climb toward the God who is our destination, but the weight of sin slows our ascent. The makers of the spiritual invoke soldierly virtues of courage and fortitude, but these are not enough. Love must be added to the list. The first stanza discloses our true end, union with God; the final stanza calls those who profess to love God to love neighbor, to take up a praxis of solidarity and compassion.

The spirituals give us access to the "experience[s], expression[s], motivations, intentions, behaviors, styles, and rhythms" of African American religio-cultural life.[26] They open a window onto the lives of the enslaved peoples and shed light on their religious, social, aesthetic, and psychological worldview. They emerge from the people's wrestling with and surrender to the power of the Spirit that set them on the "way."

A former slave become a minister of the gospel, Josiah Henson provides an example of similarly committed discipleship. In his autobiographical narrative, first published in Boston in 1849, Henson vividly recalls his conversion to Christ. Urged by his mother to go to hear preacher John McKenny, young Henson obtained permission to do so from the slaveholder Isaac Riley. Henson reports that he walked three or four miles to the place of the meeting, but upon arrival was barred because of his race from entering the building. After some effort, Henson positioned himself near the open front door to hear and see McKenny. Henson recalls:

> I saw [Mr. McKenny] with his hands raised . . . and he said: "Jesus Christ, the Son of God, tasted death for every man; for the high, for the low, for the rich, for the poor, for the bond, the free, the [N]egro in his chains, the man in gold and diamonds. . . ." I stood and heard [the sermon]. It touched my heart, and I cried out: "I wonder if Jesus Christ died for me."[27]

McKenny preached Jesus' "tender love for mankind, his forgiving spirit, his compassion for the outcast and despised, his cruel crucifixion" and reminded congregations that the message of salvation was universal. Jesus Christ died not for a select few but for all. Henson writes that these, indeed, were "glad tidings" and they were for the slave as well as the master, the poor as well as the rich, for the persecuted, the distressed, the heavy-laden, the captive; even for me among the rest, a poor, despised, abused creature, deemed by others fit for nothing but unrequited toil—but mental and bodily degradation. Oh, the blessedness and sweetness of feeling that I was loved! . . . I kept repeating to myself, "The compassionate Savior about whom I have heard, 'loves me,' 'He looks down in compassion from heaven on me. . . .' " I thought . . . "[Jesus will] be my dear refuge—He'll wipe away all tears from my eyes." "Now I can bear all things; nothing will seem hard after this." . . . Swallowed up in the beauty of the divine love, I "loved my enemies and prayed for them that did despitefully use and [mistreat] me."[28]

Meditating on this message as he returned to the plantation, Henson tells us he grew so excited that he turned into the woods nearby, knelt down, and prayed for guidance and aid. From that day forward, Henson set himself the task of climbing "Jacob's ladder" and leading others in that ascent. He soon began to gather other enslaved women and men, to speak with them about the love of the crucified Jesus, to pray with them, to exhort them, and to comfort them.

Separated by centuries, Catherine of Siena and Josiah Henson are united in committed discipleship. Both understood that Jesus of Nazareth is the absolute meaning of life for the world. He offered them a love that drew them to himself, and their love of him flowed over into a praxis of compassionate solidarity on behalf of women and men in need. Loving as Jesus loved, Catherine challenged a warring society and a fragmented church with a message of peace and reconciliation. Loving as Jesus loved, Henson confronted a slaveholding society and church with a demand for justice and transformation. Catherine and Henson took up the time-shaped challenge to love Jesus, to follow him, to live his command, to share the good news of his love, to stand in solidarity and compassion with others.

Conclusion

In this essay, I have attempted to tease out what it means to follow Jesus of Nazareth, to be his disciple, to stand as he stood at the disposal of the cross. I began with the sad spectacle of a black woman combing through the refuse bins of my apartment building. Here is a woman whose back is against the wall; her situation imposes on Christian discipleship. What can it mean to tell her that God in Jesus is also alienated, a stranger, a despised "other"? What word, what compassionate act of solidarity do we Christian disciples have for her? Moved by sight of her, I went on to examine the terrifying spectacle of the crucifixion of Jesus of Nazareth and to interrogate the cross as an indispensable condition of Christian discipleship. The experiences of Catherine of Siena and of Josiah Henson testify *both* to the unity of the mystical-political for the Christian disciple *and* to discipleship as the locus, the site, in which Christ makes himself present.

This exploration took the performative meaning of discipleship from the Lukan narrative of the story of the life, death, and resurrection of Jesus of Nazareth. Even with its ambivalent attitudes toward women, Luke's gospel affords those of us who belong to privileged groups (for example, whites or black theologians) an occasion for critical self-examination: How do we understand the relation of our own social locations to the coming reign of God? How often do those of us who belong to privileged groups conveniently overlook the incriminating criticisms of the privileged, which the narrator of Luke's gospel places in the mouth of Jesus? How often do we excuse ourselves from human communion with poor, despised hungry women and men? These are questions that any of us who would be disciples must follow in order to find the Christ of God, questions to be answered by living in search of the One whose great love for us gives absolute meaning to life.

Throughout this essay, I have kept the cross at the forefront, but in concluding I want to shift a bit. My starting point for working out the meaning of discipleship as christological locus was the sad spectacle of a black woman searching garbage. I choose the word *spectacle* deliberately, since the image of the woman leaning into stench and filth seized me, suffused my senses, entered into my theologizing, and remains vivid and authoritative in my memory. I know nothing about her: She may have fallen through the gaping cracks of the so-called safety-net established by the state of Wisconsin in its haste to eliminate welfare. Or she may have been homeless and simply, terribly hungry. Or perhaps she was poor and refrained from eating in order to feed her children. How hungry and desperate she must have been to stand in the morning sun opening bags of garbage. How hungry she must have been to endure the stares of disgust and condescension from passers-by. But to this woman scraping the dregs for life, the Lukan Jesus offers reassurance: "Blessed are you who are poor, for yours is the kingdom of God. Blessed are you who are hungry now, for you will be filled" (Luke 6:20-21).

The spectacle of a woman searching through rot for food cannot but point the Christian disciple toward the Bread of Life. This phrase, "bread of life," belongs in a special way to the Johannine Jesus, but the Lukan Jesus (like the Jesus of the Synoptics) blesses, breaks, and identifies bread with himself before he completes his way to the cross. In this gospel, the breaking of bread is the gesture that clears the tear-filled eyes of those forlorn disciples who met a stranger on their way to Emmaus (Luke 24:30-31). In *Seeing the Lord*, Marianne Sawicki comments on Luke's association of hunger with the possibility of understanding resurrection life and of recognizing the resurrected Lord.[29] This recognition, I would add, is crucial for mystical-political discipleship and for an authentic praxis of compassion and solidarity.

In Luke 14, we find Jesus on a Sabbath at table, a dinner guest of a Pharisee. Jesus bluntly tells his host: "When you give a banquet, invite the poor, the crippled, the lame, and the blind. And you will be blessed, because they cannot repay you, for you will be repaid at the resurrection of the righteous" (Luke 14:13-14). Jesus is insisting that we make space in our hearts, at our tables, in our communities for the little ones. Perhaps to drive home the point, Jesus reiterates this lesson in the parable of the great banquet. Someone invites guests to a wonderful meal, then sends a servant to summon them when all is ready. But the guests retort with excuses and rebuff his hospitality. Angry, the householder tells the servant, "Go out at once in the streets and lanes of the town, and bring in the poor, the crippled, the blind, and the lame." The servant does so and returns to report that there is still room at table. Again the host sends the servant "out into the roads and lanes, and compel people to come in, so that my house may be filled. For I tell you, none of those who were invited will taste my dinner" (Luke 14:15-24).

Hunger constitutes a possibility for mystical-political discipleship and an authentic praxis of compassion and solidarity. If we would be disciples of Jesus, we must be willing to recognize and alleviate hungers—whether for food or truth or justice, whether our own or those of others.[30] A praxis of compassionate solidarity, justice-love, and care for the poor and oppressed is a sign that we are on the "way" of Jesus. The resurrected Lord himself sends us into streets and alleys, shelters and schools, homes and hospices to find and feed those who are despised, abused, and marginalized. These children, women, and men are the only sure sign of his presence among us in our efforts to prepare a context for the coming reign of his God.

At the same time, the parable of the great banquet reiterates a warning thrown down earlier by the Lukan Jesus: "Woe to you who are full now, for you will be hungry" (Luke 6:25a). All who would be his disciples, especially those of us who have the luxury to stand and watch hungry women and men, are called to critical self-examen and a praxis of compassionate solidarity. In Luke's narrative arrangement, this parable precedes those forceful words about the fundamental condition of discipleship: "Whoever does not carry the cross and follow me cannot be my disciple" (Luke 14:27). The cross rises between the meal that Jesus shares with his disciples before he dies and the bit of grilled fish that he eats with them in Jerusalem (Luke 24:41-43). At the Passover meal, Jesus declares to his friends that he shall not eat or drink again until the kingdom of God comes (Luke 22:16-18). He promises them that when the kingdom does come, they shall sit with him at his table in places set specially for them, eating and drinking with joy (Luke 22:28-30). If we would sit at his table, we too must live in solidarity with the little ones and live at the disposal of the cross.

Notes

[1]Ched Myers, "Mark's Gospel: Invitation to Discipleship," in *The New Testament: Introducing the Way of Discipleship*, ed. Wes Howard-Brook and Sharon H. Ringe (Maryknoll, N.Y.: Orbis Books, 2002), 49. For some examples of such scholarly interpretation, see Howard C. Kee, *Community for a New Age: Studies in Mark's Gospel* (Philadelphia: Fortress Press, 1977); Ched Myers et al., *"Say to This Mountain": Mark's Story of Discipleship* (Maryknoll, N.Y.: Orbis Books, 1996); and Brian Blount, *Go Preach! Mark's Kingdom Message and the Black Church* (Maryknoll, N.Y.: Orbis Books, 1998).

[2]For some examples, see Barbara E. Reid, *Choosing the Better Part? Women in the Gospel of Luke* (Collegeville, Minn.: Liturgical Press, 1996); and Turid Karlsen Seim, *The Double Message: Patterns of Gender in Luke-Acts* (Nashville: Abingdon Press, 1994).

[3]Clarice J. Martin, "The Acts of the Apostles," in *Searching the Scriptures: A Feminist Commentary*, vol. 2, ed. Elisabeth Schüssler Fiorenza (New York: Crossroad, 1994), 770.

[4]Turid Karlsen Seim, "The Gospel of Luke," in *Searching the Scriptures: A Feminist Commentary*, vol. 2, ed. Schüssler Fiorenza, 761.

[5]Ibid.

[6]Sharon H. Ringe, "Luke's Gospel: 'Good News to the Poor' for the Non-Poor," in *The New Testament*, ed. Howard-Brook and Ringe, 65.

[7]N. T. Wright, *Christian Origins and the Question of God: Jesus and the Victory of God*, vol. 2 (Minneapolis: Fortress Press, 1996), 176.

[8]Ibid., 175.

[9]Martin Hengel, *Crucifixion in the Ancient World and the Folly of the Message of the Cross*, trans. John Bowden (Philadelphia: Fortress Press, 1977).

[10]Wright, *Christian Origins and the Question of God*, vol. 2, 482.

[11]For more on this point, see Hengel, who cites Pliny the Younger's letter to the Emperor Trajan in which he argues that the belief of Christians in a crucified God was a "pernicious and extravagant superstition" (*Epistulae* 10.96.4-8), *Crucifixion in the Ancient World*, 2.

[12]Augustine, *City of God*, ed. David Knowles, trans. Henry Bettenson (New York: Penguin Books, 1972), Book 19, Ch. 23, 884-885.

[13]Justin writes, "They charge us with madness, saying that we give the second place after the unchanging and ever-existing God and begetter of all things to a crucified man" (13.4, "First Apology," in *Early Christian Fathers*, ed. and trans. by Cyril C. Richardson [New York: Macmillan, 1970], 249).

[14]Hengel, *Crucifixion in the Ancient World*, 1.

[15]Tacitus, *Annals*,15.44.4, cited in Hengel, *Crucifixion in the Ancient World*, 26.

[16]Hengel, *Crucifixion in the Ancient World*, 22-32.

[17]In a vision, God tells Catherine of Siena, "I am infinite Good and I therefore require of you infinite desire" (104: 197, in *Catherine of Siena: The Dialogue*, trans. Suzanne Noffke [New York: Paulist Press, 1980]). This is a familiar image for Catherine and appears in her correspondence; see, Letter T74/G119, to Fratre Niccolò da Montalcino of the Order of Preachers in Montepulciano, February to April 1376, in *The Letters of Catherine of Siena*, vol. 1, trans. with introduction and notes by Suzanne Noffke (Tempe: Arizona Center of Medieval and Renaissance Studies, 2000), 313-314.

[18]For another discussion of this metaphor, see Catherine M. Meade, *My Nature Is Fire: Saint Catherine of Siena* (New York: Alba House, 1991), especially 107-128.

[19]*Catherine of Siena*, 26: 65.

[20]Ibid., 64.

[21]*The Letters of Catherine of Siena*, vol. 1, Letter T109/G41/DT51, to Bérenger, Abbot of Lézat, Apostolic Nuncio to Tuscany, January to February 1376, 266.

[22]*I, Catherine of Siena: Selected Writings of St. Catherine of Siena*, trans. Kenelm Foster and Mary John Ronayne (London: William Collins, 1980), Letter 31, 146.

[23]Ibid.

[24]*Catherine of Siena*, 13: 49.

[25]Orally transmitted for more than two centuries, the Negro or African American spirituals have a long and complicated history. These songs arose from the

spiritual striving of an enslaved community, rather than from any authorial endeavor of a single individual. I quote here one of the most familiar variants of the
spiritual, "We Are Climbing Jacob's Ladder." For readers looking for textual references, this spiritual can be found in *Lead Me, Guide Me: The African American
Catholic Hymnal* (Chicago: GIA Publications, 1987), #54.

[26]Charles H. Long, *Significations: Signs, Symbols, and Images in the Interpretation of Religion* (Philadelphia: Fortress Press, 1986), 7.

[27]Josiah Henson, *An Autobiography of the Reverend Josiah Henson*, in *Four
Fugitive Slave Narratives*, ed. Robin W. Winks et al. (Reading, Mass: Addison-
Wesley, 1968), 24.

[28]Ibid., 25.

[29]Marianne Sawicki, *Seeing the Lord: Resurrection and Early Christian Practices* (Minneapolis: Fortress Press, 1994), 90.

[30]Ibid., 90-91.

M. Shawn Copeland's "To Live at the Disposal of the Cross: Mystical-Political Discipleship as Christological Locus": A Response

Mary Ann Hinsdale

M. Shawn Copeland's provocative essay presents anyone who professes to follow Jesus with the opportunity to reflect upon his or her vocation as a disciple, particularly in terms of what it might mean to "live at the disposal of the cross." Having recently heard Professor Copeland lecture on the theme "racism and the vocation of the theologian," I approach her essay not only as a Christian who is trying to follow Jesus, but also from the perspective of my vocation as a Catholic woman religious and an academic theologian.[1] It is particularly from the vantage point of an academic theologian that I want to consider the demands that a mystical-political discipleship makes and how such a discipleship might serve as a locus for christology.

Beginning with the autobiographical anecdote in which she describes a black woman theologian doing laundry while watching a homeless black woman forage through a dumpster, Copeland attempts to theologize out of a certain *consciousness*, one that she calls "living at the disposal of the cross." This consciousness assumes the posture of a "mystical-political discipleship," one that, she argues, should be the locus for the doing of christology. Thus, she draws our attention to the theologian *as subject* in the process of theological reflection.[2] My response to her essay, to borrow a musical metaphor, is more in the realm of "dueling banjos" than a *mouvement contraire*. In other words, I consider both of us to be on the same wavelength, playing the same instrument. I want simply to take up her refrain, echo it, and add a few resonances from some other sources that I hope will suggest further

197

directions for making the cross, and the mystical-political discipleship that it entails, a locus for christology today.

Christology "From Below"

Based on Luke's gospel, Copeland reviews the ministry of Jesus
and the central motif of his preaching—the reign of God—"as a realization of truth and love, holiness and grace, justice and peace." Her
reading of Luke leads her to conclude that "Jesus made the cross an
undeniable condition for discipleship (Luke 9:23, 14:27)." In accepting his death on the cross, "Jesus *incarnated* the solidarity of God
with poor, outcast, abject and despised human persons." Clearly, this
is a christology "from below," one that begins with the Jesus of history and understands his death as intimately connected to his ministry
to the marginalized of his day. The disciples who followed Jesus heard
and responded to the words and deeds of his life—and "gradually,"
"haltingly," "fitfully," came to dedicate themselves and their living to
the concerns, commitment, and compassion of the God of Jesus. By
means of this following, disciples must necessarily put themselves
and their lives "at the disposal of the cross."

In her section on the meaning of the cross in the ancient world,
Copeland wants us to appreciate how very much at odds with the culture of the times such a discipleship will prove to be. Relying on the
work of Martin Hengel, she reminds us that crucifixion in the ancient
world was a mark of shame, the fate of criminals and slaves. For Jesus'
Jewish followers the notion of a crucified messiah was unthinkable
(as Paul points out in 1 Cor. 23); but crucifixion was abhorrent to
Gentiles as well. If we recall that Paul's context in 1 Corinthians was
one of division and quarrels within the Corinthian community, we
might view Paul's theology of the cross as one of the earliest efforts to
create "common ground" among opposing factions in the Christian
community. Even though there were many conceptions of "messiah"
in first-century Judaism, as Copeland points out, a suffering messiah
was not one of them. It took some ingenuity on Paul's part to find a
theology for this kind of messiahship. He finds it by appealing to the
Suffering Servant text of Isaiah 53 and by turning the Greek conception of wisdom on its head. This was a theological task of astounding
proportions, perhaps akin to that of answering the theodicy questions
raised by the terrorism of September 11, 2001, or of the on-going

clergy sexual abuse scandal within the U.S. Catholic Church at the beginning of the twenty-first century.

Copeland reminds us that crucifixion was a military and political punishment, reserved particularly for the lower classes, slaves, and subjugated peoples. Much like the rationalization of the death penalty in our own time, it was supposed to act as a deterrent. "Cruel and unusual punishment" was the whole point of crucifixion. She notes further that rather than being buried, the crucified body was left to be eaten by wild beasts. It might be a fruitful reflection to consider for a moment what a different account of the disposition of Jesus' crucified body might have to say to a discipleship that demands one "live at the disposal of the cross," particularly to persons who must mourn the death of loved ones without the presence of a physical body.[3] However, the controversy regarding the historicity of Jesus' burial is not at issue in Copeland's paper.[4]

What is important for her is Jesus' surrender to the will of his Father. It is this that "hallowed in him the capacity for radical resurrection-life." Jesus' death on the cross demonstrates the real cost of discipleship. It also clearly brings out an intrinsic connection between death and resurrection. In drawing our attention to this central mystery of Christianity, Copeland seeks to bring together the prophetic liberationist (political) and mystical elements of christology. Both liberationist and mystical approaches to christology have emphasized that to follow Jesus is to surrender as he did to what God asks in the concrete circumstances of our lives. Thus, "surrender" means embarking on the same sort of journey that brought Jesus to the cross. It entails being in solidarity with victims as well as participating in the very life of God. Such mystical-political discipleship requires a giving up or an expansion[5] of one's "self" that ultimately leads to personal transformation.

"Politicians"—whether civic or ecclesiastical—do not always get this connection. But here one must avoid making easy judgments. What might seem to be the case on the surface may be quite another matter from God's own point of view. The call to such largesse is likewise a lesson to be drawn from Jesus' death. Who of us knows, for example, what might be taking place in the interior life of a Bill Clinton, a Gary Condit, a Bernard Law, a Rembert Weakland, or countless others whose public stature has rendered them subject to "public crucifixion" in our own time?

I resonated quite a bit with Copeland's meditation on the theologian doing her laundry. I had a similar epiphany recently on "garbage day," when people put their trash and recyclables at curbside. Despite having spent time at a Catholic Worker house and in Appalachia, where I earned my stripes as an inveterate "trash picker," I recently caught myself becoming annoyed with the "can collectors" who rummage through my recycling bin every week. Don't they know that *I* would know better than to throw away cans and bottles that could earn deposits? *I* would not be as thoughtless as some of my lazy neighbors and actually throw out returnables! Of course, it never occurred to me that my neighbors might *deliberately* be leaving such cans and bottles for the collectors. Nor did it occur to me that collecting bottles and cans may help a homeless person feel useful, let alone provide a bit of money that could buy a sandwich. Copeland's homey example is a reminder that the vocation of the theologian is to "be at home in the world"—even the very quotidian world of laundry and recycling bins. This, after all, is where God is at work and where the cross of Jesus is to be encountered.

The Reign of God and the Cross of Jesus

Regarding the connection between the reign of God and the cross, Copeland tells us that following Jesus involves "giving all one possesses." The followers of Jesus must plan and prepare for the arrival of God in their lives, though, in fact, this cannot be planned for (as the parable in Luke notes—the kingdom comes "like a thief in the night" [Luke 12:39]). One must be "ready"—yet one cannot plan. A love that is unmeasured, unstinting, overflowing, fearless, and passionate requires an opening of life and living towards God. What was required of Jesus is required of his disciples in every time: the opening of life and living and personhood toward God, complete trust in God, belief that God will save and deliver absolutely, and, above all, love. The connection Copeland draws between God's reign and discipleship that is lived "at the disposal of the cross" is reminiscent of John of the Cross's understanding of how faith, hope, and love are existential realities in the life of the disciple.

The Carmelite Iain Matthew interprets the "night" of John of the Cross to be God's offer of encounter, which has as its main feature not suffering, but the gift of *presence*.[6] The gift that God wants to give is

God's own self. Unfortunately, human beings are unable to contain this gift without God "widening" us, in order to "make space" for this divine presence. I find this similar to what Copeland is describing as the harrowing or hallowing that "the cross" demanded of Jesus, and thus of the disciple who seeks to follow him. In order to receive the gift of Godself, the disciple is called upon to believe, hope, and love; however, the abstract-sounding words "faith," "hope," and "love" are anything but that. For example, Matthew writes,

> If given another chance to assert myself over others, I instead resist the urge to dominate, allow the others to be themselves, and say to God, "I don't need that; I need you," that is love. If someone on whose example my belief had depended ups and abandons the gospel they had taught me to embrace, and I none the less cling on to it, that is faith. If, in the face of a deep-seated defect, I do not allow cynicism ("It will never change") to close doors on the future, that is hope.[7]

Discipleship, then, for Copeland as for John of the Cross, means that Jesus is "the way." This "way" is distinctive for each person and yet it is also the same for every follower. The cross, she says, "becomes whatever exposes us, makes us vulnerable and open to the wisdom and power of God" (namely, September 11, the clergy abuse scandals, personal loss of prestige, whatever "should not be" in our lives). These experiences "hallow" in us an infinite desire and capacity for life in and with God. John of the Cross calls this the *nada*, the "nothingness" that is occasioned by the experience of the dark night. Or, to put it another way, it is God's way of "making space" in us so that the infinite desire for God that is at the heart of all human longing may indeed be filled by God—*only* God.[8]

The Following of Jesus

Another resonance that I hear in Shawn Copeland's proposal to make living "at the disposal of the cross" the heart of mystical-political discipleship and the locus for doing christology is Jon Sobrino's epistemological principle of "the following of Jesus." Articulated first in *Christology at the Crossroads* (1978), Sobrino has developed this notion further in *Jesus the Liberator* (1993) and in *Christ the Libera-*

tor (2001).[9] Basically, to understand "the following of Jesus" as an epistemological principle, as Sobrino does, means:

> We do not get to know him personally by reading the witnesses to his words and deeds, or hearing sermons, or taking solid courses. The only way to get to know Jesus is to follow after him in one's own real life; to try to identify oneself with his own historical concerns; and to try to fashion his kingdom in our midst. In other words, only through Christian praxis is it possible for us to draw close to Jesus. Following Jesus is the precondition for knowing Jesus.[10]

Copeland draws upon the example of Catherine of Siena and her image of the staircase of Christ's crucified body as "the way." I was struck by Catherine's imagery—again, the perspective is clearly "from below," from the perspective of those at the foot of the cross, who, we might remember, were mostly women. Presented here is a beautiful summary of the essential truths of the spiritual life:

1. the first stair ("the feet" of Christ) is self-knowledge;
2. the second stair ("the heart" of Christ) causes us to realize how open God is to us, so open that we find ourselves to be "in" God;
3. the final stair ("the mouth") is the realization that one's contemplation is not for oneself alone, nor for its own sake, but for becoming a true shepherd (one who lays down one's life). Thus, being a disciple is ultimately being "for" others.

Copeland ties the vision of Catherine of Siena to the African American spiritual "Jacob's Ladder," which she also sees as a meditative dialogue about growth in the life of the Spirit. The continuing promise "I am with you" is a disclosure of God's constant presence. In drawing this connection, Copeland is saying that this conviction is what enabled Jesus to surrender to the inevitable consequence of his life and ministry. The unfailing belief, hope, and experience of God's constant presence provide the connection between Jesus' preaching and embodying the kingdom of God message and the cross.

Christology from Within

Catherine's "staircase" and Jacob's "ladder" are metaphors that recall similar images from other mystics: for example, the "dwelling places" of Teresa of Avila's *Interior Castle*, or the "thicket" of John of the Cross's *Spiritual Canticle*. For all of them, Jesus is "the way" and it is only union with him that will satisfy the heart's deepest desire. I am reminded here of Mark McIntosh's study of Hans Urs von Balthasar's christology, which McIntosh calls "christology from within."[11] This is an approach that seeks a mediation of Christ not based upon merely external imitation, but one that "includes a profound sharing of Jesus' own consciousness."[12]

The anecdote with which Shawn Copeland began her reflection, drawn from "the hidden life" of the theologian, the struggle to bring together one's own experience and the wisdom of the tradition, raised the question: What is a theologian called to do regarding a classical doctrine of our Christian tradition—"What does belief in Jesus as truly God and truly human have to say to a homeless woman searching through the garbage?" Copeland's answer is that christology needs to begin with the *cross* and, more specifically, with a discipleship that puts one "at the disposal of the cross." It is the cross that brings out most starkly that the "cost" of discipleship is not adherence to metaphysical or ontological statements about Jesus, but about adherence to an existential statement about God; namely, that "God is for us." What is revealed in Jesus' ministry and in his death and resurrection is that all who are "other" deserve a place at the table in the reign of God. For the theologian who would also be "disciple," the task that awaits us is more than simply adopting the view of the victims. The task, as both Copeland and Sobrino suggest, involves a "fusion of horizons" between the faith of victims and that of theologians. Sobrino captures this fusion:

> In the suffering of oppression and the hope of liberation both forms of faith, historically and existentially different, can converge. Then in solidarity with victims, in mutual support in faith, the eyes of the non-victims are opened to see things differently. Whether this new vision can ever coincide completely with that of the victims is something that I do not think we shall ever know. But I do believe that our perspective can change sufficiently for the victims to give us a specific light in which to "see" what we call the objects of theology: God, Christ, grace, sin. . . . The poor and the victims bring theology something more important than contents; they bring light by which we can see the contents properly.[13]

Notes

[1]Copeland's essay itself inspires a "confessional" response. Her recent work on "the vocation of the theologian" (see "Racism and the Vocation of the Theologian," *Spiritus* 2 [2002]: 15-29) and her choice of the theme "The Vocation of the Theologian" for the 2003 Catholic Theological Society of America annual meeting serve to remind us that personal reflection on discipleship, once quite a common practice among theologians, as is illustrated in the writings of Augustine, Aquinas, Luther, Barth, and Rahner, seems to have fallen out of vogue. One recent exception is Sallie McFague's introduction to *Life Abundant: Rethinking Theology and Economy for a Planet in Peril* (Minneapolis: Fortress Press, 2001). Unfortunately, in our own day, the phrase "the vocation of the theologian" more frequently calls to mind Cardinal Ratzinger's 1990 "Instruction on the Ecclesial Vocation of the Theologian" (see *Origins* 20 [July 5, 1990]: 117-26). This statement, far from encouraging the voice and religious experience of the theologian and his or her community to enter into the theological project, reduces theology to parrot-like repeating of what the official magisterium has taught.

[2]While not articulated explicitly, Copeland's anecdote reflects her understanding that the theologian-disciple is always a subject-in-relation to a *community*: the poor—and more specifically, poor women of color. At the same time, her relationality is not solely defined by this particular communal context, because she also sees herself as part of the privileged community of academically educated theologians. Thus, in sharing her personal struggle to discern what it means "to live at the disposal of the cross" *as a theologian*, she also reveals a Duboisian double (and as a black *woman*, triple) consciousness, or "hybridity," which is not always apparent to the dominant culture of professional, academic theologians.

[3]One thinks, for example, of those who lost family and friends in the World Trade Center disaster, the nameless victims of war, genocide, and other atrocities.

[4]John Dominic Crossan has raised this issue in *Who Killed Jesus? Exposing the Roots of Anti-Semitism in the Gospel Story of the Death of Jesus* (San Francisco: HarperCollins, 1996). Crossan takes issue with Raymond Brown and others in viewing the passion story as a matter of "prophecy historicized," with many of the details surrounding Jesus' trial, execution, and burial creatively constructed from Hebrew scriptures, including the "hopeful idea" of his burial by enemies (cf. Deut. 21:22-23), which eventually evolved into a burial by friends. See *Who Killed Jesus?*, 7-13 and 160-88.

[5]Iain Matthew, whose reading of John of the Cross I rely on in this essay, continually points out that God is an "inflowing God" who wants to "make space" in us for the gift of Godself. Since this gift is none other than Christ himself, I prefer the term "expansion of" rather than "giving up" the self to describe the transformation process called for by the approach of God. See Iain Matthew, *The Impact of God: Soundings from St. John of the Cross* (London: Hodder & Stoughton, 1995), 35-50.

[6]Matthew, *The Impact of God*, 28-34.

[7]Ibid., 94.

[8]Ibid., 72.

[9]Jon Sobrino, *Christology at the Crossroads*, trans. John Drury (Maryknoll, N.Y.: Orbis Books, 1978); idem, *Jesus the Liberator: A Historical-Theological Reading of Jesus of Nazareth* (Maryknoll, N.Y.: Orbis Books, 1993); idem, *Christ the Liberator* (Maryknoll, N.Y.: Orbis Books, 2001).

[10]Sobrino, *Christology at the Crossroads*, xiii. See also *Christ the Liberator*, 323: "The following of Jesus consists . . . in remaking his life and praxis, and this remaking can bring about 'an inner knowledge' (as the mystics say) that is not simply based on texts concerning Jesus, which always remains to a certain extent extraneous to our reality."

[11]Mark A. McIntosh, *Christology from Within: Spirituality and the Incarnation in Hans Urs Von Balthasar* (Notre Dame: University of Notre Dame Press, 2000).

[12]Ibid., 22.

[13]Sobrino, *Christ the Liberator*, 7-8.

"At the Disposal of the Cross": Discipleship, Julian of Norwich, and What Bartimaeus Saw

Anthony J. Godzieba

First of all, I want to thank Professor Copeland for her thought-provoking paper. It is an evocative exercise in Christian religious imagination that sees christology, spirituality, and liberative praxis in an essential unity.

As a context for my comments, let me say that I am in fundamental agreement with her on all the issues that she raises here. As I understand her paper, the "way of Jesus" is to be appropriated by the disciple who would follow Jesus. It is a way of suffering and vulnerability, "emptiness and failure," but also the development of "infinite desire and capacity for life in and with God." Both *how* that "way" has been embodied by Jesus and *what precisely* the disciple must do to follow Jesus are summed up in the cross of Christ. The cross incarnates the "unimaginable love" with which God has taken up our lives and our sufferings in order to redeem them. The disciple's cruciform way of life in imitation of Jesus is itself a locus for christological reflection.

What I would like to offer in my commentary are some ways that Copeland's argument and imaginative vision can be supplemented and perhaps even deepened. First, I am in complete agreement with her overall thesis: "To live as Jesus' disciple means to live at the disposal of the cross—exposed, vulnerable, open to the wisdom and power and love of God. . . . [Discipleship] requires a praxis of solidarity and compassion as well as surrender to the startling embrace of Divine Love" (p. 180). The key here is the understanding of discipleship as a *practice* or as an ensemble of practices linked in a reciprocal way to knowledge: one knows who Jesus is by following him, and one follows him because one knows that he is the human face of God.

Elsewhere I have made a strong fundamental theological case for a quite similar model of interpretation. I have argued that the New Testament is best understood along the lines of a musical score to be performed rather than as a text to be read, and that the kingdom of God as announced by Jesus can *only* be understood by us in performance, when we actively articulate the values of the kingdom of God in our own lives.[1] If one views discipleship as essentially "performing the score," then one is not only mindful of the risks involved in every performance. One also sees clearly how the essential revelatory character of Jesus' proclamation of the kingdom of God and of the New Testament itself is bound up with issues of incarnation and temporality, with the messiness of history that the kingdom of God has assumed as its performing stage.

Second, Copeland leans heavily on the Gospel of Luke for her reconstruction of the praxis and message of Jesus, so much so that at times there is a danger that we will conflate some of the specifics of Luke's developed theology of discipleship with the *ipsissima intentio Jesu*. The relationship between the various historical quests for the "aims" of Jesus and christology is a delicate one, and too complex to go into here.[2] But since we need to rely on interpreted experiences of Jesus, I am surprised that she makes very little use of the one gospel most obviously concerned with the character of discipleship, the Gospel of Mark. Mark offers us rich resources for understanding the connection between cross and discipleship, and an appeal to Mark could only strengthen her case. At the very least, the entire second half of the gospel depicts the intentionality of discipleship as being pointed squarely in the direction of the cross. The episode where the blind Bartimaeus is healed (Mark 10:46-52) leaves us in no doubt about this. Mark's redaction of this miracle story into a discipleship story is a corrective to the completely inadequate and perhaps pernicious understanding of discipleship articulated by James and John in the previous pericope (Mark 10:35-45). According to Mark, they and the other members of Jesus' inner circle (those whom we would expect would know precisely what being a disciple involves) equate discipleship with eschatological power and control. In the Bartimaeus pericope this definition is swept aside and the true nature of discipleship is again revealed; the question-answer ping-pong effect of the concluding dialogue of Jesus and Bartimaeus (10:51-52) directly equates "sight" with "faith," and therefore with spiritual insight. It is with both physical sight and spiritual insight, then, that Bartimaeus, at the close of the episode, "followed him on the way" (10:52), the way that leads to Jerusalem, to suffering, to the cross. Authentic discipleship is embodied in Bartimaeus and in his faith that this truly is the way to God.

One should also pay attention to the conclusion of the passion story, where the pent-up emotion of the gospel's intense meditation on the suffering and dying Jesus bursts forth as an epiphany in the centurion's confession (15:39). Here, the cross reverberates as the point of convergence for all the claims that have to do with Jesus. Only here, Mark tells us, at the foot of the cross, at the end of Jesus' earthly journey, can the truth of Jesus as "the Son of God" be proclaimed and known.

Third, Copeland's claims concerning Jesus' understanding of the kingdom of God ("Jesus envisioned life lived under the reign of this God as a realization of truth and love, holiness and grace, justice and peace") stand alongside her reflection on the meaning of the cross ("Jesus incarnated the solidarity of God with abject and despised human persons"). But the relationship between the two is more hinted at than made explicit. In our theology and spirituality we always need to make this connection more explicit, lest we wind up with a christology no better than that of the Neo-Scholastic manuals, where the life of Jesus and the salvific meaning of the cross were only extrinsically related.[3] In this matter, one could take a page from N. T. Wright, whose *Jesus and the Victory of God* attempts to discern the meaning of Jesus' crucifixion by situating his life and story within Israel's wider overarching story of exodus, exile, and eschatology.[4] This flows directly from Wright's fundamental principle that "stories are one of the most basic modes of human life" and that "worldviews, the grid through which humans perceive reality," have "an irreducible narrative element."[5]

In the present case, one needs to show how the "story" of the kingdom of God necessarily includes the cross as one of its "chapters." In order to do this, the kingdom of God needs to be described more fundamentally. In the gospels, the revelation of God's reign through the words and actions of Jesus is portrayed as an action of *reversal,* the transformation of situations of negativity, suffering, and dehumanization into situations of positivity, joy, and human flourishing beyond any human achievement—a fundamental reversal of circumstances that could be accomplished only by God, Jesus' Abba. As suggested by Jesus' parables, God's reign makes the offer of love and reversal open to all without qualification and, in doing so, surpasses human expectations and standards. That this reversal of negativity and restoration of human well-being is truly God's salvific will is confirmed by the resurrection of Jesus, which is the definitive reversal, the reversal of death into life.

Right here is the connector that we need to highlight. The resurrection is God's reversal of the evacuation of meaning, which is the cross. The cross, in turn, is the consequence of the judgment leveled against Jesus for his "radical" kingdom preaching, whether that radical character is located in his "open commensality" (J. D. Crossan), his prophetic critique of the Temple as the primary symbol of the codes of purity and economic oppression that Jesus sought to undermine (P. Fredriksen), or his reorienting of Israel's story so that it pointed to him as the focal point through whom YHWH would act to end Israel's sufferings (N. T. Wright).[6] The cross, so to speak, is the second act, following upon the first act of Jesus' life, praxis, and message in service to the kingdom of God. It is meaningful because it is assumed and reversed by God in order to show, in connection with the resurrection, that Jesus' claim to represent God's salvific will is true.

But before we ourselves appropriate this meaning, before we experience the ecstatic release of Easter Sunday, we must live through Good Friday, we must first linger and experience the cross's terrible power, as did the first disciples. That terror comes from its threatening ambiguity, seen from the vantage point of Good Friday: Is the crucifixion of Jesus truly the incarnation of the solidarity of God with the poor and despised, or is it rather the negation of that promise of solidarity-in-love and a reversal of that salvific reversal proclaimed by Jesus as a reality? Only the resurrection will begin to help us tell the difference. The cross as visible negation, the cross as surd, the cross with no easy solution accompanied by the flicker of hope in God's power to conquer the seemingly almighty power of death—these all must be experienced in relation to the kingdom of God, if we are in any way to understand the depth of the kingdom's truth as God's reversal, and the participative power of our own performance of the reversal by living according to kingdom values, the way of discipleship that we believe will be approved by God through our own resurrection.

Lastly, I am very much moved by the recollection of Catherine of Siena's image of the staircase of Christ's crucified body that Catherine offers as a guide to the mystical and praxical intensification of discipleship. The contemplative attentiveness and rapturous experience of Christ's love recall a long medieval tradition of meditation upon the wounds of the crucified Savior, as in the *Rhythmica oratio* (*Membra Jesu nostri*) attributed to Bernard of Clairvaux. Its stanzas are progressive meditations on the crucified's "members" (his feet, his knees, his hands, his side, and so on).

I would frame this image alongside another that comes from Catherine's near-contemporary, Julian of Norwich. The image is shattering because it seems so counter-intuitive, and yet I would suggest it as a necessary prelude to the journey that Catherine suggests to us. In the midst of her meditation upon the crucifix, a meditation so intense that those around her thought that she had died,[7] Julian has this experience:

> Here I saw a great union between Christ and us; for when he was in pain, we were in pain. And all creatures who were capable of suffering, suffered with him. And as for those who did not know him, their suffering was that all creation, sun and moon, withdrew their service, and so they were all left in sorrow during that time. And thus those that loved him suffered for love, and those that did not love him suffered from a failure of comfort and from the whole of creation.
>
> At this point I wanted to look away from the cross, but I dared not, for I well knew that while I contemplated the cross I was safe and sound; therefore I was unwilling to imperil my soul, for beside the cross there was no safety, but the ugliness of fiends. Then a suggestion came from my reason, as though a friendly voice had spoken, "Look up to his father in heaven." Then I saw clearly with the faith that I felt, that there was nothing between the cross and heaven which could have distressed me, and either I must look up or I must answer. I answered and said, "No, I cannot, for you are my heaven." I said this because I did not wish to look up, for I would rather have suffered until Judgement Day than have come to heaven otherwise than by him; for I well knew that he who redeemed me so dearly would unbind me when he wished.
>
> Thus I chose Jesus as my heaven, though at that time I saw him only in pain.[8]

Julian refuses to look away, refuses to take any short-cut to heaven and to mystical fulfillment. "No," she says, "you"—the crucified Savior, the bleeding and dying Jesus—"you are my heaven." For Julian there is no way to union with God without the cross, without her identification with the sufferings of Jesus and with all of creation that suffers with him and through him. The intensity of personal identification with Jesus opens out into an embrace of all creation.

Why Julian's image as a prelude to Catherine's? In Catherine's staircase imagery, forward progress is made. There occurs a deepening of love for and identification with the Crucified and with his care for souls (as the spiritual "Jacob's Ladder" says, "If you love him, why not serve him?"); our overwhelming yearning for God already finds the beginnings of its fulfillment. But in Julian there is no progress. Rather there is the overwhelming realization that one must stay with the cross despite all temptation to do otherwise. One must be present to the cross and all it represents, and must stay present with patient (recalling all senses of *patior, passus*) attention and attachment. One's yearning is for happiness of heaven, surely, but heaven is also to be identified with the redeeming love revealed on the cross. This is not masochism; Julian is clear that desire's true and ultimate goal is God, and that one's fundamental wish is to be "unbound." But her image is one of exquisite equipoise: one waits by the cross in solidarity with Jesus and all creation, suspended between the negativity of pain that is before our eyes and the hope for the fulfillment of God's promise that "all manner of things shall be well."[9]

Today we are far away from the social and economic optimism of the 1970s and the late 1980s, and even farther from the euphoria that swept through the church in the immediate post-Vatican II period of the late 1960s. If anything, we have witnessed the failure of one "certainty" after another. Our faith in the Enlightenment myth of progress has been shattered. Who would have guessed that the fall of the Berlin Wall in 1989 and the dream of a "new world order" would serve as the prelude to an unbridled flood of genocide? Who would have predicted the extent to which economic globalization has pushed the Two-Thirds World deeper into poverty and despair? Who would have predicted that the waning days of a papacy praised on all sides for being an uncompromising moral icon would be beset by a moral crisis so shattering—a crisis whose roots are within the hierarchy itself—that the very credibility of Catholicism is threatened? The groaning of a world in pain has become only more intense. From where shall come our help?

Our present bewilderment and our desperate need for the reversal that is God's reign is why Julian's image of discipleship at the disposal of the cross is the necessary accompaniment to Catherine's. Julian's loving gaze upon the cross, carried out in the space between visible suffering (which mocks our hopes) and faith in the unseen fulfillment of God's promise of salvation, is the starting-point of a portrait of discipleship in our age. Catherine then portrays in detail the progressive intensification of this discipleship, a mystical pedagogy that forms and intensifies one's following of Jesus and readies the disciple for "a praxis of solidarity and compassion": confronting the self, experiencing the revelation of divine love in the pierced heart of Jesus, identifying oneself with that love, and loving all those for whom the Savior was crucified.

Is this perhaps the portrait of a contemporary disciple who can see what Bartimaeus saw? The true disciple is one who can see to Golgotha but no further, who can see that there are no human guarantees on the way with Jesus to Jerusalem, and yet sets out on the way with him and is crucified with him. The disciple at the disposal of the cross believes that the love of God will prevail even over Golgotha's verdict, that the reversal that the Father performed on behalf of the Son will also be a reversal performed for us if we faithfully perform the life-giving values of the kingdom of God.

Notes

[1] Anthony J. Godzieba, "Method and Interpretation: The New Testament's Heretical Hermeneutic (Prelude and Fugue),"*Heythrop Journal* 36 (1995): 286-306.

[2] On this issue, see especially Ben F. Meyer, *The Aims of Jesus* (London: SCM Press, 1979); Elizabeth A. Johnson, "The Theological Relevance of the Historical Jesus: A Debate and a Thesis," *The Thomist* 48 (1984): 1-43; Francis Schüssler Fiorenza, "The Jesus of Piety and the Historical Jesus," *Catholic Theological Society of America Proceedings* 49 (1994): 90-99; Anthony J. Godzieba, "Christology: Contemporary Issues," *Handbook of Catholic Theology,* ed. Wolfgang Beinert and Francis Schüssler Fiorenza (New York: Crossroad, 1995), 91-96; Elizabeth A. Johnson, "The Word Was Made Flesh and Dwelt among Us: Jesus Research and Christian Faith," in Doris Donnelly, ed., *Jesus: A Colloquium in the Holy Land* (New York: Continuum, 2001), 146-66.

[3] Cf. Edward Schillebeeckx, *Church: The Human Story of God,* trans. John Bowden (New York: Crossroad, 1990), 120: "We may not isolate the death of Jesus from the context of his career, his message and his life's work; otherwise we

are turning its redemptive significance into a myth, sometimes even into a sadistic and bloody myth. . . . The death of Jesus is the historical expression of the unconditional nature of his proclamation and career, in the face of which the significance of the fatal consequences for his own life completely paled into insignificance."

[4]N. T. Wright, *Christian Origins and the Question of God, Vol. 2: Jesus and the Victory of God* (Minneapolis: Fortress Press, 1996), esp. 540-611.

[5]N. T. Wright, *Christian Origins and the Question of God, Vol. 1: The New Testament and the People of God* (Minneapolis: Fortress Press, 1992), 38.

[6]John Dominic Crossan, *The Historical Jesus: The Life of a Mediterranean Jewish Peasant* (San Francisco: HarperCollins, 1991); Paula Fredriksen, *Jesus of Nazareth, King of the Jews: A Jewish Life and the Emergence of Christianity* (New York: Vintage, 2000), esp. 197-200; N. T. Wright, *Jesus and the Victory of God* (n. 4); idem, *The Challenge of Jesus: Rediscovering Who Jesus Was and Is* (Downers Grove, Ill.: InterVarsity Press, 1999), esp. 74-95.

[7]Julian of Norwich, *Revelations of Divine Love,* trans. Elizabeth Spearing (London/New York: Penguin, 1998), 16 (short text, Showing 10).

[8]Ibid., 17 (short text, end of Showing 10 and beginning of Showing 11).

[9]Ibid., 24 (short text, Showing 15).

Feminists' Christs and Christian Spirituality

Linda S. Harrington

Feminist theologians have argued that many of the images of Jesus Christ presented by the Christian tradition have been used to justify and to reinforce women's subjugation and oppression in family, society, and church.[1] Christian feminist theologians have written much about how these traditional images are inadequate and how one might think of the Christ more appropriately. This re-imaging effort is of primary importance since our images of Christ are the foundation from which both the Christian community and the individual believer respond to the experience of the divine present and active in our midst. They are also the foundation from which theology, the formal reflection on that experience, arises. Christian feminist theologians have presented images of Christ that address the distressingly patriarchal and misogynist aspects of the Christian tradition that would deny women their full potential as human beings.

The Christian feminist discussion encompasses doctrinal and ethical aspects of Christian life as well as liturgical and spiritual aspects. Feminist theologians argue convincingly that images of Christ that devalue embodiment are too easily distorted into a denigration of women.[2] They argue convincingly that an emphasis on Jesus of Nazareth's maleness to the exclusion of the other particularities of his existence has distorted the incarnation into a denial of women's ability to image God or Christ.[3] And they argue convincingly that images of Christ such as Lord and King have been too easily distorted into the idea that hierarchical structures of power that allow one group to oppress another are divinely ordained.[4] All of these arguments have been accompanied by suggestions for alternative ways of thinking about Christ that could counter the patriarchal, androcentric bias that permeates the tradition, particularly as it is harmful to women. Yet in all these re-imaging attempts, necessary as they are, it seems as if one question never is asked about the images of Christ they present. It is that question that I wish to raise in this paper.

From the earliest years of the Christian era, the Christian community has gathered in Christ's name and offered praise and worship to God in, through, and with Christ, in union with the Holy Spirit. Paul's letters, the earliest written record we have of Christian practices, are filled with references to this action "in Christ." Contemporary Christian communal practice still is to pray to God "in Jesus' name" or "through Christ" in union with the Holy Spirit.[5]

Each person's participation in that community is predicated on the individual receiving the sacrament of baptism. Whether the decision for baptism is made by one's parents during infancy or one makes a fully conscious decision to seek membership in the Christian community as an adult, baptism is personal. One person, no matter the stage of physical, emotional, or spiritual development, becomes part of the community of believers who worship together in Jesus' name in the unity of the Holy Spirit. One person has decided (or must eventually decide, in the case of infant baptism) to accept the message of salvation that is mediated through the Christian community. Christian spirituality, the response to the Christian experience of the divine, therefore has two aspects, personal and communal. The community's worship, especially in the Eucharist, is (or at least ought to be) both a response to and a mediation of the community's experience of God through Christ in the Spirit[6]; and each Christian's personal prayer, begun in the personal act of accepting baptism and joining the community at prayer, is a reflection of and a response to the individual's own personal experience of God through Christ in the Spirit.

The question that I wish to bring to the images of Christ and the description of Jesus presented by Christian feminist theologians is twofold, corresponding to both the communal and individual aspects of Christian spirituality. At the communal level, it seems that one must ask if the Christ whom Christian feminists describe can be the one through whom, with whom, and in whom the community worships God in union with the Holy Spirit. And at the individual level, it seems that one must ask if the Christ whom Christian feminists describe is one with whom the Christian believer could develop a personal relationship that leads to and includes a relationship with God in the Holy Spirit.

In order to explore these questions, it will first be necessary to examine the images of Christ offered by Christian feminist theologians. I have chosen Rosemary Radford Ruether, Rita Nakashima Brock, Jacquelyn Grant, and Elizabeth Johnson as much for their influence on contemporary feminist Christian theological discourse as for their role in my own theological formation.[7]

Feminist Christology

Rosemary Radford Ruether

One of Rosemary Radford Ruether's many contributions to Christian feminist theology is an historical analysis of how patriarchy arose and how it has defined woman as "other," an object to be manipulated and controlled.[8] Her christology is shaped by two theses that rise out of that analysis.[9] The first is that sin is not the hubris of pride that rebels against some divinely ordained hierarchy; rather it is the violation of the basic relations that sustain life on earth, preventing everyone (and everything) involved from developing fully.[10] The primary form that sin takes among human beings is sexism, an unnatural structure that secures male domination over female by defining woman solely in terms of her sexuality. Bolstered by a mythology that makes woman responsible for the advent of evil and that turns female evil into an ontological principle,[11] patriarchal family, social, and cultural systems sustain and perpetuate this primordial sin. Because sexism deforms the most fundamental human relationship, that between man and woman, from mutuality into domination, it is the root of all other relations of domination, whether it be one ethnic group over another, one class over another, or humanity over the rest of creation.[12]

Ruether's second thesis is that classical christology has betrayed both the message and the person of Jesus of Nazareth.[13] He lived and taught an iconoclastic, prophetic reversal of cultural, social, and familial systems of domination and subjugation. "Jesus renew[ed] the prophetic vision whereby the Word of God does not validate the existing social and religious hierarchy but speaks on behalf of the marginalized and despised groups of society."[14] He called for his disciples to become servants of God in the same way that he was, so that they could be freed from every other bond of servitude and would instead become brothers and sisters.[15] Jesus also rejected the nationalistic revenge model of messianic hope and called for the repentance that would bring a time of justice and peace for all peoples.

The community that Jesus gathered around himself and the earliest Christian communities embodied this egalitarian ideal.[16] Rooted in the Hebrew hope for a "Year of the Lord," when God's blessings on Israel would be restored in this world, the hope of Jesus and his followers was for a "this-worldly era of peace and justice,"[17] "a dawning new age in which God's will is done on earth."[18] However, as the Christian movement spread, it took on the Greek philosophical dualism that separated soul from body and that turned redemption into some future escape of the spiritual soul from the imprisonment of the material body. The original message and mission of Jesus were further betrayed when Christianity became the Roman imperial religion; the Christ as *logos* came to be equated with the existing imperial hierarchical order.[19] By identifying the man Jesus of Nazareth with the Logos/Christ, and by eventually attaching the imperial order of the Roman empire to this male Christ, Christianity succumbed to and perpetuated patriarchy's sin of sexism. No longer a prophetic challenge to religious and political institutions, the Christ symbol became the apex of a hierarchical pyramid that again oppressed women, the poor, and the outcast. "[P]atriarchy, hierarchy, slavery, and Greco-Roman imperialism have all been taken over and baptized by the Christian church."[20]

Turning to what she understands as the original message and mission of Jesus, Ruether writes that Christianity must affirm Jesus in every aspect of his particularity—Jewishness, maleness, first-centuryness—and in that affirmation recognize the limitations of Jesus' particularity. What is important is not Jesus' biological particularity, but his person as lived message and practice.[21] Jesus did the work of the Christ, proclaiming to the poor the good news that God loves and liberates those whom society has despised and discarded; he showed the way to live that message by confronting the oppressive religious and social systems of his time, even at the risk of his own life. Jesus enters into the condition of every despised person, suffering with them, becoming a victim like them.[22] He is "the foundational representative of this way of the cross and liberation, [but] he is not its exclusive possibility. Each Christian must also take up this same way . . . becom[ing] 'other Christs.' "[23]

Christ's work continues in the Christian community that still proclaims and lives that good news.[24] Christ takes on the face of every person and every group and every struggle for liberation; therefore, the "one who is to come" cannot be the returning Jesus of Nazareth, glorified and exalted at the right hand of God.[25] This image, too, is contrary to Jesus' own vision and expectation of "the human one" who is to come.[26] Jesus of Nazareth is the paradigmatic example of those who accept and proclaim the redemptive message of God's love for the poor and who live that message by challenging oppressive social and religious structures.[27] But he is only *one* such example. Christ continues as redemptive person and Word of God in the Christian community that looks forward to the redeemed humanity that "goes ahead of us, calling us to yet incompleted dimensions of human liberation."[28]

Redemption means that mutuality is restored and domination ceases to be the norm in human relationships; it happens here on this earth, not in some future "a-historical departure from history and embodied existence."[29] Redemption happens in and through the community of those already redeemed. Just as Jesus accepted baptism by John and became redeemer to those who responded to his message, so each redeemed person is called to become another's redeemer by communicating and living the good news.[30]

Rita Nakashima Brock

Like Rosemary Ruether's, Rita Nakashima Brock's christology is heavily influenced by her understanding of sin.[31] Building on her own experience of abuse and racism and on her work with those who have suffered abuse, she describes sin, not as some universal human condition of guilt or willful disobedience, but as the symptom of brokenheartedness, the damage inflicted to our "original grace" of vulnerability. "Sin is not something to be punished, but something to be healed." [32] Every child is born with the need for and the ability to respond to the kinds of loving, non-damaging relationships that promote and nurture self-awareness and self-acceptance. This original grace reveals itself when the vulnerable heart is free to exercise what Brock calls our erotic power for love. This "fundamental power of life, born into us, heals, makes whole, empowers, and liberates."[33] This is the love that touches others without damaging, and that allows connection and interdependence with other vulnerable, open selves.[34]

Yet there are few, if any, people who reach adulthood without their original vulnerability and trust having been damaged. The patriarchal family, structured around an understanding of power that relies on relationships of domination and dependency to maintain control and authority, is the primary source of that damage. Because the struggle to maintain control and authority always involves coercion, it produces the brokenheartedness that characterizes human existence. Unhealed brokenheartedness is passed from one generation to the next in an unrelieved cycle as each generation's forced dependency on the previous becomes its own domination of the next.[35]

Christianity has taken up the patriarchal understanding of power as domination and authority over others and, like the patriarchal family, Christianity has equated love with obedience to authority.[36] The patriarchal understanding of the human being as guilty of disobedience from the beginning means that Christianity "misplace[s] divine incarnation and human redemption in someone else's perfection and heroic action."[37] The patriarchal understanding of power means that divine presence in the world uniquely manifests itself in the "life of one heroic historical person who is singly identified as Christ."[38] Patriarchal preoccupation with a nostalgic image of father as both loving and punitive means that the hero who saves is the perfect son who is sent to suffer for the rest.[39] Brock writes that as long as Christianity is captive to patriarchy, its central claims (that each person is created in the divine image, that God is love in its fullness, and that the community of believers is a community of justice and peace) are put to the lie.[40] Christologies that are based solely on the divinized hero Jesus of Nazareth are inadequate for transforming patriarchy or healing suffering.[41] "We must find the revelatory and saving events of Christianity in a larger reality than Jesus and his relationship to God/dess."[42]

Brock contends that the reality of human life is that no person comes to be outside of relationship.[43] Like every other human being, Jesus' connections with the world and with other people are constitutive of his being. Jesus loved only because he had first been loved; Jesus was redeemed and liberated only because he belonged to a community of mutual liberation.[44] The community and the healing interconnectedness of those in the community, not Jesus, are the center of Christianity. "What is truly christological, that is, truly revealing of divine incarnation and salvific power in human life, must reside in connectedness and not in single individuals. . . . Jesus neither reveals [the relational nature of erotic power] nor embodies it, but he participates in its revelation and embodiment."[45]

The manifestation of divine power, liberating and moving each person to action for love, justice, and peace in the interconnection of mutuality, is located in what Brock names the Christa/community.[46] The Christ is found not in a single person but in the interconnectedness of the self-aware, self-accepting members of the Christa/community where the abusive power structures that define the patriarchal family are rejected and where the brokenheartedness those structures cause is healed. Shifting the center of Christianity from the person of Jesus to the community of which he was a part exposes the traditional image of Jesus (the perfect, self-sacrificing, and obedient child) as the attempt to maintain and justify the abusive structures of the patriarchal family that it is. The one perfect child does not save by taking on the punishment that the Father would inflict on the others, nor does the Father simply allow that perfect child to get caught up in the punishment that the others deserve.[47]

Jesus' death is not what saves.[48] It is the resurrection community— those who stayed with Jesus as he died and who returned to his grave to care for his body in spite of the risks—that saves. The power of love incarnate revealed in this remnant is not obedience but mutuality, not innocence but responsibility for each other, not fear alone but hope in spite of fear.[49] "Christ is the community remembrance of the Jesus who lived on earth. . . . Jesus' followers refused to let death have the final word. The community bears witness to divine power in us, power in the passion of living persons committed to survival, to giving life to each other, and to a vision of life-as-it-can-be-lived."[50] Christa/community, not the self-sacrificing death of Jesus, is the "revelatory and redemptive witness of God/dess' work in history."[51]

Jacquelyn Grant

Jacquelyn Grant's christological reflections rise out of African American women's experience of oppression and their experience of Jesus' presence as co-sufferer, as liberator, and as equalizer in their struggles to cope with that oppression.[52] Faith in Jesus as God incarnate has been the force that enables African American women to survive the troubles of the world and to move beyond them. For, like African American women, Jesus has been imprisoned by the threefold oppression of sexism, racism, and classism.

In regard to sexism, Grant writes: "Jesus has been imprisoned by patriarchy's obsession with male supremacy."[53] Men in power have defined Christ so as to validate their own positions of privilege in church and society. In the patriarchal view of reality, the divine is most often imaged in terms of what it means to be male; the resulting association between the divine and the male is so pervasive that Jesus' maleness becomes paramount. The emphasis on Jesus' maleness gives rise to a "negative Christology" that distorts both Jesus' personality and Christianity's interpretations of the Christ.[54] Those in power have also exploited Christianity's images of Jesus and God, as well as the imagery for good and evil, in not-so-subtle ways to support white supremacy. Jesus and God have nearly always been pictured as white men; sinlessness and goodness are often associated with the color white. Jesus has been imprisoned by those who would use his supposed whiteness to legitimate the status quo of racial inequality.[55]

Finally, the image of Jesus as servant has been misused consistently to equate the Christian religious ideal of service to others with the socio-political servanthood to which patriarchal systems relegate people who are not of the dominant class. "Servanthood language existentially functions as a deceptive tactic to keep non-dominant culture peoples and the non-privileged of the dominant culture complacent."[56] Jesus, imaged in the white skin of the dominant culture, is imprisoned in a privileged bourgeoisie. He has been made into the image of those "servants of the church" who expect to be served in their positions of privilege, while those who actually are servants, the poor and the oppressed at the margins of society, are disenfranchised.[57]

The predominant image of Jesus in the Christian tradition as privileged, white, and male has functioned to place African American women three steps away from the divine image (as women, as black, and as pressed into socio-economic servanthood).[58] Even so, Jesus has been a central figure in the lives of African American women.[59] By imaging Jesus as co-sufferer and equalizer, as liberator and source of freedom,[60] African American women have liberated Jesus from his imprisonment in the distortions of the tradition just as he has liberated them from their own undeserved suffering. African American women "identified with Jesus because they believed that Jesus identified with them."[61] Because he was also persecuted and made to suffer, Jesus and African American women are able to identify with each other in their cross experiences. Because Jesus is God incarnate, their identification with the suffering Jesus gives African American women the immediate connection with the divine that the tradition has tried to deny them.[62] Because he suffered for all, Jesus Christ makes all people equal and invalidates the oppressive limitations imposed on some by others.[63] As liberator, Jesus Christ empowers African American women, and all oppressed people, for active participation in the struggle for liberation; his message of freedom for captives, whether they be captive to psychological, cultural, and social oppression, or to political and economic oppression, is the grounding for all liberation and protest activities.[64]

Womanist theology does not diminish the role of Jesus of Nazareth in salvation, but instead describes the realities of Jesus' life, his ministry and preaching, his death and resurrection, as the events in which the absolute God becomes concrete.[65] In his ministry and preaching, Jesus identified with the lowly of his own time and he continues to do so in our time.[66] In the American context, those lowly are African American women. Just as Jesus' resurrection meant that there is more to his life than the cross, Jesus' solidarity with the lowly means that African American women's suffering is not the end. Suffering is merely the context within which oppressed people strive to experience hope and liberation.[67]

Grant stresses: "Jesus Christ thus represents a three-fold significance: first he identifies with the 'little people,' African American women, where they are; secondly he affirms the basic humanity of these, 'the least'; and thirdly, he inspires active hope in the struggle for resurrected, liberated existence."[68] This means that as savior of all people it is not Jesus Christ's maleness that is significant, but his humanity, for it is in the humanity of Jesus that God becomes concrete. And it is not only in the man Jesus that the absolute becomes concrete, but "in the lives of those who will accept the challenges of the risen Saviour the Christ."[69] Therefore, the Christ image for today can be found in the experiences of African American women; in fact, Christ can most appropriately be imaged as an African American woman. She is, as much as any, the Suffering Servant who is despised and rejected by men, one who is acquainted with grief, yet is mother, wife, nourisher, sustainer, and preserver of life.[70]

Elizabeth Johnson

For Elizabeth Johnson,[71] the starting point for christology is always the search, undertaken in our present situation within the living tradition of the Christian community as well as within a particular human culture, for a way to articulate the experience of Jesus of Nazareth as the concrete foundation of salvation from God through the power of the Holy Spirit.[72] In the past, Jesus Christ's identity has been "interpreted within a patriarchal framework with the result that the good news of the gospel for all has been twisted into the bad news of male privilege."[73] Searching our "inherited discourse and seek[ing] its scattered rays of truth, hoping to accomplish a critical retrieval in the light of women's coequal humanity,"[74] Johnson finds in the Wisdom tradition a set of symbols and images with which one can interpret Jesus of Nazareth in a way that is indeed good news for women as well as for men.

Wisdom, the personified aspect of God used to signify God's presence and action in the world, has the greatest depth and magnitude of any of the Old Testament images for God. Even though a feminine image, it is the only Old Testament personification that carries the weight of divinity,[75] and it is among the first of the Old Testament symbols that were attached to Jesus.[76] Understanding Jesus as the one who spoke Wisdom's words and who embodied Wisdom's ways meant understanding Jesus as the one who personifies God's own self, coming toward the world, dwelling in it, and ever active for its well-being. Jesus came to be understood as God's only-begotten only after he was identified with Wisdom.[77] Wisdom categories also enabled the early Christian communities to give cosmic significance to the crucified and risen Christ; Jesus Christ's saving deeds were in continuity with Wisdom's activity in history.[78]

The narrative memory of Jesus' life, death, and resurrection and of the pouring out of the Holy Spirit that has been preserved by the Christian community is the framework within which Jesus can be recognized as the concrete foundation of salvation. He shows us the way of divine compassion in the midst of historical sin, death, and defeat. The community's living memory and remembrance of Jesus give hope for the future by showing that God is present in the continuing struggle against suffering and oppression.[79]

However, the community's narrative and memory have been distorted by an anthropology that relies on gender dualism. Such dualism results in a christology that makes Jesus' maleness an ontological necessity, that gives the male sex greater dignity as the normative way of being human, and that leaves women's salvation in jeopardy.[80] A remedy for this distortion can be found by turning to the feminine figure of Wisdom.[81] Describing the man Jesus as the incarnation of the feminine Wisdom subverts gender dualism and supports a more egalitarian and inclusive anthropology.[82] Such an anthropology recognizes the reality that each human person is the embodiment of a unique combination of essential human characteristics (of which sexuality is only one) who exists in mutuality and reciprocity with other human persons who incarnate their own unique combination of those characteristics.[83] This human "interdependence of difference" means that Jesus' maleness, while part of his historic personal identity, cannot be made determinative for his identity as Christ. Nor can Jesus' maleness be made into the normative Christian identity.[84] "[T]he typical stereotypes of masculine and feminine are subverted as female *Sophia* represents creative transcendence, primordial passion for justice and knowledge of the truth while Jesus expresses these divine characteristics in an immanent way relative to bodiliness and the earth."[85]

Jesus is the one who announces that God wills the wholeness and full humanity of every person, especially those who are poor and oppressed. He makes concrete Sophia's drawing near in his preaching, healing, and exorcisms. He embodies Sophia's inclusiveness by expanding the table community to include those who are most disvalued and by forming those who follow him into a discipleship of equals.[86] Jesus' death was not required by God as repayment for sin; it was, rather, "a dialectic of disaster and powerful human love through which the gracious God of Jesus enters into solidarity with all those who suffer and are lost."[87] Evil, however, does not have the last word, for the crucified one is not abandoned; Sophia-God gathers her child into the "new, transformed life that is the promise of a future for all the dead and for the whole cosmos itself."[88]

Jesus in his historical, physical, and spiritual reality has been raised into glory by the power of the Spirit.[89] The glorified Jesus, animating the body which is the whole church, is the Christ, and the community of believers shares in Jesus' Christhood since it too participates in Christ's living and dying and rising.[90] The body of the risen Christ cannot be limited to the one man Jesus of Nazareth, nor can it be limited to select members of the community; all, regardless of ethnicity, gender, or class, are one in Christ.[91] All the particularities of earthly existence are brought together in life with God through the risen Christ.[92]

These thumbnail sketches of four examples from the body of feminist work in christology do not begin to do justice to the complexity of each person's work. However, they do give an idea of the images of Christ in each woman's work and why each has described the Christ the way that she has. But before we can ask any questions regarding the kind of spirituality they might support, it will be helpful to describe briefly the aspects of Christian spirituality that will shape those questions.

Christian Spirituality: Grounded in Christ

Spirituality is that aspect of human life that gives evidence of the innate human capacity for self-transcendence; it is a capacity for reaching out to others from the center of one's own self in love, freedom, and truth. In a religious context, that capacity for self-transcendence is set into motion by what a person considers to be of ultimate value. In the specifically Christian religious context, it is the experience of God in Jesus Christ by the gift of the Spirit that brings the human capacity for self-transcending knowledge, love, and commitment to actuality.[93]

Spirituality involves the whole person in every dimension of life. For many people, it may be a largely unconscious, unexamined pattern of behavior that takes its form from convention or social expectations. But for many others, spirituality is a conscious, explicitly reflected upon and developed movement toward psychological and spiritual maturity. Anne Carr helpfully stresses that in the Christian context that movement toward integrated wholeness rests on "the conviction that God is indeed personal and that we are in immediate personal relationship to another, an Other who 'speaks' and can be spoken to, who really affects our lives."[94] As such, Christian spirituality often involves an intensely personal relationship with God; yet, because it affects every aspect of human life, Christian spirituality inevitably finds expression in one's response to the situations, individuals, and communities that make up the concrete context of each person's life. One's personal movement toward self-transcendence augments and is augmented by (or diminishes and is diminished by) the movement of the communities and relationships of which one is a part.

For women, the movement toward self-transcendence, toward holiness, toward integrated maturity, takes place within a community whose own self-expression has risen out of a cultural bias against the female that is so pervasive as to be as invisible as the air we breathe.

Mature spirituality depends on the full development of the whole human being. Yet women's development as human beings has been restricted by an anthropology that holds up the male as the normative way of being human and that either completely dis-values the qualities it assigns to the female or makes the female so "other" from the male that she is considered only for her role in reproduction.[95] Christian teaching and practice have exacerbated the problem of women's restricted development by holding up as virtuous the kind of self-effacing, self-denying behavior that in reality stunts a person's growth, and by condemning as sinful in a woman behavior that is actually a sign of her being a mature, self-aware, emotionally stable person.[96] Women's development has been further hampered by the distortion of biblical revelation that ignores both the feminine images for God and the central fact of God's existence as Spirit, who is neither male nor female. The result is that everyone, male and female, absorbs only masculine images for God. Without feminine (or at least non-masculine) images, women lack any context in which to value and affirm themselves as truly being in the image of God.[97]

Christian spirituality, as Anne Clifford rightly notes, "reaches toward the God revealed in Jesus Christ, through the grace of the Holy Spirit."[98] It is a response to the invitation to intimacy with God offered through Jesus Christ. It is a way of life, undertaken by individuals in company with others who respond to that invitation. It is a response to the person Jesus Christ who is mediated by the community, especially when gathered in worship, and who is encountered in personal prayer. It is discipleship.[99] Yet images of Christ from the tradition have distorted the person of Jesus Christ and thus the community of disciples who are also the Body of Christ, exalting the male over the female, the Caucasian over the colored, the Greek (or European or North American) over the Jew (or African or Asian or South American). Thus, the work of feminist theologians on re-imaging God and Christ is an important element of reclaiming the vision that in Christ there is no more division, that every person's gifts are recognized, valued, and accepted for the good of the whole community, the church that is the Body of Christ.

Conclusion

The question is whether the images of Christ proposed by the four feminist theologians discussed in this essay "work" as a basis for Christian spirituality. They do address the anthropological distortions that have functioned to keep women from a participation in the life of the Christian community that truly reflects their own dignity as *imago Dei*. But will they also bring to actuality the capacity for self-transcendence in each individual, especially in women? Will they also bring to actuality the capacity for self-transcendence in the community of believers as a whole? Do they reflect "the conviction that God is indeed personal and that we are in immediate personal relationship to another, an Other who 'speaks' and can be spoken to, who really affects our lives?"[100] Do they foster a personal, intimate relationship with Christ that leads to and includes a relationship with God in the Holy Spirit?

Returning to the images discussed earlier, recall that Rita Brock describes Jesus as one of the many who participate in the revelation and embodiment of divine, salvific power in human life. Christ, that revelation and embodiment in which Jesus and his followers participate, is the inter-connectedness among the members of the Christa/community that heals brokenheartedness and overcomes the damage inflicted by the patriarchal family with the healing power of erotic love. In her effort to counter the classical christology that she says relies on and perpetuates the abusive parent/submissive child model characteristic of the patriarchal family (the powerful father-God demands that the perfect, submissive son take on the punishment of his disobedient siblings), she diminishes the role of Jesus. His role is really no different from that of any other Christian who finds her true self in the context of a community of self-aware and self-affirming selves, and then invites others to enter into the healing relationships that community offers. In Jesus, "[w]e claim a distant partner who participates in our search for life whole and healed."[101]

With Jesus as a "distant partner" and the Christ located in the relatedness of Christa/community, one must ask where is the person with whom the individual believer can develop the personal relationship that grounds Christian spirituality. Developing the kind of intimate relationships that make up Christa/community may indeed activate the capacity for self-transcendence in both the individual and the community as a whole. However, Brock has presented such an abstract image of Christ, an image that is so separated from the person of Jesus of Nazareth, that one must ask how an intimate, personal relationship with that Christ could be possible.

Rosemary Ruether describes Jesus as the iconoclast prophet, the historical figure who showed the way to live without acquiescing to one's own oppressive privilege. It was his example of standing and suffering in solidarity with the despised and outcast, not his death, that brought the hope of salvation into the world; that hope was not for deliverance from death, but deliverance from unjust suffering and premature violent death.[102] Like all human beings, Jesus' death meant that his "existence cease[d] as individuated ego/organism and dissolve[d] back into the cosmic matrix of matter/energy from which new centers of individuation arise."[103] And like every other earth creature, Jesus is resurrected when the physical components of his body "disintegrate into the earth so that another may arise from its womb."[104] The Christ, liberated humanity, redemptive person, and Word of God, continues in the community of those who follow in Jesus' way.[105]

Ruether presents Jesus as an example from times past who challenges us to follow in his footsteps, confronting oppression and evil even at the risk of life and limb. Such an example can and does actuate both the individual's and the community's capacity for self-transcendence. However, because Jesus' continued personal existence is something about which we must be agnostic,[106] the Christ becomes an abstract ideal associated more with the community than with the concrete person Jesus of Nazareth. Even though Ruether describes Jesus as more than a "distant partner," she still abstracts Christ from the person of Jesus in a way that leads one to question whether a personal relationship with Christ that brings one to relationship with God in the Holy Spirit is possible.

The images of Christ that Rosemary Ruether and Rita Brock describe do address the anthropological problems that come from emphasizing the maleness of Jesus. They address the distortion of authority and power that rise out of Christianity's absorption of patriarchal systems. And they address Christianity's appropriation of Greek philosophical systems that devalue the material world while at the same time associating women with that materiality. In the process of addressing those problems, however, the connection between Jesus of Nazareth and the Christ becomes so tenuous that the Christ appears to be some impersonal, idealized vision of relationship in community or of liberated humanity.

On the other hand, the womanist christology described by Jacquelyn Grant and the Wisdom christology described by Elizabeth Johnson indicate ways that the Christ can be imaged that both affirm women in their full humanity and do not diminish the role of Jesus. Their recon-structions of christology retain an explicit connection between him and the Christ without denying the members of the community of dis-ciples their own christic character. The two sets of images that come out of those christologies—Christ as co-sufferer, equalizer, and lib-erator, and Christ as Wisdom incarnate—also address the anthropo-logical and philosophical issues of gender and dualism, as well as the cultural issues of classism, racism, and sexism.

Held together, these sets of images present a Christ who does actu-ate the human capacity for self-transcendence. Christ as co-sufferer and liberator is one with whom any person or community who struggles against oppression and injustice can develop a personal relationship of mutuality and reciprocity. Christ as Wisdom of God incarnate is one through whom, with whom, and in whom the individual and com-munity can give thanks and praise to God in union with the Holy Spirit. This Christ, still intimately connected with Jesus, is personal rather than an abstract ideal. And it is this personal Christ who supports "the conviction that God is indeed personal and that we are in immediate personal relationship to another, an Other who 'speaks' and can be spoken to, who really affects our lives."[107]

Epilogue

This essay is prompted by the sense of disconnect that has arisen between my own experience and the theology that I have read. That disconnect is the classic locus for feminist theological reflection; how-ever, the theology in this case is not that of the classic Christian tradi-tion (although there is a disconnect there as well), but feminist theol-ogy. And the experience from which that theology is disconnected is my personal spirituality, my personal encounter with the divine present and active in my life in prayer. Of course, it is entirely possible that my spirituality is not yet truly mature and for that reason I find Christ as described by Rosemary Radford Ruether and Rita Nakashima Brock too impersonal. Yet, my spirituality is no unreflective, pie-in-the-sky spirituality; it is the result of a lifelong search for the appropriate re-sponse to encounters with the divine—and the not-so-divine—in my own quite ordinary situation (Caucasian, middle-aged, middle-class, mid-western American, Roman Catholic). It is a spirituality that has grown and sustained me in the difficulties and joys of being daughter and sister, friend and wife, mother and grandmother, career person, victim of sexual assault, and caretaker and deathbed companion for elderly parents.

Rosemary Radford Ruether and Rita Nakashima Brock have provided me with the concepts and vocabulary with which to understand and to articulate my own experience. Their reflections on how relationship and community might be re-visioned so as to recognize and increase God's saving power in the world ring true with my own experience of relationship and community. Their exposure of the ways that nearly every human institution perpetuates sexism, racism, and classism is on target. Still, there is that nagging sense of disconnect between my own experience of the divine in a rather ordinary life and their theological systems. Comparing the Christ images presented by Ruether and Brock with those presented by Jacquelyn Grant and Elizabeth Johnson points to the source of that disconnect: the way each woman describes the relationship between Jesus of Nazareth and the Christ. It seems that only a personal Christ, anchored in time and space by a strong connection with Jesus of Nazareth, can support the spirituality that grows out of my own prayerful reflection on experience. However, there must be an on-going dialogue between theology and experience, a dialogue that questions theological reflection in light of one's own experience of the divine, and then continues to use the insight of that reflection to question the cultural, social, and personal elements that shape one's experience. This essay is but one phase of that continuing dialogue.

Notes

[1]Examples from the authors who shape this essay: Rita Nakashima Brock, *Journeys by Heart: A Christology of Erotic Power* (New York: Crossroad, 1988), especially chap. 3; Jacquelyn Grant, *White Women's Christ and Black Women's Jesus: Feminist Christology and Womanist Response*, AAR Academy Series 64 (Atlanta: Scholars Press, 1989), especially chap. 2; Elizabeth A. Johnson, "Redeeming the Name of Christ" in *Freeing Theology: The Essentials of Theology in Feminist Perspective*, ed. Catherine Mowry LaCugna (San Francisco: HarperSanFrancisco, 1993), 115-37; Rosemary Radford Ruether, "Can Christology Be Liberated from Patriarchy?" in *Reconstructing the Christ Symbol: Essays in Feminist Christology*, ed. Mary Ann Stevens (New York: Paulist Press, 1993), 7-29.

[2]See Rosemary Radford Ruether, *Introducing Redemption in Christian Femi-*

nism, Introducing Feminist Theology, vol. 2, ed. Mary Grey et al. (Cleveland: Pilgrim Press, 2000), 90-1.

[3]See Rosemary Radford Ruether, *Sexism and God-Talk: Toward a Feminist Theology* (Boston: Beacon Press, 1983) 122-26; Elizabeth A. Johnson, *She Who Is: The Mystery of God in Feminist Theological Discourse* (New York: Crossroad, 1992), 151-54.

[4]See Rosemary Radford Ruether, *To Change the World: Christology and Cultural Criticism* (New York: Crossroad, 1983), 24-6.

[5]One has only to page through service books for any Christian denomination to find a myriad of examples, from fundamentalist to ultra-liberal, of how Christians continue the tradition described in Romans 8:15 and Galatians 4:6 of praying to God in Jesus' name in the power of the Spirit who enables Christians to "cry out 'Abba, Father!' "

[6]While not every communal act of worship is eucharistic, Eucharist, breaking bread and sharing the cup in memory of Jesus, is the uniquely Christian form of worship. It is true that many find Eucharist to be painful and alienating; not only are some excluded from ordained ministry simply because of who they are, but the ritual tradition is permeated with hierarchical, patriarchal overtones and undertones that only serve to reinforce a climate of domination and control within the Christian community beyond the immediate experience of the eucharistic banquet. Nevertheless, Eucharist has been and is the definitive Christian communal celebration. One can only hope that every person called to share in the meal in whatever capacity will eventually find the seat that has been prepared for her.

[7]These four women were among the speakers at a symposium on feminist christology at Creighton University in 1992 that was my introduction to Christian feminist theology. Each has made significant contributions to feminist theological discourse: an analysis of the development of patriarchy and the results of its objectification of woman (Ruether), an analysis of the use of Christian symbols to sacralize the abuse fostered by patriarchal family structures (Brock), the necessity of recognizing that racism and classism are equally sinful distortions of Jesus' message of salvation (Grant), and the ways that feminine images might be retrieved from the Christian tradition and used to speak of the triune God (Johnson). The papers from that symposium have been collected in Stevens, ed., *Reconstructing the Christ Symbol.*

[8]Rosemary Radford Ruether identifies herself as a Catholic Christian feminist who is also a white, middle-class American. See *Disputed Questions: On Being a Christian* (1981; Maryknoll, N.Y.: Orbis Books, 1989) for Ruether's autobiographical account of the development of her thought. Also see *Women and Redemption: A Theological History* (Minneapolis: Fortress Press, 1998), 221-24.

[9]The themes discussed here run throughout Ruether's work. See *To Change the World,* especially 45-56; *Sexism and God-Talk,* especially 116-38; *Introducing Redemption,* especially 81-94; and the entire essay "Can Christology Be Liberated?"

[10]See *Sexism and God-Talk,* chap. 7, especially 173-83, and *Introducing Redemption,* chap. 5, for extended discussions of sin and evil.

[11]Ruether, *Sexism and God-Talk*, 168.

[12]Ruether, *Introducing Redemption*, 73.

[13]See *Sexism and God-Talk*, chap. 5, especially 116 and 122-26, for Ruether's assessment of the development of christology. See also *To Change the Earth*, 17-18, 24, and 45-53, and "Can Christology Be Liberated?" 17-20.

[14]Ruether, *Sexism and God-Talk*, 136; see also *Introducing Redemption*, 93, and "Can Christology Be Liberated?" 23-4.

[15]Ruether, *Sexism and God-Talk*, 121; see also *To Change the World*, 53-5.

[16]See *Women and Redemption*, 14-24, for Ruether's description of the egalitarian nature of the first communities of the Jesus movement. See also *Introducing Redemption*, 17-20.

[17]Ruether, *To Change the World*, 14.

[18]Ruether, *Sexism and God-Talk*, 138.

[19]Ruether, *To Change the World*, 24-5, 48-9; *Sexism and God-Talk*, 124-25.

[20]Ruether, *To Change the World*, 48-9.

[21]Ruether, *Sexism and God-Talk*, 137-38; *Introducing Redemption*, 93-94; and "Can Christology Be Liberated?" 23-25; see also *To Change the World*, 38-39.

[22]Ruether, *Introducing Redemption*, 67.

[23]Ruether, "Can Christology Be Liberated?" 24; see also *Introducing Redemption*, 93.

[24]Ruether, *Sexism and God-Talk*, 138; *Introducing Redemption*, 93-94.

[25]Ruether, *Introducing Redemption*, 94.

[26]Ruether, *Sexism and God-Talk*, 121-22.

[27]Ruether, *Introducing Redemption*, 93.

[28]Ruether, *Sexism and God-Talk*, 138.

[29]Ruether, "Can Christology Be Liberated?" 20.

[30]Ruether, *Sexism and God-Talk*, 138.

[31]Rita Nakashima Brock is a mixed-race Asian American and an ordained minister in the United Church of Christ. *Proverbs of Ashes: Violence, Redemptive Suffering and the Search for What Saves Us*, with Rebecca Ann Parker (Boston: Beacon Press, 2000), contains several autobiographical essays that trace Brock's theological development. She develops her christology most fully in *Journeys by Heart: A Christology of Erotic Power*. See also "Losing Your Innocence, But Not Your Hope" in *Reconstructing the Christ Symbol*, 30-52; "And a Little Child Will Lead Us: Christology and Child Abuse," in *Christianity, Patriarchy and Abuse: A Feminist Critique*, ed. Joanne Carlson Brown and Carole R. Bohn (Cleveland: Pilgrim Press, 1989), 42-61; and "The Feminist Redemption of Christ" in *Christian Feminism: Visions of a New Humanity*, ed. Judith L. Weidman (San Francisco: Harper & Row, 1984), 55-74.

[32]See Brock, *Journeys by Heart*, 7.

[33]Ibid., 25.

[34]Ibid., 23-24.

[35]See "And a Little Child Will Lead Us," 43-50, and *Journeys by Heart*, 9-16, for Brock's description of the ways that patriarchal family structure damages the child.

[36]Brock, "Losing Your Innocence," 37-38; see also *Journeys by Heart*, 49 and 54.

[37]Brock, *Journeys by Heart*, 9.

[38]Ibid., 53.

[39]Ibid., 55-56; see also "Losing Your Innocence," 37-38.

[40]Brock, *Journeys by Heart*, 50.

[41]Ibid., 51; see also "The Feminist Redemption of Christ," 68-71.

[42]Brock, *Journeys by Heart*, 68; see also "The Feminist Redemption of Christ," 68-69.

[43]Brock, *Journeys by Heart*, 62-63.

[44]Ibid., 66-67.

[45]Ibid., 52.

[46]See ibid., 66-70, for Brock's development of the notion of Christa/community. This is similar to her description of the "resurrection community" and the "saving remnant" in "Losing Your Innocence," 50-51.

[47]Brock, *Journeys by Heart*, 55.

[48]Brock, "Losing Your Innocence," 50; see also *Journeys by Heart*, 51-52.

[49]Brock, "Losing Your Innocence," 50; see also *Journeys by Heart*, 98-100.

[50]Brock, "The Feminist Redemption of Christ," 70; see also *Journeys by Heart*, 100-04.

[51]Brock, *Journeys by Heart*, 69.

[52]Jacquelyn Grant is an African American theologian who is also an ordained elder in the African Methodist Episcopal Church. *White Women's Christ and Black Women's Jesus: Feminist Christology and Womanist Response* is the fullest development of her christology. See also "'Come to My Help Lord, For I'm in Trouble': Womanist Jesus and the Mutual Struggle for Liberation" in *Reconstructing the Christ Symbol*, 54-71, and "Jesus and the Task of Redemption" in *We Belong Together: Churches in Solidarity with Women*, ed. Sarah Cunningham (New York: Friendship Press, 1992), 30-42.

[53]Grant, "Come to My Help, Lord," 58.

[54]Grant's analysis of the role of patriarchy in christological discourse may be found in "Come to My Help, Lord," 57-59, and *White Women's Christ and Black Women's Jesus*, 68-74.

[55]See "Come to My Help, Lord," 59-63, for Grant's analysis of racism in Christian theology in general, and *White Women's Christ and Black Women's Jesus*, 199-205, for her analysis of racism in feminist theology.

[56]Grant, "Come to My Help, Lord," 65; see also *White Women's Christ and Black Women's Jesus*, 209-10.

[57]See "Come to My Help, Lord," 63-66, and *White Women's Christ and Black Women's Jesus*, 209-10, for Grant's assessment of the relationship between religion and classism.

[58]Grant, "Come to My Help, Lord," 65-66; *White Women's Christ and Black Women's Jesus*, 209-10; "Jesus and the Task of Redemption," 39-40.

[59]Grant, *White Women's Christ and Black Women's Jesus*, 212; "Come to My Help, Lord," 55-56; "Jesus and the Task of Redemption," 39.

[60]These four images (co-sufferer, liberator, equalizer, and source of freedom) are developed in "Come to My Help, Lord," 66-69. See also *White Women's Christ and Black Women's Jesus*, 213-18, and "Jesus and the Task of Redemption," 39-40.

[61]Grant, *White Women's Christ and Black Women's Jesus*, 212; see also "Come to My Help, Lord," 67, and "Jesus and the Task of Redemption," 40.

[62]Grant, "Come to My Help, Lord," 67; see also *White Women's Christ and Black Women's Jesus*, 212-14, and "Jesus and the Task of Redemption, 40.

[63]Grant, "Jesus and the Task of Redemption," 41.

[64]Grant, *White Women's Christ and Black Women's Jesus*, 214; "Come to My Help, Lord," 69; "Jesus and the Task of Redemption," 41.

[65]Grant, *White Women's Christ and Black Women's Jesus*, 214; "Come to My Help, Lord," 69.

[66]Grant, *White Women's Christ and Black Women's Jesus*, 215.

[67]Ibid., 217.

[68]Ibid.

[69]Ibid., 220.

[70]Ibid., 218, citing William Eichelberger, "Reflections on the Person and Personality of the Black Messiah," *The Black Church II* (n.d.): 14-16.

[71]Elizabeth A. Johnson is a member of the Congregation of the Sisters of St. Joseph, Brentwood, New York. She identifies herself with these words: "I write in the context of white, academic, middle-class, American culture, yet I seek to be aware of the sufferings of all women in this country and around the world" ("Redeeming the Name of Christ," 118). Her treatment of christology may be found in "Wisdom Was Made Flesh and Pitched Her Tent among Us" in *Reconstructing the Christ Symbol*, 95-117; "Redeeming the Name of Christ: Christology" in *Freeing Theology: The Essentials of Theology in Feminist Perspective*, 115-27; and "Jesus-Sophia," in *She Who Is: The Mystery of God in Feminist Theological Discourse* (New York: Crossroad, 1996), 150-69. See also *Consider Jesus: Waves of Renewal in Christology* (New York: Crossroad, 1990); "Jesus and Salvation," *CTSA Proceedings* 49 (1994), 1-18; and "The Word Was Made Flesh and Dwelt among Us: Jesus Research and Christian Faith" in *Jesus: A Colloquium in the Holy Land*, ed. Doris Donnelly (New York: Continuum, 2001), 146-66.

[72]Johnson, "Jesus and Salvation," 2 and 18.

[73]Johnson, "Redeeming the Name of Christ," 118.

[74]Johnson, *She Who Is*, 10.

[75]Johnson, "Redeeming the Name of Christ," 121; see also "Wisdom Was Made Flesh," 98-102.

[76]Johnson, "Redeeming the Name of Christ," 121; "Wisdom Was Made Flesh," 103-05.

[77]Johnson, "Wisdom Was Made Flesh," 105-06; "Redeeming the Name of Christ," 121.

[78]Johnson, "Redeeming the Name of Christ," 120-21; "Wisdom Was Made Flesh," 105.

[79]Johnson, "Jesus and Salvation," 18.

[80]Johnson, *She Who Is*, 151-54; "Redeeming the Name of Christ," 118-20.

[81]Johnson, "Redeeming the Name of Christ," 122; *She Who Is*, 154.

[82]Johnson, "Wisdom Was Made Flesh," 108; "Redeeming the Name of Christ," 127-28.

[83]See Johnson, *She Who Is*, 154-56, for a discussion of multipolar anthropology.

[84]Ibid., 156.

[85]Johnson, "Wisdom Was Made Flesh," 108. See also "Redeeming the Name of Christ," 128, and *She Who Is*, 165.

[86]Johnson, *She Who Is*, 157-58; see also "Wisdom Was Made Flesh," 106-10.

[87]Johnson, *She Who Is*, 159.

[88]Ibid., 159.

[89]Ibid., 163.

[90]Johnson, "Redeeming the Name of Christ," 128.

[91]Johnson, *She Who Is*, 161-62.

[92]Johnson, "Redeeming the Name of Christ," 128.

[93]See Joann Wolski Conn, "Toward Spiritual Maturity—Spirituality" in *Freeing Theology: The Essentials of Theology in Feminist Perspective*, ed. Catherine Mowry LaCugna (San Francisco: HarperSanFrancisco, 1993), 235-37. See also her essay "Women's Spirituality: Restriction and Reconstruction" in *Women's Spirituality: Resources for Christian Development*, ed. Joann Wolski Conn (New York: Paulist Press, 1986), 9-10.

[94]Anne E. Carr, "On Feminist Spirituality" in *Horizons on Catholic Feminist Theology*, ed. Joann Wolski Conn and Walter E. Conn (Washington, D.C.: Georgetown University Press, 1992), 136.

[95]Conn, "Women's Spirituality," 10-11.

[96]Ibid., 11-12. For influential discussions of the way that traditional, androcentric definitions of sin and virtue harm women, see Valerie Saiving Goldstein, "The Human Situation: A Feminist Perspective," *The Journal of Religion* 40 (1960): 100-12, and Judith Plaskow, *Sex, Sin and Grace: Women's Experience and the Theologies of Reinhold Niebuhr and Paul Tillich* (New York: American University Press, 1980).

[97]Conn, "Women's Spirituality," 14-17; see also Sandra Schneiders, "The Effects of Women's Experience on Their Spirituality" in *Women's Spirituality: Resources for Christian Development*, 41-44.

[98]Anne M. Clifford, *Introducing Feminist Theology* (Maryknoll, N.Y.: Orbis Books, 2001), 210.

[99]Lawrence S. Cunningham and Keith J. Egan, *Christian Spirituality: Themes from the Tradition* (New York: Paulist Press, 1996), 9-14.

[100]Carr, "On Feminist Spirituality," 136.

[101]Brock, "The Feminist Redemption of Christ," 69.

[102]Ruether, *Introducing Redemption*, 106.

[103]Ruether, *Sexism and God-Talk*, 257. See also *Introducing Redemption*, 118-19.

[104]This, for Ruether, is "the only resurrection of the dead" (*Introducing Redemption*, 120).

[105]Ruether, *Sexism and God-Talk*, 137-38.

[106]Ibid., 256-58. Ruether's discussion of personal eschatology is not explicitly applied to Jesus of Nazareth; however, since Jesus is human, one may presume that her description of the end of human life applies to him.

[107]Carr, "On Feminist Spirituality," 136.

The Practice of Teaching Christology

The Evolution of an Undergraduate Christology Course

Patricia A. Plovanich

Introduction

The practice of teaching engages a professor in an endeavor that builds bridges between the teacher's scholarly understandings and the students' learning. Ten years of teaching christology to undergraduates at the University of San Diego has led to these reflections on the progressive dynamics of that "bridge building" and how my christology course has evolved. I suspect that many teachers of christology will see in the process some reflection of similar dynamics in their own courses.

The course evolved through four stages. At the first stage the professor, with a newly minted doctorate, is faced with the question of how to adapt the course model and content studied in graduate school for use with undergraduates. This stage may require relinquishing that pattern altogether in favor of a model better suited to undergraduate teaching. The second stage brought further adaptation: incorporating elements gleaned from graduate education as well as tailoring the course to the models and syllabi of department colleagues. Then, in time, teaching experience and recent publications in the field prompt experimentation with the course model, resulting in a third stage.

The last stage begins when one's grasp of the christological literature fosters a course that more effectively builds a bridge between the teacher's understanding and the students' learning. While committed to presenting major developments in the christological tradition and incorporating elements from current scholarly discussions, the course at this last stage draws on the intellectual capital of graduate education but is also oriented to the life and faith experience of the students. This requires that attention be given to how their geographical and cultural locations shape their lives.

In what follows, I will trace the changes that have yielded my present course in christology, taking into account the course's developmental stages as well as the influences that prompted them.

"Jesus in Christian Tradition"—A Course History

Stage 1: From Graduate Student to Professor

As a graduate student at Fordham University in the 1970s, I took courses in christology in which the professors used several approaches. One model favored the study of contemporary authors, such as Rudolf Bultmann and Karl Rahner. Another used a chronological approach, tracing the topic's historical development through the study of historical texts. Assigned to teach christology at the University of San Diego in 1990, I was given a course entitled "Jesus in Christian Tradition" with this catalogue description: "a critical investigation of the person and ministry of Jesus in light of scripture and the Christian tradition." Since neither graduate model fit this design, abandoning them was necessary; I hoped, nonetheless, that they would provide intellectual capital for future course development.

Stage 2: Adapting the Courses of Colleagues

My first course adopted the outline and some texts from a colleague's syllabus. The course model used a triadic structure of the historical Jesus, the Christ of high christology, and a contemporary reconsideration of Jesus the Christ. The schema required teaching students a new vocabulary that would distinguish between the historical Jesus and the Christ of faith, and ascending (low) and descending (high) christologies. Students read the Gospels of Mark and Matthew along with Günther Bornkamm's *Jesus of Nazareth* for the latter component. St. Athanasius' *On the Incarnation* provided an apt example of high christology and the dogmatic view of Christ. The text selected for study of a contemporary view of Jesus' life and meaning was

Monika Hellwig's *Jesus, the Compassion of God*.[1] When time permitted, the course ended with student proposals about contemporary ways
to explain Jesus Christ's historical and dogmatic reality.

The course design presumed an internal logic that effectively served
pedagogical issues and provided a careful study of Jesus of Nazareth.
In an abbreviated way, it communicated a sense of the tradition's historical sequence as a unitary interpretative trajectory. The sequence of
topics and texts also supported the goal of learning the terminology
and different approaches (high, low, biblical, dogmatic, and so on) of
contemporary christologies. In general, I judged the model successful.

Student response was favorable. Exams and course essays showed
a general comprehension of course content. Still, viewpoints expressed
in student work hinted that perspectives taught were only minimally
comprehended. Some students revealed a tenacious dedication to the
high christology of their childhood religious education in their tendency to distinguish gospel events, even the infancy and resurrection
narratives, as alternately demonstrating Jesus' humanity and divinity.
Other students took an adoptionist stance, distinguishing the high/low
models with phrases such as "before Jesus became the Christ," or they
interpreted Jesus using the paradigm of other memorable historical
figures. These problems still did not alter my commitment to the model,
and I retained the syllabus outline and texts without major modifica-
tion for several years.

My confidence in the model's validity, however, was shaken by
questions raised in other contexts, questions related to scholarship on
the historical Jesus and the use of scripture. Discussions with a rabbi
who teaches a course on Judaism challenged my presentation of the
historical Jesus, which made no reference to the Jewish context and
cast of Jesus' life and historical world. Mary R. D'Angelo's article
"*Abba* and 'Father': Imperial Theology and the Jesus Traditions"[2] challenged Jesus' *Abba* relationship with God, a common feature in historical Jesus studies. D'Angelo cautioned further that gospels do not
offer direct access to Jesus but instead represent early Christian communities' memories and constructions; she urged theologians to be
more attentive to the factual biblical and historical heritage of
christology. These considerations prompted my first major effort to
redesign the course.

Stage 3: A Course in Transition

My first decision was to select new texts to support topic alteration. One concern was finding texts that establish the Jewish context of historical Jesus study. Another was determining sources that provided a broader study of New Testament christology. Experimentation with these concepts and with new texts signaled the topical revisions of this stage. Bernard Lee's texts, *The Galilean Jewishness of Jesus* and *Jesus and the Metaphors of God*,[3] seemed apt studies of Jesus, but most students could not grasp their theoretical perspectives. Two other works provided reviews of biblical christology and of Christ images in later tradition. *Who Is This Christ?*[4] by Reginald Fuller and Pheme Perkins offered a broad review of New Testament christologies as well as references to the issues of cultural change and world religions. To explore later tradition, I used Gerald Sloyan's *The Jesus Tradition* and Jaroslav Pelikan's *Jesus through the Centuries*[5] in alternate semesters to provide useful surveys of the historical development of Christ images. *The Clowns of God*[6] by Morris West offered an interesting reflection on contemporary Christ images for one class, but the work did not elicit much interest from students living in an era of prosperity and peace. For the course's final unit (contemporary interpretations of Jesus Christ), I eventually wrote summaries of new contextual christologies, explaining the concerns of these works and their links to the tradition.

These changes provided broader examples of the christological tradition than did the first model. The reflection on Judaism was a particularly rewarding perspective for thought about Jesus of Nazareth. The historical selections illustrating christology's biblical and historical development were well received. In concept, however, the original course goals and the outline emphasizing a unitary development of the christological tradition remained unchanged, although the new model featured a four-part sequence: the historical Jesus, the New Testament Christ of faith, the Christian tradition's doctrinal Christ, and contemporary interpretations of Jesus Christ. I used this third model for four years.

Eventually, I turned to two new studies because juggling three or four books proved awkward. Both promised a way to consolidate important elements in one text. William P. Loewe's *The College Student's Introduction to Christology*[7] permitted retention of the four-part structure. It consolidated the historical viewpoint in one text written for the undergraduate reader. Loewe's work clearly delineates the ascending/ descending approaches to christology. It provides a remarkably readable summary of the historical Jesus enterprise and an insightful review of different Christian responses to the quest. The author's own construction of the historical Jesus is an interesting summary of scholarly discussions, and students easily followed his delineation of the historical move from biblical to dogmatic interpretation. In general, Loewe's work well served many of my evolving goals for the course. However, it did not address all of my concerns, especially my commitment to make the students aware of the Jewish context of Jesus, nor did it seem to take sufficiently into consideration the diverse christological traditions of the New Testament.

To address these concerns, I adopted Gerald O'Collins's *Christology*,[8] which provided a complete and well-crafted review of the tradition's development and diversity. However, its dense topical presentation proved too technical for my students and it lacked attention to a recent development in scholarly literature that interested me, namely, the contextual approaches to christology. I used this text for only one semester, but its value lay elsewhere. O'Collins's dedication to describing the variety of christologies throughout history confirmed a shift in my own thinking. I adopted an approach favoring a review of the tradition's diversity in a chronological format instead of the unitary historical model of the first- and second-stage courses.

Stage 4: My Own Course

After a decade of experimentation, course development has progressed to what I call a fourth stage: it emphasizes the faith tradition's past and present factual diversity as the foundational principle in course method and content. This stage represents more than a course design based on scholarly developments in christology. It is, in fact, a course that consolidates principles learned from graduate school models into a design reflecting current literature, and it is also appropriate for undergraduate study in my cultural location of southern California.

The model retains the four-unit format. The first unit considers first-century witnesses about Jesus Christ (gospels and epistles, pre-New Testament images, and apocryphal literature, for instance). The second unit surveys representative texts and images from selected moments in the tradition: some early patristic and normative dogmatic texts, one medieval text in spirituality, and a brief review of Reformation christologies. The new model retains the historical Jesus study but does so in the third course segment as an example of the modern effort to understand Jesus of Nazareth, using the best historical methods our era provides. This unit presents the quest for the "historical Jesus" not as a skeptical enterprise, but as an examination of that person who is the Christian tradition's ultimate presupposition.

The first and final weeks are devoted to the fourth component, which considers contemporary challenges to Christianity's absolute conviction about revelation and salvation in Jesus Christ. Noted here are the secular rejection of belief, the different convictions of other religions, the divergent and sometimes exclusive interpretations of Jesus Christ among various Christian communities. The final classes return to this topic to permit students to address these issues and to suggest ways of interpreting the christological tradition for our era.

Although the course emphasis is on the christological tradition's diversity throughout history, it heeds Walter Kasper's principle that theology must attempt to determine the tradition's inherent continuity in the discontinuity of history. Course texts that support this model are Richard Longenecker's *New Wine into Fresh Wineskins: Contextualizing the Early Christian Confessions* for New Testament christology, and E. P. Sanders's *The Historical Figure of Jesus*[9] for that topic. I compose the surveys and selections for the middle unit on christologies in the tradition but am guided by Roger Haight's *Jesus Symbol of God.*[10]

Although most academic goals of the earlier course models are retained, recognition of the tradition's diversity is a new course goal, and this course has had strong success in student mastery of that goal. Because the issues are complex, students often express frustration at the semester's beginning. At the semester's end, however, most students produce competent descriptions of several Jesus traditions. They can identify the New Testament origins of selected traditions and trace their development through at least three historical eras. Student-written comparisons show their understanding of the complementarity of the traditions. Working with a model that attends to the diversity of traditions, students grasp better the *de facto* pluralistic situation of individual and denominational views of Jesus Christ represented in any class session. Secure in the location of their own Christ image in the spectrum of traditions, they acknowledge that all Christians do not imagine or understand Jesus or church traditions in the same way. They are then able to respond positively to differences in beliefs with a modicum of understanding and respect. Given the course emphasis on the plurality of traditions, students are surprised to discover the many commonalities and convergences in the Jesus traditions and are then better prepared for the final reflection on the challenges to christology today. As for those tenaciously held personal images mentioned above, using this course model, a student who expresses a position is able to recognize it for what it is.

Influences and Challenges

Why abandon a successful and familiar course pattern in favor of a more complex and pedagogically challenging model? Four factors influenced my continuing reflections on christology and the issue of how to teach it: Walter Kasper's theology, the wisdom of my departmental colleagues, the religious and cultural backgrounds of the students, and developments in the topic.

Theological Foundations

Walter Kasper's theology provides the primary model for my reflections on theology and its methods. In the monograph *The Methods of Dogmatic Theology*,[11] Kasper explains theology as guided by two realities: God's word in scripture (the very "soul of theology," *Dei Verbum*, #24) and questions raised in our contemporary situation. Although theology focuses on biblical texts, this focus is directed by the life questions of people, both believers and nonbelievers. Since revelation is comprised of sacred scripture and tradition, any attempt to achieve a cogent exposition of revelation for people today requires the theologian also to engage in historical theology. The purpose of studying the history of the christological tradition is not to hastily choose one final authoritative answer for a particular question, but to attend to the labyrinthine diversity of traditions that has emerged during Christianity's long history. Having done this, one can then probe them for the *one* unarticulated tradition underlying them. This requires the avoidance of a rush to judgment by patiently listening to many witnesses and carefully examining conceptual frameworks, concepts, and symbols for their theological intent and scope.

The Influence of Colleagues

Conversations with colleagues in my department and professional societies continue to reinforce and shape my application of Kasperean principles. Significant influences have been the expertise provided by the biblical scholars at the University of San Diego and its historical and Latino theologians. The decisive influence on decisions about the course's present stage, however, has been the cultural context of the University of San Diego with its diverse student body.

Kasper proposes scripture as the foundation of theological reflection. Thus it is from biblical scholars and historians that I learn about new methods for interpreting scripture. Conversations with the department's biblical scholars revealed that my first course's emphasis on the historical Jesus favored study of the synoptic gospels to the neglect of other New Testament traditions, among them Pauline and Johannine theologies, which were profoundly enduring influences on the Jesus tradition. They helped me recognize the distinction between historical Jesus studies and the Christ images unique to each gospel. Their influence prompted my awareness of the historical Jesus enterprise as a modern quest intended to produce a pure historical portrait of Jesus removed from the context of faith. This supported my recognition that the course's historical Jesus component had eclipsed other christological traditions in the New Testament and supported my decision to alter my course model.

Kasper's dedication to the testimony of the church's diverse historical tradition provided a second methodological consideration. Colleagues who are historical theologians assisted my reading of past traditions. They cautioned that systematic theologians tend to craft synthetic reviews of history that obliterate the historical uniqueness and diverse character of faith and theological reflection found in the documents of earlier eras. This wisdom has fostered my interest in presenting a selection of Christ images from various historical periods.

Kasper's concerns about contemporary persons have also influenced me. Colleagues who are Latino theologians guide my understanding and application of that principle in an academic institution whose culture and demographics reflect the cultural complexity of Mexican border and Pacific Rim communities. Orlando Espín's reflections on the faith of the people, the significance of popular Catholicism, and the uniquely concrete religious symbols various peoples employ as carriers of the tradition[12] provided invaluable assistance to my efforts to design class segments that explore the concrete Christ symbols treasured by each student and his or her religious community. Thus, the christology course is shaped to foster awareness of the culture of the university and its community, a milieu comprised of very specific ethnic and religious communities, as well as to attend to scholarly topical issues.

The Influence of Students

Central to the goal of building a bridge between sound scholarly understandings of Jesus Christ and the students' lives is the commitment to attend to their faith convictions and cultural backgrounds. This is an essential component in any decisions made about the content and pedagogy of the course. The region's human, cultural, and religious diversity is clear in student names and faces. It is reflected in the several languages heard on campus where English, Spanish, and Vietnamese are the neighborhood tongues. The differing faith convictions now evident in the larger Catholic community are reflected in the attitudes of the class's Roman Catholics. Equally evident are the Christ images from the ethnic traditions of their home parishes, religious education, and family traditions. The cultural make-up of the classroom is made more complex by the university's large non-Catholic population. Viewpoints from other mainline Christian denominations, from evangelical Christians eager to give witness to their beliefs, from members of the Church of Jesus Christ of Latter Day Saints, and from Christian Scientists must be given a hearing, along with the perspectives of the unchurched and the occasional Buddhist or Hindu. Without question, any teacher must consider the experience of course participants while designing the structure and content of a course; when dealing with matters of belief, such as christology, the religious and cultural diversity of student experience has vital relevance.

The cultural situation of the students was the decisive influence on my effort to restructure the course around the Jesus tradition's diversity, not its unity, and to include class discussions about the unity and diversity of faith experiences. It remains a concern in planning course assignments, which assist student mastery of the technical course components, and also imagining exercises, which help them identify the theological foundations of the Jesus symbols encountered in local worship, religious education, and popular Christianity.[13]

Assessing Course Changes

The new model appears to bring clear gains: appreciation of the historical perspective and acceptance of the common tradition's rich diversity are inestimable benefits. One clear outcome is student awareness that diversity has caused Christian divisions but that it is not an insurmountable obstacle to respect and unity among churches whose Christ traditions differ. This model permits exploration of theological traditions neglected in the first model's emphasis on the historical Jesus, doctrines that can illuminate contemporary issues. The doctrine of Jesus Christ's pre-existence becomes interesting when linked to the doctrine of creation and to ecological concerns. Exemplar christologies ground a comparison of Jesus with the founders and great figures in other religions. Thus the new model can assist reflection on the encounter of the Christian tradition with contemporary culture and the challenge of global awareness. A final achievement is the sense each class member gains about the location of her or his personal and denominational Christ images within the inherited christological tradition.

There are also clear losses in the new course design. Due to time constraints, valuable aspects of the study of the historical Jesus addressed in the third stage had to be sacrificed. Foremost among these are the detailed study of Jesus' Jewish context and of the New Testament's roots in the Hebrew scriptures. These are now treated in a much more cursory manner. Because attention is given to the labyrinthine diversity evident in the christological tradition, some Christian students have lost their earlier confidence in the unity of the Christ tradition transmitted in church history. This is not necessarily a deficiency, but it is a concern as I attempt to build bridges that link christological scholarship and students' lives. Also, in the current model clear foundational philosophical categories that link topical units are weaker, making integration of the material more challenging for students as a whole. The course's new emphasis on religious diversity also contributes to students' conception of differences in faith convictions and beliefs as identical with the tendency to cultural relativity that this generation tends readily to adopt.

Changes in course design were not achieved in a vacuum. Concerns and questions that fostered each period of experimentation reflected shifts in theological literature over the past two decades. One notable change in biblical christology is found in texts that examine the diversity of the historical Jesus quests or explore the diversity of Christ images in the New Testament as a whole.[14] The second is the appearance of christological studies that re-image Jesus with reference to concrete local cultures or other religions. A third change is found in comprehensive studies that build around the commonalities in the Christ tradition but expose a plurality of images in different eras of that same tradition. O'Collins's *Christology* is one such work. Roger Haight's *Jesus Symbol of God* is another. Tracing several trajectories of Christ traditions (as christology or soteriology) starting with biblical origins, Haight establishes a common framework of christology across the ages. However, the plurality of biblical and traditional christological images provides both a warrant and a model for contextualizing christology today. In different ways, these two works model a new type of christological construction, the contours of which resemble Walter Kasper's early recommendations about theological method.

This reflection on teaching christology by noting changes in course concept and design does not argue that all courses should follow the model of christological diversity. It does not guarantee that my own course will retain the current outline to the exclusion of other designs. Revisiting past course designs, I now note the value of modified versions of syllabus two, course models that study Jesus and the early Christ traditions with a reference to the culture and faith of Judaism. Recent publications on the historical Jesus, including Paula Fredriksen's *Jesus of Nazareth: King of the Jews* and *From Jesus to Christ*,[15] provide content more sensitive to this issue than their predecessors because they do not preclude linkage between the historical Jesus and the Christ of faith; they are also suitable for my final model.

In summary, thinking about teaching christology and reviewing the literature of the field suggests that two models remain permanent options for constructing the christology course. One model conceives the topic in the mode of a unitary historical trajectory grounded in the study of the historical Jesus and then explores the interpretative traditions that derive from his life. In the second model, the historical Jesus topic is not absent, but it does not dominate the study. This model accepts the diversity of the Jesus tradition as its starting point and structures a course design that reviews the story of Jesus' life and then explores the diversity of traditional Christ images as symbols of faith's richness and as the basis for interpreting Christ images for the concrete cultures and historical circumstances of the present day. In light of the diverse possibilities of approach and content featured in contemporary christological literature, we are no longer obligated to confine ourselves to one course model; thus the consideration of one's cultural location can now weigh in as a significant factor in determining how the course should be constructed.

Notes

[1]Günther Bornkamm, *Jesus of Nazareth* (San Francisco: Harper & Row, 1960); St. Athanasius, *On the Incarnation* (Crestwood, N.Y.: St. Vladimir's Orthodox Theological Seminary, 1982); Monika K. Hellwig, *Jesus, the Compassion of God: New Perspectives on the Tradition of Christianity* (Wilmington, Del.: Michael Glazier, 1988).

[2]Mary Rose D'Angelo, "*Abba* and 'Father': Imperial Theology and the Jesus Traditions," *Journal of Biblical Literature* 111/4 (1992): 617-622.

[3]Bernard J. Lee, S.M., *The Galilean Jewishness of Jesus: Retrieving the Jewish Origins of Christianity* (New York: Paulist Press, 1988); *Jesus and the Metaphors of God: The Christs of the New Testament* (New York: Paulist Press, 1993).

[4]Reginald H. Fuller and Pheme Perkins, *Who Is This Christ? Gospel Christology and Contemporary Faith* (Philadelphia: Fortress Press, 1983).

[5]Gerard S. Sloyan, *The Jesus Tradition: Images of Jesus in the West* (Mystic, Conn.: Twenty-Third Publications, 1986); Jaroslav Pelikan, *Jesus through the Centuries: His Place in the History of Culture* (New Haven: Yale University Press, 1985).

[6]Morris West, *The Clowns of God* (New York: Morrow, 1981).

[7]William P. Loewe, *The College Student's Introduction to Christology* (Collegeville, Minn.: Liturgical Press, 1996).

[8]Gerald O'Collins, S.J., *Christology: A Biblical, Historical, and Systematic Study of Jesus* (New York: Oxford University Press, 1995).

[9]Richard Longenecker, *New Wine into Fresh Wineskins: Contextualizing the Early Christian Confessions* (Peabody, Mass.: Hendrickson Publishers, 1999); E. P. Sanders, *The Historical Figure of Jesus* (New York: Penguin Books, 1993).

[10]Roger Haight, *Jesus Symbol of God* (Maryknoll, N.Y.: Orbis Books, 2000).

[11]Walter Kasper, *The Methods of Dogmatic Theology*, trans. John Drury (New

York: Paulist Press, 1969). See chaps. 3 and 4 for Kasper's explanation of the use of scripture, history, and the contemporary situation. A succinct explanation of Kasper's position on concrete historical reality and diversity is given in "Die Welt als Ort des Evangeliums" in *Glaube and Geschichte* (Mainz: Matthias Grünewald, 1970), 209-23. Also see articles in *Theology and Church* (New York: Crossroad, 1989) for more recent discussions of theological method and models.

[12]Orlando Espín, *The Faith of the People: Theological Reflections on Popular Catholicism* (Maryknoll, N.Y.: Orbis Books, 1997). There are now a number of valuable studies of Jesus Christ in reference to local cultures. Among these are: Anton Wessels, *Images of Jesus: How Jesus Is Perceived and Portrayed in Non-European Cultures,* trans. John Vriend (Grand Rapids: Eerdmans Publishing, 1990), and Volker Küster, *The Many Faces of Jesus Christ: Intercultural Christology* (Maryknoll, N.Y.: Orbis Books, 1999).

[13]I have experimented with exercises to help students grasp this viewpoint and have had classes tour the parish church on campus to study the portrayal of Jesus in liturgical art. Recently I designed a research assignment titled "Jesus on the Web" in which students examine Christ images on two church web-sites, then select and describe two other Jesus sites that interest them. Last semester's project entitled "Bumper Sticker Jesus" required students to choose a genre of popular religion (hymns, popular prayers, family traditions, bumper stickers) and then select ten images in the chosen category and identify the traditional Christ concept implied in each popular image. Far from trivializing course content, the exercises permit students to note popular symbols and to analyze them in relationship to a traditional image. They discover then the pervasive and enduring character of the tradition's Christ images, even in popular modalities.

[14]See Frank J. Matera, *New Testament Christology* (Louisville: Westminster/John Knox Press, 1999), for an example of this approach. The classical study that grounds this method is the work of James D. G. Dunn, *Unity and Diversity in the New Testament: An Inquiry into the Character of Earliest Christianity* 2d. ed. (Valley Forge, Penn.: Trinity Press International, 1990).

[15]Paula Fredriksen, *Jesus of Nazareth, King of the Jews: A Jewish Life and the Emergence of Christianity* (New York: Vintage Books, 1999); see also *From Jesus to Christ: The Origins of the New Testament Images of Jesus* (New Haven: Yale University Press, 1988).

The Practice of Teaching Christology

Christology as Introduction

Elena G. Procario-Foley

"Always be prepared to make a defense to any one who calls you to account for the hope that is in you, yet do it with gentleness and reverence" (1 Pet. 3:15b). The author of 1 Peter offers sage counsel to the one who teaches christology to undergraduate students. Both the topic and the students deserve gentleness and reverence. My response to the question "How do you teach christology?" requires a brief word on the social location of my students, a disclosure of my pedagogical and theological commitments, a description of the course, "Images of Jesus throughout History," and selected critical questions that are raised by a related course, "Jesus and Judaism." In so doing I hope to account for the hope that is in me when I present the questions of christology to undergraduate students.

Demographic Profile

A total of 3,417[1] undergraduate students were enrolled in my institution during the academic year 2001-2002, of whom 11 percent were non-traditional returning adult students. The average SAT score for the entering class of 2001 was 1017. The student body, at present, is drawn predominantly from the New York metropolitan region, with only 15 percent of students from out-of-state. It is reasonably diverse, with 26 percent of the population self-reporting as Black, Hispanic, or Asian. Religious diversity, however, is minimal. While the institution does not collect data on religious affiliation, experience reveals that in a class of 30 to 35 students, there is likely no more than one non-Christian; frequently, classes are homogeneously Christian. Finally, it is important to note that a significant number of students are first-generation college students, though such statistics are not presently maintained.

All students are required to take two courses in religious studies. The core course, "The Introduction to the Study of Religion," is mandatory and students may elect any 300 or 400 level course as a second course. Consequently, the christology course (listed as 401) is populated by sophomores, juniors, and seniors; their preparation for the academic study of Jesus is widely varied.

Commitments

Edward Schillebeeckx's approach to christology has indelibly affected my own orientation to christological questions. His work provides both an interpretative horizon and a set of implicit goals for the design of a christology course. At the end of *Jesus: An Experiment in Christology* (the original Dutch subtitle reads, "the story of a living one"[2]), Schillebeeckx argues that in order for a contemporary christology to be credible for a contemporary believer (or potential believer), it must engage a combination of stories, theology, and praxis. He writes, "[t]hen and only then will theory, story and parable—hand in hand with the praxis of the kingdom of God—be for this world an invitation to make a reply, in real freedom and on its own behalf, to the question: 'But you—you who read this—whom do you say that I—Jesus of Nazareth—am?' "[3] His christological achievement with the trilogy *Jesus*, *Christ*,[4] and *Church*[5] accomplishes just such a combination. The historical criticism of the first volume yields a narrative of the first Christians' experience of Jesus and therefore, for Schillebeeckx, an echo of the earthly Jesus. The literary criticism of the second volume produces a theological interpretation of that experience, while the third volume's critical correlation of tradition and situation, especially with respect to suffering, results in a call for praxis that alleviates suffering in anticipation of the full reign of God.

Schillebeeckx's project depends on the dialectical relationship between experience and thought. Schillebeeckx maintains that one's history provides a constant context and interpretative structure within which one has and evaluates experiences. He writes, "On the one hand, thought makes experience possible, while on the other hand, it is experience that makes new thinking necessary. Our thinking remains empty if it does not constantly refer back to living experience."[6] Thus, the dialectical relationship between experience and thought gives rise to the three christological elements of story, theology, and praxis.

I am persuaded by Schillebeeckx's three-fold approach to christology. Though I do not explicitly present the christology course to my undergraduates in terms of story, theology, and praxis, these elements provide the foci of the course. Some of my stated course objectives imply the importance of these elements:

- To engage a new appreciation of Jesus in his Jewish context;
- To gain a knowledge of the tradition of creeds concerning Jesus;
- To encounter the plurality of positions concerning the identity of Jesus;
- To develop and articulate one's own christology.

The first objective cultivates interest in the story of Jesus through historical and biblical explorations. Biblical presentations of Jesus, however, are conditioned by a theology even as they purport to tell a story; therefore, the attempt to understand Jesus in his Jewish context involves the experience-thought dialectic. The second and third objectives, similarly dependent upon the interpretative horizon of the experience-thought dialectic, indicate theological reflection upon the story and experience of Jesus. Finally, the last objective is an attempt to involve students in the christological process through, as Schillebeeckx notes, the necessary integration of story, theology, and praxis.

Course Structure

When I was in graduate school, the course "Introduction to New Testament" began with the professor vehemently stating: "We don't know who the gospel writers are, when they wrote, for whom they wrote, or what they meant! I am going to *de-familiarize* you with everything you thought you knew!" On the other hand, *my* experience in the classroom has been the opposite, and I have quickly learned that I need to *familiarize* students with what *I* thought they knew. A recent article in *Religious Studies News* titled "Moses Who?" recounts the extent of biblical and religious illiteracy among undergraduates.[7] The author reminds us that the rudimentary facts of the basic narratives of the Jewish and Christian traditions are unfamiliar to and/or garbled for many students, even those who come from religiously practicing homes and/or parochial schools. For example, in response to my question, "What did God give Moses and the people in the desert?" (Exod. 16), one student responded "manna and small coconuts."

I view the christology course as introduction to the Bible, to Jesus, to what the church says about Jesus, and to the diversity of positions regarding the meaning and identity of Jesus. By the end of the course, students should be able to comprehend the basic creedal affirmations of the church well enough to be able to recognize how a particular christology may emphasize different aspects of the church's definitions as well as to discuss intelligently the sacred texts that provide the first attempts "to put Jesus into words"—William Loewe's wonderful description of christology.[8]

The first section of the course introduces the Bible in two ways: by discussing the formation of the biblical canon and by briefly comparing the gospels. Spending time on canon formation introduces students to the idea that Jesus was Jewish and his sacred texts were *not* the New Testament. In order to engage the element of story in christological reflection, students need to understand that the Tanakh exists, that it is not identical with the Old Testament, and that the order and structure of the two canons tell different stories for different communities. Indeed, when students realize that 2 Chronicles concludes the Tanakh but it is Malachi that completes the Old Testament, they begin to glimpse the implication of a biblical canon: story and theology are dialectically related.

An introduction to the gospels is necessary to ground the story component of the christological trajectory, to provide an introduction to Jesus, and to disabuse students of the idea that the gospels are historical biography. Developing a level playing field of shared readings is essential. Required readings include the Gospel of Mark, the infancy narratives, the passion narratives, and the resurrection appearances. For students, an explanation of the Modified Two-Source Theory accounts for the differences in the stories but, more importantly, the comparisons illustrate the idea of christology as an articulation of the meaning and identity of Jesus for a community. Such a discussion often introduces the more general idea of the experience-thought dialectic that is manifest in the formation of the gospels.

At this point in the course, Raymond Brown's *An Introduction to New Testament Christology* is a helpful guide.[9] Technical terms such as functional christology and ontological christology can be broached, and students can begin to explore the variety of incipient christologies in the New Testament from pre-existence to Parousia, from boyhood to public ministry. The biblical section thus establishes christology as an ongoing dynamic project.

The second section of the course begins with an introduction to christological doctrine and how contemporary Christians variously interpret it. In order to facilitate student understanding of christology as a process of reflection on Jesus by people of faith, I use John Cobb's *Doubting Thomas: Christology in Story Form.*[10] In a pithy book of barely one hundred pages, Cobb weaves the tale of straight-laced Thomas Atherton, a Protestant seminarian and chaplain-intern who is experiencing a crisis of faith and vocation in reaction to the preaching of his very liberal chaplain supervisor Janet Levovsky who maintains an extremely low christology. The tense dialogue between Thomas and Janet quickly introduces students to the christological debate about humanity and divinity; the epistemological question about the starting point for christology (in other words, is Jesus known through the Bible, through doctrine, or through experience, and does it make a difference where one starts?); and the theological question about the uniqueness of God's incarnation in Jesus. The profound initial disagreements between Janet and Thomas immerse students in the dynamics of the interaction of story, theology, and praxis without abstract description.

With the help of a variety of type-cast characters ranging from fellow seminarian Chan-Hie to a Dorothy Day-esque radical Christian, Thomas considers the development of the creeds, the challenge of religious pluralism, feminist theology, liberation theology, the christological roots of anti-Semitism, and the implications of the gospel Jesus for praxis. By journeying with Thomas, students learn fundamentals of the tradition and questions posed to the tradition today. Thus, they begin to develop the ability to identify a christology in basic terms (for example, is it high or low?) and to articulate the starting point for that christology (as noted above, is it the Bible, doctrine, or experience?).

The rest of the course (approximately one-half to two-thirds) is devoted to delving more deeply into these questions and the earlier biblical material by turning to William Loewe's *The College Student's Introduction to Christology.* Loewe's introductory explanation of a low-ascending approach to christology involving historical knowledge, religious dimensions, and contemporary interpretation[11] offers students an immediate counterpoint to the high-descending approach represented by the character Thomas. Through a presentation of the results of historical Jesus research, Loewe provides a context for students within which they can begin to understand why some people would acclaim Jesus as Christ while others would seek his execution. Loewe's approach allows students an entry into the story, theology, and praxis of Jesus and secures a foundation for them to begin to evaluate christological positions.

Additionally, Loewe's text affords the opportunity to further elucidate for students the relationship between Tanakh and the New Testament as a *christological* moment. Of course, this often does not have the intended effect. First, students have difficulty understanding that Jewish-Christians would read scripture in light of their experience of Jesus. Second, that such an experience-thought dynamic could condition the writing of the New Testament seems at times a Gordian knot for students.

The following student response to a final exam question demonstrates the difficulty in asking students to identify characteristics of Jesus' idea of the reign of God using images available to Jewish-Christians from the Tanakh: "I think *Isaiah* is right on target here and does a great job of being non-partisan and showing both a high and low approach to christology." Though this particular student missed the christological integration of story, theology, and praxis sought by the question, the answer sheds light on the need to view teaching christology as introduction—again, minimally, to the Bible and to historical context.

IMAGES OF JESUS

Introduction to the Bible
  • Canon and Theology
  • New Testament Christologies
Beginning Christological Thought
  • Faith and Experience, Doctrine and Interpretation
  • High and Low Approaches
  • Nicea and Chalcedon: Winners, Losers, Issues
Who Is Jesus?
  • Results of Historical Jesus Research
  • A Tentative Christological Portrait
Contemporary Questions and Perspectives

Course Evaluation

With the structure of the course (above) as a backdrop, it is appropriate to indicate what types of assignments have been more or less successful and to consider possible additions to the course as currently outlined.

Assignments

Not surprisingly, assignments that require students to do more sustained work with scholarly resources do not usually yield clear christological thought. Shorter assignments that involve a more interpretative response based largely on class discussion and lecture are more successful. For instance, the strategy of student dyads presenting chapters of Pelikan's *Jesus through the Centuries* to their peers is not advisable.[12] Small group work, however, analyzing Christmas carols can yield good results, especially since that exercise helps to demonstrate that a difference in the christological starting point does not have to produce a different doctrinal result. (The carol assignment, though, involves an important caveat: all verses of the carol must be used if the progression of christological thought is to be fully manifest. Some of the effectiveness of this assignment results from students reflecting on unfamiliar verses.) Christmas carols also have the benefit of integrating the christological elements of story and theology in a particularly vivid way.

An additional productive assignment is to require e-mail journal entries. The journal prompts students to achieve incremental steps in christological thought. The questions posed to the students follow an alternating pattern of fact-based and interpretative inquiry. The fact-based questions probe the students' basic understanding of the material, and the interpretative queries (for example, asking students to explain their preference for one christological formulation to another) challenge students to engage in christological argumentation. Similarly, a research paper that requires an exegesis of a New Testament passage as the basis for an articulation of the student's own christology encourages students to think christologically while weaving together story, theology, and praxis. The results of the paper, however, are not as widely positive as those from the e-mail journal, and the benefits of the assignment are more difficult to assess.

Additions

Two amplifications would strengthen the course. "Images of Jesus" would be more successful, in terms of both student interest and in moving students from fact to understanding to insight,[13] if it involved extensive use of the arts. Film, painting, sculpture, music, poetry, novel, and dance can open wide windows into the process of christological integration that class lecture and discussion of texts only barely crack. The film *Roses in December*, for example, portrays the missionary work of four American women (three religious, one lay) in El Salvador in the late 1970s and 1980. Their efforts to organize the poor in El Salvador and to provide for their basic health, educational, and catechetical needs were terminated by the brutality of rape and murder. Does the integration of story, theology, and praxis in the lives of the women in *Roses in December*—now known simply as Ita, Dorothy, Maura, and Jean—ring true christologically for students? Or, perhaps more provocatively, how might the young, innocent, tragic hero of the recent *Pay It Forward*, a Hollywood feature devoid of explicit religious commitments, challenge students' christological imaginations? If the students' overwhelmingly positive reaction to doing oral presentations based on *The National Catholic Reporter's Jesus 2000* art competition is any indication, then a more deliberate use of the arts seems warranted.

The praxis component of the course's rationale also requires a meaningful expansion. If a stated objective of the syllabus is for students to be able to articulate a christology of their own, then supplementing their understanding of the meaning of the praxis of Jesus Christ is in order. Story and theology can be best understood through application, as praxis emerges at the center of christology. A service-learning module that engages students in service to the poor, outcast, and forgotten of our society brings Jesus' preaching of the reign of God to life before their very eyes and through the work of their hands, albeit in a fragmentary way. Biographies and autobiographies—Romero, King, Day, Bonhoeffer, Kolbe, Wallenberg—on their own or as both preparation for and guided reflection after a service-learning experience may also be helpful in intensifying students' understanding of praxis.

A Cognate Course: Some Critical Reflections

Shortly after my first experience teaching christology, I was directed by the dean's office to create a cross-disciplinary program in

Jewish-Catholic studies. As part of the curriculum development facet of the program, I introduced the course, "Jesus and Judaism." The course is an introductory exploration of the life of Jesus and his Jewish world set within the wider historical context of Jewish-Catholic relations. The course description states: "This course examines the life of Jesus in its Jewish context in an effort to uncover more accurate trajectories of continuity and discontinuity between Judaism and Christianity. An examination of key texts in the development of Jewish-Catholic relations since 1965 provides a contemporary perspective on the theological developments of and after the first century C.E."

Key objectives are:
- Develop a basic knowledge of the formation of the Bible;
- Provide insight into the anti-Jewish uses of the New Testament;
- Develop a basis for the inter-religious dialogue between Jews and Catholics;
- Provide interpretations for increased understanding about the crucifixion of Jesus;
- Focus attention on the climate created by two thousand years of theological anti-Judaism as a cause of the *Shoah*.

The course proceeds, as the description and objectives indicate, quite literally from Jesus to Hitler. Paula Fredriksen's *Jesus of Nazareth*[14] is a central course text for both formal and material reasons. On a formal level, her text, though not easy for undergraduates, is more accessible than Sanders' classic *Jesus and Judaism*.[15] Early in the text, Fredriksen employs the device of "preludes," which might be described as dramatic interludes. The first prelude renders a vivid account of the destruction of Jerusalem (based on Josephus' description in *Bellum Judaicum*), while the second offers a story about how a young Galilean boy, Yehoshua, learns from his family about purity laws, feasts such as Pesach and Sukkot, and pilgrimage to Jerusalem. The preludes provide a dramatic foreground for Fredriksen's historical analysis as well as an engaging point of reference for students as they navigate her argument. Her historical and logical method affords students a strikingly clear structure to assist their assimilation of large amounts of new information (even if the results her method yields are not unassailable). Materially, her quest to discover a reasonable explanation both for Jesus' crucifixion and the fact that his followers were spared this penalty offers students important foci for (re)examining the life of Jesus and the trajectories of responses to Jesus, some of which lead to anti-Jewish attitudes that have ramifications for their study of the religious background of the *Shoah.*

From the experience of teaching "Jesus and Judaism" and of developing the larger program in Jewish-Catholic studies, I am convinced that a christology course needs to confront the christological roots of anti-Semitism as well as Jesus in "relationship to his contemporaries in Judaism."[16] The *Shoah* is about as significant for students as the French and Indian War. In fact, students have admitted that they thought *Schindler's List* was simply a fiction of Spielberg's fertile imagination. Further, students, in an undergraduate population that is predominantly Christian, by no means universally know that Jesus was Jewish, and have even less understanding of ancient or contemporary Judaism.

JESUS AND JUDAISM

Judaism and Catholicism: The State of the Question
- *Nostra Aetate* and Post-Vatican II Documents
- The Jewish Response

Tanakh, Christian Bible, Covenant
- Canon and Theology
- Promise/Fulfillment v. Supersessionism
- Covenant and Anti-Judaism

Late Second Temple Judaism
- Politics, Society, Religion
- Jesus in His Time

Anti-Judaism and the Gospels, Anti-Semitism and the *Shoah*

Christological Roots of Anti-Semitism

Cobb's text provides some introductory material and Loewe only obliquely approaches the issue in his concluding two pages about Jesus and the world religions. Consequently, two sessions have been added to address this topic.

These adjustments seem woefully inadequate, however, given the importance of the questions involved and the passionate responses of some students. For example, in the class on "Images of Jesus" one student was shocked to recognize that she had appropriated, unawares, the teaching of contempt for Jews and never understood the relationship between Christianity and anti-Semitism. She was moved to focus her exegetical paper on Matthew 27, focusing on the idea of the "culprits of Jesus' death." She concluded, "It seems inappropriate and unjust to blame all of the Jewish population for the death of Jesus." A student from the "Jesus and Judaism" course studied the Gospel of John and observed, "Everything negative in the Gospel of John involves the Jews. If this is true, the Gospels helped fuel Hitler's message and can be considered partially responsible for the death of six million innocent Jews. . . . The 'Good News' isn't good at all."

If christology as an integration of story, theology, and praxis is to be meaningful for potential or contemporary believers, then the darker integrations must be included in classroom instruction and the harsh reality of the trajectory from gospel anti-Judaism to the *Shoah's* anti-Semitism must be illuminated.[17] It is powerful and transformative for students. Though there is not enough space in a one-semester course to add two entire books to "Images of Jesus," carefully selected portions of *Pain and Polemic: Anti-Judaism in the Gospels*[18] and *Hope Against Hope: Johann Baptist Metz and Elie Wiesel Speak Out on the Holocaust*[19] could be imported from "Jesus and Judaism" to structure discussion about the christological roots of anti-Semitism.

Jesus and His Religious Contemporaries

Research into Jesus and his religious contemporaries leads to two questions that are equally important to christological reflection. A student "blooper" sheds light on the first question: "Jews were a great spiritual people of the past and the Jewish religion was misplaced by Christianity." Fredriksen, Sanders, and others advance the position that if Jesus had been so different from his Jewish contemporaries, his message would not have received a hearing; others argue as if Jesus had "misplaced" his Judaism. How do Christian theologians interpret the evidence, such as that presented by Fredriksen, that Jesus was *a traditionally observant Jew*?[20] Does this make a difference for christology?

At the end of his positive review of Fredriksen's *Jesus of Nazareth*, Jon Levenson, a professor of Jewish studies at Harvard University, put the case this way: "Jesus himself lived a traditional observant life. How the Church can integrate that insight into its life and teachings today is a question [Fredriksen does not] address. It is not a question that is likely to go away."[21] This question needs to be part of deliberations about the pedagogy of christology.

The second question involves the significance of vastly divergent interpretations of what are considered incontrovertible facts about Jesus' life gleaned from historical research; such divergences beg the classic questions of the legitimacy, possibility, and necessity for such research and their import for christology. Juxtapose, for example, two approaches to the cleansing of the Temple. Fredriksen maintains that *even if* Jesus actually caused a disturbance in the Temple, it would have been noticeable to a very few and thus cannot be established as a cause of Jesus' execution.[22] By contrast, in *Rabbi Jesus*, Bruce Chilton describes a premeditated, significant, and armed attack on the Temple and causally links it to the execution.[23] Admittedly, Chilton's is a very different type of text from Fredriksen's, bordering more on "fiction than . . . with painstaking historical scholarship,"[24] but it still serves to raise the question: Does the manner of Jesus' life and death make a difference for christology? If so, then how do we as teachers make sense for our students of such different hypotheses derived from presumably the same data? Surely the scholarly community's tradition of review and debate will help narrow the field of plausible options but the question remains open: "How much of the debate can we and should we incorporate into undergraduate christology courses?"

Monika Hellwig writes that "for systematic Christology, the research into the Hebrew context for the life, teaching, and actions of Jesus still holds immense possibilities for transcending the apparent gridlock on the way to contemporary intelligibility. . . . "[25] Despite the difficulties inherent in historical Jesus research and in incorporating it into undergraduate christology courses, we must make the effort to integrate story, theology, and praxis in order to excite students about the christological question. Works such as Fredriksen's, for example, are also necessary as part of an effort to eradicate some of the christological roots of anti-Semitism and the caricature of Jesus as always over and against his Jewish contemporaries. Schillebeeckx writes: "[f]aith in search of historical understanding is an intrinsic consequence of the fact that Christianity is not merely concerned with a decisive message from God but, at the same time, it centers on the person of Jesus Christ, someone who appeared in our history and who, therefore, must be given a place within the whole of the history of God with us."[26]

Notes

[1]Data in this section are derived from the Iona College Self-Study prepared for the Commission on Higher Education Middle States Association of Colleges and Schools, "Aspirations and Achievements: Iona College in the New Millennium" (November 2002), 26-31. Indications about religious diversity (or a lack thereof) and first-generation college students are anecdotal and based on experience since the institution does not track such trends.

[2]*Jesus: An Experiment in Christology*, trans. Hubert Hoskins (New York: Crossroad, 1979). Originally, *Jezus, het verhaal van een levende* (Bloemendaal: H. Nelissen, 1974).

[3]*Jesus*, 673.

[4]*Christ: The Experience of Jesus as Lord*, trans. John Bowden (New York: Crossroad, 1981). Originally, *Gerechtigehid en liefde: Genade en bevrijding* (Bloemendaal: H. Nelissen, 1977). The Dutch title translates as "Justice and Love: Grace and Liberation."

[5]*Church: The Human Story of God* (New York: Crossroad, 1990). Originally, *Mensen als verhaal van God* (Baarn: H. Nelissen, 1989). The title translates as "Human Beings as the Story of God."

[6]*Christ*, 32.

[7]Bruce Grelle, "Moses Who? Literacy, Citizenship, and the Academic Study of Religion in the Schools," *Religious Studies News* 17 (March 2002): 9, 11-12.

[8]William P. Loewe, *The College Student's Introduction to Christology* (Collegeville, Minn.: Liturgical Press, 1996). See, for example, 177 and 202.

[9]Raymond E. Brown, *An Introduction to New Testament Christology* (New York: Paulist Press, 1994). I would not recommend this book as a course text, but, depending on the skill level of the students, judicious selections may be in order as required reading.

[10]John Cobb, *Doubting Thomas: Christology in Story Form* (New York: Crossroad, 1990).

[11]Loewe, *The College Student's Introduction to Christology*, 2-4.

[12]Jaroslav Pelikan, *Jesus through the Centuries: His Place in the History of Culture* (New Haven: Yale University Press, 1985). Pelikan's text assumes too strong a knowledge-base for it to advance understanding for undergraduates attempting independent projects in an introductory course in christology.

[13]I am moved by Jacob Neusner's articulation: "Ours is a privileged field of

learning, for when we devote our lives to the academic study of religion, the very nature of the documents that we examine and the ideas that we try to understand change our work, transforming facts into insight and insight into wisdom" ("Scholarship, Teaching, Learning: Three Theses for the Academic Study of Religion," *Religious Studies News* 12:3 [September 1997]: 22).

[14]Paula Fredriksen, *Jesus of Nazareth, King of the Jews: A Jewish Life and the Emergence of Christianity* (New York: Knopf, 1999). It is pertinent to note that Fredriksen is an adult convert to Judaism.

[15]E. P. Sanders, *Jesus and Judaism* (Philadelphia: Fortress Press, 1985). Fredriksen's acknowledgments and notes reflect a certain debt to, if not dependence on, Sanders's approach to historical Jesus research. See, for example, xvi-xvii and 276.

[16]Sanders, *Jesus and Judaism*, 1 and passim.

[17]A classic text in this regard is Rosemary Radford Reuther's *Faith and Fratricide: The Theological Roots of Anti-Semitism* (New York: Seabury Press, 1974).

[18]George M. Smiga, *Pain and Polemic: Anti-Judaism in the Gospels* (New York: Paulist Press, 1992).

[19]Ekkehard Schuster and Reinhold Boschert-Kimmig, eds., *Hope Against Hope: Johann Baptist Metz and Elie Wiesel Speak Out on the Holocaust* (New York: Paulist Press, 1999).

[20]See Fredriksen, 106-109 and 200-201, wherein she redirects the reader's attention to overlooked details of familiar pericopes. Thus, instead of focusing on the faith of the woman cured from the hemorrhage and Jesus' lack of concern for purity after being touched by an "unclean" woman, Fredriksen points out that the Levitical or ritual impurity incurred by the touch was easily dispensed with a "wash and wait" ritual; moreover, the *tzitzit* or tallit that Jesus wears marks him as a traditionally observant Jew (see Mark 5:25-34; Matt. 9:20-22; Luke 8:43-44; for "fringe" or *tzitzit* see Matt. and Luke above and Mark 6:56). For Fredriksen, such a view moves us away from what she calls two "traditional characteristics of New Testament historiography: the conviction of Jesus' singular moral excellence and a long cultural habit of 'explaining' Christianity by having Judaism be its opposite" (Fredriksen, "What You See Is What You Get: Context and Content in Current Research on the Historical Jesus," *Theology Today* 52 [April 1995]: 75-97).

[21]Jon Levenson, "Divine Dilemma," *National Review* (December 20, 1999): 63.

[22]See Fredriksen, *Jesus of Nazareth*, 207ff and 225ff.

[23]Bruce Chilton, *Rabbi Jesus: An Intimate Biography* (New York: Doubleday, 2000).

[24]The description is attributed to Donald Senior in Gary M. Burge, "A Jesus Quest without a Compass?," *Evangelical Quarterly* 74:1 (2002): 59. Other reviews questioning Chilton's historical methodology include Zachary Karabell, "A Perplexing Reinterpretation of Jesus' Life," *The Los Angeles Times* (December 23, 2000), B.2, and *Publishers Weekly* 247:39 (September 25, 2000), 109.

[25]Monika K. Hellwig, "Historical Jesus Research: Its Relevance to Thoughtful

Christians and to Systematic Theologians," in *The Historical Jesus through Catholic and Jewish Eyes*, ed. Bryan F. Le Beau, Leonard Greenspoon, and Dennis Hamm (Harrisburg, Penn.: Trinity Press International, 2000), 91.

[26]Edward Schillebeeckx, "Can Christology Be an Experiment?," *Proceedings of the Catholic Theological Society of America* 35 (1980): 10.

The Practice of Teaching Christology

Teaching Christology: History and Horizons

Terrence W. Tilley

Introduction

My presentation is divided into three parts.[1] First, I will suggest that we must "begin at the beginning," that is, with the christologies we find embedded in and expressed by the documents of the New Testament. Whatever we might think the center of christology, these documents are our primary sources and we must start there. Second, I want to take a position on what I will call "traditional christologies," that is, the christologies that emerge from further reflection on the person, work, and significance of Jesus *after* the New Testament period, especially in (but *not* limited to) conciliar documents from Nicaea and Chalcedon. The conciliar texts provide a set of boundaries or principles for orthodox christologies. However, substantive, effective, faith-filled christologies are found elsewhere. Third, I want to consider two items on today's christological horizon: the "historical-Jesus"[2] and the issues of Jesus and the Living Faith Traditions. Numerous other items might be considered, especially many forms of liberationist christology, but these two items seem to me the more fundamental issues. If we reach some conclusions about them, they will affect how we can do more substantive christologies, including liberationist christologies and others that evoke a particular standpoint.

Two preliminary points: First, the course I teach is a Master's level christology seminar. My approach may be adaptable for advanced undergraduates, but other approaches may be superior in other contexts. Second, I have argued elsewhere that christology begins in the imaginations of disciples.[3] To begin christology elsewhere is to begin in the wrong place—but that does not mean that one ought not visit those "other places." A christology that began in, never left, and ended in the imagination would be indistinguishable from fantasy.

New Testament Christology

The New Testament presents multiple images of Jesus. Many of these are captured in the vehicles of the imagination, visual arts, music, and popular images. Jesus is a healer-exorcist, a teacher, an eschatological prophet, a law-giver, messiah, king, and so on. He is recognized in his actions as God's son in his conception, birth, baptism, healing, fellowship, death, resurrection, and—most powerfully—as the stranger on the road to Emmaus. In my view, the "first rule" of christology is not to forget the multiplicity of images of this first-century Jew from Nazareth. No single image or concept fits him like a glove. Even when Peter, in the Caesarea Philippi scene, gets the "word" right by imagining him as the Anointed One of God, he so gets the story wrong that Jesus finally rebukes him as a "satan." No single image, no single christology is rich enough to capture him. In our christology seminar, the first assignment for the students is to do "quick and dirty" reports on the christology of a New Testament author, text, or set of texts. This brings the diversity of New Testament christologies front and center.

The significance of the multiplicity in New Testament—and subsequent—christology can be seen by reflecting on the title of "Son of God" and the stories that the evangelists tell to make sense of this title.[4]

In fact, there are at least two dominant patterns in the stories that give meaning to New Testament "Son of God" christologies. One can be summarized like this: "God made a man God's Son." As noted above, Jesus is made or recognized as God's son at a number of different times in the synoptic gospels and the Pauline corpus. The content of this pattern can be identified as a "low, ascending" christology. The most obvious problem to be associated with this approach is "adoptionism." The other pattern can be summarized

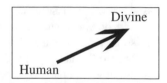

Low, Ascending Christology

like this: "God made the Son a man." This pattern can be found in the prologue to the Gospel of John and in some of the hymns found in the New Testament. The content of this pattern can be called a "high, descending" christology. The obvious problem connected with this approach is "monophysitism." Nonetheless, it is

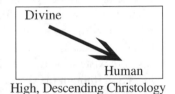

High, Descending Christology

clear that these are two different patterns, representing two different narratives saying what it means for Jesus to be the Son of God. The two patterns cannot be simply combined, but must be held in some way in creative tension.

Traditional Christologies

These images lead us into the area I have identified as traditional christologies. As later Christians came to reflect on the significance of Jesus, they valorized the title "Son of God." Among the christologies developed after the New Testament are, first, those that are inadequate or heretical. Some patterns are

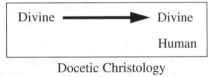

Docetic Christology

"gnostic" or "docetic." In these christologies the divine never really encounters or never fully enters into the human; the Creator remains isolated from the creation, not incarnated into it. Jesus is conceived of as "God," but his humanity is ignored or downplayed. In contrast, some patterns are Arian or humanistic or (arguably) adoptionist. Jesus the Christ is seen as a creature, even as the incar-

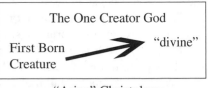

"Arian" Christology

nation of the "first born of all creation," like God, but not God—never fully divine or as "divine" as the Father, never really one in being with the Creator or Mind of the universe.[5] Both patterns fail to hold in tension the two scriptural narratives of the "Son of God," but capitalize on one to the neglect of the other.

Second, I would argue that the classic orthodox christology offers

us a complex story attempting to hold together in tension the two patterns for the "Son of God."[6] First, it begins with the earthly Jesus that
we meet in scripture and in the community. He is truly human. Second, it infers that to be who he is, he must have been from God in a
special way. Classic traditional christology images him as in some
sense preexistent with God. This is profoundly metaphorical. He is
God's Son (though the Creator does not have procreative equipment)
or God's Word (though the Unoriginate One does not have vocal cords).
Fourth, the Word, Wisdom, or Logos of God is seen as descending to
be present in the life, ministry, death, and resurrection of the earthly
Jesus. Fifth, Jesus is exalted or raised up to return to God the Father.[7]
Thus:

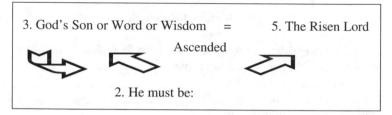

3. God's Son or Word or Wisdom   =   5. The Risen Lord

Ascended

2. He must be:

What this approach illustrates is that there is no such thing as
"christology from above." We always start with "where we are" and
"where we imagine Jesus the Christ to be." The popular distinction
between "from above" and "from below" christology obscures the
fact that christology always arises in disciples' imaginations.[8] We start
with Jesus as he is perceived on this earth even if we choose to start
the story as if it began in heaven.

These patterns, however, do not provide a substantial christology.
Even orthodox conciliar formulae simply provide acceptable patterns
(as heterodox patterns are deemed "unacceptable") for orthodox
christologies to follow. In fact, real christologies are also much more
diverse.[9] Three examples will illustrate this.

First, ascetics saw Jesus as the one who "embodied the passionless
humanity that they worked to attain."[10] He showed them the way and
walked with them. He had been in the desert resisting temptation; so
did they, from Anthony onward. He became indifferent to suffering
and death; so would they. He was their model and trainer or coach
who would empower them to reach that perfectly human state of
"passionlessness," *apatheia*, undistorted by the tugs of passion but

filled to the brim and flowing over with love for God and God's creation. As he was perfectly divine in majesty and perfectly human in *apatheia*, so would they be.

Second, martyrs saw Jesus as the proto-martyr, tortured and executed undeservedly, as they also were. Christ was their present companion, suffering with them. Christ was so present that he "did in and with them what he had once done for them."[11] The martyrs were "other Christs," witnesses to and embodiers of the justice and mercy of Christ, even agents of salvation. From Steven to Polycarp to Blandina and beyond, martyrs do not merely mirror or follow Christ, but they become as he was.

Third, activists saw Jesus as the one who would lead in the revolution/transformation of this world into God's place of reign. In 1832 Hugues Robert Félicité de Lamennais imaged Christ as "the saving Christ, the liberating Christ, the Christ who pities the poor, the weak, the miserable, and who breaks the sword over their oppressor."[12] Lamennais's Christ, like Dostoevsky's in "The Grand Inquisitor" episode in *The Brothers Karamazov*, was the incarnation of liberty, a liberty suppressed by kings and prelates on the thrones of this world. Christ was present in the world in the masses who were both agents and receivers of freedom (a perspective in some ways echoed more recently in Oscar Romero's prophetic word that he would rise again in the Salvadoran people).

The second section of the christology seminar, then, is devoted to a brief look at classic christological debates, but spends the bulk of its time on actual, popular christologies. For Nicaea and Chalcedon are not really responses to the christological question, "Who do you say that I am?" but guides to how concrete answers can be given to these questions. Of course, some of the images are shallow,[13] and all of them need to be qualified both by being "jostled" by other images and by being critically analyzed. But real christology effective in the community of disciples is rarely constructed of conciliar formulae.

The "Historical-Jesus"

I believe that the quests for the historical-Jesus were an outgrowth of "traditional" christology. Disciples—and others—sought to create and validate images of Jesus. I will not rehearse the quests here, but make three points about them.[14] First, the first questers (and possibly some in the second) seemed to want to find a "foundation" in history for faith. Their failure is well known—and, arguably, should have been known to them. The shifting results of historical investigations are hardly bedrock foundations for religious faith.[15] Second, some questers have sought to find a foundation from which religious faith could be undermined. History would reveal the "facts" of the matter and show how faith was really "fantasy." While they have, perhaps, had some success in popular circles, their failure should be as obvious as the other questers' failure. The "historical-Jesus" is clearly a construct of historians, an image that they have developed, whether as members of a "Jesus Seminar," as disciples, or as critics. While historical investigations and disciplines need to correct the excesses of the religious imagination, the methods of history cannot provide the "facts" that will upset or establish religious belief. Third, just as the early church used the tools it had to understand who Jesus was and what he did for them, so we must use the tools of our own age, including those of historical investigation. The question is how to use these tools in christology.

My approach is to take the historical investigations of Jesus to provide us with a "touchstone" for our images of Jesus the Christ.[16] Along with Luke Timothy Johnson, I see no reason to accept historians' reconstructions of Jesus' "self-presentation" as any better than those of the evangelists. However, historical investigations can provide some insight into what components of our images of Jesus might well be fantasy—and what in the evangelists' constructs we might also have to consider fantasy. Legitimating each of these claims would take a long book, not a panel presentation, so I will merely lay them out apodictically.

First, we ought to begin with Jesus' actions.[17] We know he was crucified. We have good reason to think that he was arrested and dispatched because of the incident of the cleansing of the temple, a religio-political act.[18] He was baptized by John. He was an itinerant. He healed people of illness. He exorcised some as part of that healing. He had commensality with various people whom some might find socially marginal. He developed a movement in Judaism that would carry on his way, members of which testified to his postmortem appearances. Other actions are, of course, possible, but this core seems to me very secure.

Second, his distinctive speech acts were remembered and rehearsed.

He preached turning one's life to/into God's reign. He challenged people, especially in parables, which still have power to startle people today. He lived in a time with eschatological hopes and very likely used eschatological images in his prophetic teaching. How creative and distinctive his speech acts were is open for debate, but, in any event, they were challenging and memorable.

While I do not think that there are hard evidential grounds for two issues about Jesus' "style," I think it likely that Jesus was in some sense "political" and "inclusive." Both "fit" with the actions supported as historical, but are clearly interpretive. First, I see no reason why we ought to think that Jesus was *not* in some significant sense "political." The proper question is not whether he was political, but how he was political. Clearly he was concerned with the nation of Israel, and although his political views and tactics may not parallel ours, to say he was "only" a religious or social reformer denies the evident challenge he laid to some of his contemporaries, reflected in the gospels (sometimes distortedly, of course; for example, Pilate sending Jesus to Herod in the midst of the trial scene as Luke 23:6-12 reports). To deny political relevance to Jesus serves all too well the interests of those who would deny political teeth to contemporary Christianity.[19]

Second, I see no reason why we ought to think that Jesus was not in some sense "inclusive." The arguments Elisabeth Schüssler Fiorenza has made for a shift to a basic vision of Jesus' community as a discipleship of equals as a revealing historical possibility have not been undermined.[20] While "Jesus the feminist" pictures are ludicrous, finding patriarchal structures and policies originating in his life and work serves all too well the entrenched interests of those men who are comfortable to sit in the boys' clubs of the higher reaches of ecclesial structures.

In short, I think, first, that the "historical-Jesus" cannot provide a foundation for faith or unfaith, but provides a touchstone for our commitment and our imagination. Second, I feel we need to recognize that "quests" for the historical-Jesus as opposed to the "Christ of faith" are privileged by a disenchanted culture. Such a culture values information over wisdom and verifiable certain data over a sacramental vision of the universe and so deserves only qualified support and wary use. Third, understanding the research that goes into the quests for the "historical-Jesus" can nonetheless be a gift to challenge our complacency as Jesus' disciples.

Jesus and the Living Faith Traditions

Finally, the relationship of Jesus to the other living faith traditions is a currently "hot" horizon. My students read an article or text addressing these issues. However, after nearly a decade of working somewhat sporadically on these issues,[21] I am inclined to think that these issues are not soluble in theory, at least given the present formulations of theory—and any alternatives I can envision. What I say here can be taken as a promissory note for future work.

Basically there are about six propositions in this area that have to be affirmed by Christians. One version of them would run like this:

1. Salvation is available before Jesus was born.
2. God's will is the salvation of each and every creature.
3. Sin—as tendency (original) and act—is real.
4. Salvation, grace, and faith are correlated.
5. The salvation brought by Jesus the Christ is constitutive and sufficient for all.
6. Other religious traditions *qua* traditions are not independent sources of salvation, yet are intrinsically worthwhile, part of God's creation, and have much to teach Christians (and Christianity) about practice and belief.

While any one of these propositions might well be disputed or refined, it is my judgment both that no theory yet developed can hold these propositions together consistently and that they—or some perfected and clarified version of them—are undeniable by Christian disciples today. The various strands of the major explanatory theories wind up denying or killing by a thousand qualifications one or more of these propositions. "Exclusivism" denies 1 and/or 2 and often 6. "Inclusivism" denies 4 and, in some strands, 5. "Pluralism" denies 4 and 5 and, in some strands, 2 and/or 3.

It is my opinion that rather than developing a theory to harmonize these views, what is needed is a defense of their consistency,[22] coupled with a *praxis* of solidarity in working together with those of other traditions for social justice and ecological sustainability. Even if we cannot finally *say* how all this fits together in theory, we can *show* (a) how these claims are not an inconsistent set of beliefs, and (b) what is

our commitment to God and God's creatures by the *praxis* that transforms strangers and enemies into guests for our celebrations, friends
in the struggle, and colleagues seeking understanding. Warrants for
this opinion remain to be developed.

Conclusion

I am terribly conscious of how truncated this panel presentation is
and how *ex cathedra* many of its pronouncements seem. Nonetheless,
if christology begins in disciples' imaginations, then teaching
christology means to develop our students' imaginations through the
discipline of understanding biblical and traditional forms developed
by the christological imagination and how these forms may be used to
address some key contemporary issues. There is much more that could
be said, of course, but if we are to do christology as disciples, we must
fire our own imaginations and those of our students so that we and
they can continue the disciples' practice of inventing the christological
tradition.

Notes

¹The present essay is based on a brief "PowerPoint" presentation. Many of the
illustrations do not transfer to this format. I have tried to preserve the relatively
informal style of the presentation and some of the simpler visual images here.

²I have come to adopt this typographical convention from Elisabeth Schüssler
Fiorenza, *Jesus and the Politics of Interpretation* (New York: Continuum, 2000).

³See my "O Caesarea Philippi: On Starting Christology in the Right Place,"
Theology and Sacred Scripture, CTS Annual Volume 47, ed. Carol J. Dempsey
and William P. Loewe (Maryknoll, N.Y.: Orbis Books, 2002), 135-161.

⁴For further development of this approach, see my *Story Theology* (Wilmington,
Del.: Michael Glazier, 1985), chap. 7.

⁵Recent Patristic scholarship has suggested that some of the differences among
early Christians were due to different conceptions of divinity and of how salvation
could be accomplished. Moreover, in the Greco-Roman world, divinity was not a
single definite quality, but a quality with a continuum of applications or grades
from (at least) the Emperor to "Nous," the God beyond the gods who never inter-
acted with the world. Many now find Nestorius's christology to be orthodox, a
view rejected in the Patristic era, and Cyril of Alexandria to be something of a
proto-Arian. It is far beyond the scope of this presentation to lay out these classic
disputes. Indeed, in a general christology course it is hard to do more than visit
them briefly.

⁶One way of doing this is to form a "descending, ascending" christology. I

first understood this as articulated by Reginald H. Fuller, *The Foundations of New Testament Christology* (New York: Scribner's, 1965). The proposal here takes the epistemological shape of the imagination, rather than the images we produce, as determining the shape of christology and thus of how we ought to use "above" and "below" in christology. I find the usual use of "from above, from below" obscuring rather than illuminating. Whatever image we may have, we always must start "from below."

[7]One of the confusions regarding Roger Haight, *Jesus Symbol of God* (Maryknoll, N.Y.: Orbis Books, 1999), is the claim that he denies or downplays the resurrection. Haight locates Jesus' exaltation in the crucifixion (124-26) and does minimize the "legends" of the empty tomb. But this is not a denial of resurrection, but a claim about the best way to understand Jesus' being raised up (in itself a metaphorical image). The claim, of course, is arguable: there may be better ways to image God's raising Jesus to new life, but merely asserting it is not denying the resurrection.

[8]This is the thesis of my next major research and writing project. I anticipate it in "O Caesarea Philippi."

[9]At this point I rely especially on William H. Clebsch, *Christianity in European History* (New York: Oxford University Press, 1979), and Jaroslav Pelikan, *Jesus through the Centuries* (New Haven: Yale University Press, 1985). Pelikan's and Clebsch's interests are primarily historical; my own forthcoming work attempts to mine similar sources for their theological insights.

[10]Clebsch, *Christianity in European History*, 82.

[11]Ibid., 60.

[12]Clebsch, 257, citing Peter N. Stearns, *Priest and Revolutionary: Lamennais and the Dilemma of French Catholicism* (New York: Harper & Row, 1967), 165, citing Lamennais, December 15, 1832, to Comtesse de Senfft von Pilsach.

[13]Many come to mind, but Robert Lee Scott, Jr.'s *God Is My Co-Pilot* (New York: Scribner's, 1943) seems to stand out as an example.

[14]The literature on the quests is legion. I will mention only three recent studies. Schüssler Fiorenza provides an important and compelling criticism of the whole enterprise of the third quest. Luke Timothy Johnson, *The Real Jesus: The Misguided Quest for the Historical Jesus and the Truth of the Traditional Gospels* (San Francisco: HarperSanFrancisco, 1996), offers a frequently incisive, if truculent, critique of the quest, especially of those scholars who develop portraits of Jesus that exclude an eschatological/apocalyptic component in his ministry. I fully agree with Johnson on this latter point. Paula Fredriksen, *From Jesus to Christ: The Origins of the New Testament Images of Christ*, 2nd ed. (New Haven: Yale University Press, 2000) is very accessible. It also includes some "retractations" of some of her earlier views.

[15]See my "Practicing History, Practicing Theology," *Horizons* 25/2 (Fall 1998): 258-275; a slightly different version is published as "Introduction: Practicing History, Practicing Theology," *Theology and the New Histories*, College Theology Society, vol. 43, ed. Gary Macy (Maryknoll, N.Y.: Orbis Books, 1999), 1-20, for an outline of my view of the matter.

[16]The oral presentation included a fairly standard presentation of the expanded (to include John) two-source hypothesis and some "second quest" criteria, which have to be modified considerably. The criteria of multiple attestation, dissimilarity, and coherence can still serve as rough guidelines (not criteria) for thinking about what we can know about the actual man Jesus. Some who have rejected or "transcended" the second quest have thrown the gold out with the tailings in their excessively absolutist rejections of the (admittedly problematical) theory that makes these disposable rules of thumb into hard and fast criteria. An analysis and evaluation of the variety of approaches that the third questers use is beyond the scope of this paper.

[17]I found E. P. Sanders, *Jesus and Judaism* (Philadelphia: Fortress Press, 1985), convincing on the strategy of starting with Jesus' acts rather than his teaching. Of course, I also find "speech act theory" the best account of language use—understanding language use starts with understanding the acts we perform in speaking; see *The Evils of Theodicy* (Washington, D.C.: Georgetown University Press, 1991), chaps. 1-3.

[18]Sanders thinks that Jesus thus is best understood as a charismatic, autonomous prophet. Many see him as wanting to restore authentic worship and life in opposition to the Temple authorities. Such reconstructions are possible, but evidence for Jesus' purpose in this act is too thin to build such theories on. We can say, however, that his is a serious act challenging religious and political leadership. Paula Fredriksen has argued that this act is better understood as a creation of the Christian community rather than an historical event (see *From Jesus to Christ*, 2nd ed., and *Jesus of Nazareth, King of the Jews: A Jewish Life and the Emergence of Christianity* [New York: Knopf, 1999] for her arguments). I find her arguments unconvincing. First, they take away any reasonable motivation for the execution and make Jesus a *de facto* scapegoat. Pilate may have been arbitrary, but arguing against the historicity of such an incident belies the intrinsic plausibility it has as part of the passion narrative (and if it were not known as an incident, why would John include it early on in his gospel?). Second, Fredriksen tries to explain Jesus' execution as "exemplary" in part because he was executed alone rather than with his disciples. However, the gospels already explain Jesus' being alone by noting the disciples' immediate flight. Why reject that account in favor of one that has no textual support and is speculative? Third, Fredriksen's arguments are based in part on the physical layout of the Temple so that even those nearby might not know about the disturbance and the arrest. This view, analogized by Fredriksen in her plenary address to being in Logan Airport, is not convincing. Given the number of people in Jerusalem, a city ruled by the Romans, for Passover and the number likely at the Temple, a mob scene at a soccer match, ready to explode at the slightest spark, seems much more likely as an analogy than a crowd in Logan Airport; Jesus could have been whisked off quickly to prevent the dry tinder of oppression from catching fire. That the cleansing of the Temple may have been a small "hit and run" event (as the synoptics hint by their narration of Jesus' exit) or may have been quickly contained by soldiers is not implausible. Fourth, Fredriksen's argument implies that politico-religious opposition between Jews-for-Jesus and other

Jewish "sects" or "groups" of the late first century was not anticipated or insti-
gated in part by Jesus in his own time. While the "anti-Judaism" in the New Testament is the harsh rhetoric of "sibling rivals," why would one not think that there
was some serious opposition between Jews-for-Jesus and others earlier as well?
While the second quest completely overdid its distinguishing Jesus by the use of
the criterion of "dual dissimilarity," Fredriksen's reconstructions nearly collapse
Jesus into his background, making him an insignificant figure, a tactic that seems
just as problematical. If Jesus was so much like his contemporaries that he didn't
stand out at all, the Jesus movement catching fire is nearly as miraculous as the
incarnation. For these, and for other less significant reasons, I find Fredriksen's
reconstruction unconvincing—too much that is plausible in the gospel stories and
in the reconstructions of recent critics has to be explained away to have her reconstruction make more sense than the consensus view of contemporary questers (that
the incident happened) or even the basic testimony of the gospels that survives the
historians' investigations.

[19]In this I am suggesting that contemporary images of a non-political Jesus are
not really warranted by the New Testament and are more likely the product of
disciples' imaginations motivated by being in comfortable social locations. This is
one way in which we should use the New Testament as a "touchstone" to check
our imaginations.

[20]See her *Discipleship of Equals: A Critical Feminist "Ekklesia-logy" of Liberation* (New York: Crossroad, 1993). As she notes in *Jesus and the Politics of
Interpretation*, passim, many attempted rebuttals have addressed caricatures of
her argument and have left the major points unscathed. While I find her style
difficult and have trouble discerning what all her warrants for some of her claims
are, I think her main points are indeed intact.

[21]I have addressed these issues in *The Wisdom of Religious Commitment* (Washington, D.C.: Georgetown University Press, 1995; reprint 2002), especially in chap.
5 and the epilogue; *Postmodern Theologies: The Challenge of Religious Diversity*
(Maryknoll, N.Y.: Orbis Books, 1995), esp. chap. 11; "A Recent Vatican Document on 'Christianity and the World Religions,'" *Theological Studies* 60/2 (June
1999): 318-337; and "Why We Need Both Stories" (a response to Robert Krieg,
"Who Do You Say I Am? Christology: What It Is and Why It Matters"),
Commonweal CXXIX/6 (March 22, 2002): 16-17.

[22]This is a strategy analogous to that of constructing a *defense* of the compatibility of beliefs about God and the reality of evil and of eschewing constructing a
comprehensive *theodicy* that offers a theory that tries to explain how it is that God
allows evil in the world. For elucidation of this point and its significance, see my
"The Use and Abuse of Theodicy," *Horizons* 11/2 (Fall 1984): 304-319, and *The
Evils of Theodicy*, chap. 5.

Contributors

Anne M. Clifford, C.S.J., is Associate Professor of Theology at Duquesne University. Author of *Introducing Feminist Theology* (Orbis Books, 2001) and a contributing editor for the second edition of the *New Catholic Encyclopedia* (Gale Group and Catholic University of America Press), articles by her have appeared in *Horizons, The Journal of Feminist Studies of Religion, Dialog, A Journal of Theology,* and *World Vision International.*

M. Shawn Copeland is Associate Professor of Systematic Theology at Marquette University and (adjunct) Associate Professor of Systematic Theology at the Institute for Black Catholic Studies, Xavier University of Louisiana, New Orleans. Professor Copeland currently serves as convenor of the Black Catholic Theological Symposium (BCTS) and is president-elect of the Catholic Theological Society of America (CTSA).

Paula Fredriksen is the William Goodwin Aurelio Professor of the Appreciation of Scripture at Boston University. Among her publications are *From Jesus to Christ: The Origins of the New Testament Images of Jesus,* 2nd edition (Yale, 2000), *Jesus of Nazareth, King of the Jews: A Jewish Life and the Emergence of Christianity* (Knopf, 1999), and articles in *The Journal of Theological Studies* and *Theology Today.*

Anthony J. Godzieba is Associate Professor of Theology and Religious Studies at Villanova University. His publications include "Prolegomena to a Catholic Theology of God between Heidegger and Postmodernity" (*The Heythrop Journal,* 1999) for which he won the College Theology Society 2000 award for best article. His essays have appeared in *Theological Studies, The Heythrop Journal, Philosophy and Theology, Horizons,* and *Augustinian*

Studies. He is a contributor to the second edition of the *New Catholic Encyclopedia* (Gale Group and Catholic University of America Press).

Roger Haight, S.J., is Professor of Theology at Weston Jesuit School of Theology in Cambridge, Massachusetts. He is a past president of the Catholic Theological Society of America and the author of *The Experience and Language of Grace, An Alternative Vision: An Interpretation of Liberation Theology* (both from Paulist Press), *Dynamics of Theology,* and *Jesus Symbol of God* (both published by Orbis Books).

Linda S. Harrington is a doctoral candidate in the School of Religious Studies at The Catholic University of America in Washington, D.C. She is also an adjunct instructor of theology at Briar Cliff University, Sioux City, Iowa.

Mary Ann Hinsdale, I.H.M., teaches constructive theology and directs the Pastoral Institute at Boston College. She co-authored (with Helen Lewis and Maxine Waller) *"It Comes from the People": Community Development and Local Theology* (Temple) and co-edited *Women and Theology* (with Phyllis Kaminsky) (Orbis Books) and *Faith That Transforms* (with Mary Jo Leddy) (Paulist Press).

Peter A. Huff holds the T. L. James Chair of Religious Studies and is chair of the Religious Studies Department at Centenary College of Louisiana. He has published articles on fundamentalism and interreligious dialogue in journals such as *Horizons* and *Cross Currents.*

James F. Keating is currently a member of the Department of Theology at Providence College. He has written about the theological issues surrounding the quest of the historical Jesus in various journals.

Robert Masson is Associate Professor of Theology at Marquette University. The editor of the Rahner Papers in *Philosophy and Theology* (1995-2002), he specializes in Catholic systematic and fundamental theology with particular interest in how the character of language and understanding affects theological convictions and argumentation.

Michael E. O'Keeffe is Assistant Professor in the Department of Religious Studies at Saint Xavier University in Chicago. Articles by him appear in *Horizons* and in *New Theology Review.*

Patricia A. Plovanich is Assistant Professor of Theology and Religious Studies at the University of San Diego, where she teaches christology, ecclesiology, and U.S. Catholic history. Her specialization is the theology of Walter Kasper and of the Catholic Faculty of the University of Tübingen. At present, she is engaged in a study of the work of twentieth-century Tübingen theologians.

Jacquelyn Porter, R.S.H.M., is Associate Professor of Theology at Marymount University, Arlington, Virginia. She has recently published a translation of Stanislas Breton's *The Word and the Cross,* which includes an introduction to his works.

Elena G. Procario-Foley is Assistant Professor of Religious Studies and John G. Driscoll Professor of Jewish-Catholic Studies at Iona College, New Rochelle, New York.

Gloria L. Schaab, S.S.J., is a doctoral candidate at Fordham University, New York. Her essays on feminist theological methodology and on trinitarian theology have been published in *Theological Studies* and *THEOFORUM.*

Terrence W. Tilley is Professor in the Department of Religious Studies at the University of Dayton. He chaired that department from 1994 to 2003. His most recent book is *Inventing Catholic Tradition* (Orbis Books, 2000). He has received an NEH Fellowship to work on the relationships of history and theology in 2003-2004 and has planned a book on that topic and yet another on christology for the near future.